THE BATTLE FOR IRAQ

THE BATTLE FOR IRAQ

BBC News Correspondents on the War against Saddam

Edited by
Sara Beck and Malcolm Downing

The Johns Hopkins University Press
Baltimore, Maryland

This book is dedicated to the memory of BBC cameraman
Kaveh Golestan and translator Kamaran Muhamed, and to all
other journalists killed and injured reporting this war.

**Library
University of Texas
at San Antonio**

© BBC Worldwide Limited 2003
Chapter eight © John Simpson 2003
All rights reserved.
First published 2003 by BBC Worldwide Limited, London
Johns Hopkins edition published 2003
Printed in the United States of America on acid-free paper
9 8 7 6 5 4 3 2 1

The Johns Hopkins University Press
2715 North Charles Street
Baltimore, Maryland 21218-4363
www.press.jhu.edu

0-8018-7936-1

Library of Congress Control Number: 2003113115

Cartographer: Angela Wilson, All Terrain Mapping

Picture credits: Page 2 Rex/Sipa; 18 © BBC; 51 Associated Press/Brant Sanderling;
65 Popperfoto/Kevin Lamarque; 78 AP/Denis Poroy; 104 EPA/Tim Reeves; 132 AP;
179 AP/Ian Waldie; 192 Press Association/Matthew Fearn; 203 AP/Murad Sezer;
210 AFP/ Karim Sahib.

CONTENTS

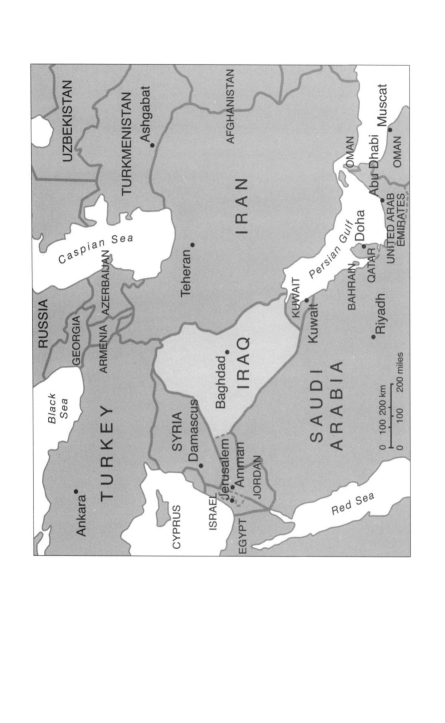

8

TURKEY

0   100   200 km

0   100   200 miles

36th parallel

Mosul

Arbil

SYRIA

Suleimanieh

Tigris

Kirkuk

Tikrit

IRAN

IRAQ

Euphrates

BAGHDAD

33rd parallel

JORDAN

Karbala

32nd parallel

Najaf

al-Faw
peninsula

Nasiriya

SAUDI
ARABIA

Basra

Umm Qasr

KUWAIT

▨ Area controlled by Kurds

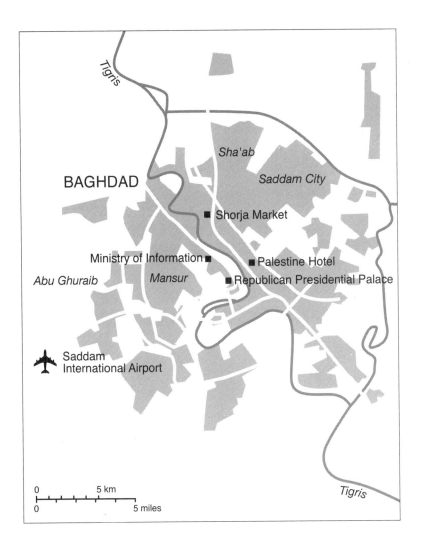

BAGHDAD

Tigris

Sha'ab

Saddam City

■ Shorja Market

Ministry of Information ■

Abu Ghuraib

Mansur

■ Palestine Hotel

■ Republican Presidential Palace

✈ Saddam
International Airport

0 — 5 km
0 — 5 miles

Tigris

9

CHRONOLOGY

1979 **16 July** Saddam Hussein becomes president of Iraq, after forcing the resignation of Ahmad Hassan al-Bakr.

1980 **22 September** A border dispute between Iran and Iraq escalates into full-scale war.

1988 **16 March** Saddam uses chemical weapons against the Kurdish town of Halabjeh.
20 August The Iran–Iraq war ends in stalemate. A ceasefire comes into effect, to be monitored by the UN.

1990 **2 August** Iraq invades Kuwait. The invasion is condemned by UN Security Council Resolution 660, which calls for a full withdrawal.
6 August The UN imposes economic sanctions on Iraq.
29 November Resolution 678 authorizes 'all necessary means' to uphold Resolution 660.

1991 **16 January** Operation Desert Storm is launched by the US and her allies. A six-week air campaign is followed by a short ground war.
27 February Kuwait is liberated.
3 March Iraq accepts the terms of a ceasefire.
March–April Iraqi forces suppress rebellions in the north and south of the country. Retribution against the Marsh Arabs is particularly severe.
6 April Iraq accepts a UN resolution requiring it to end production of weapons of mass destruction and to allow monitoring by a UN inspection team.
10 April A UN 'safe haven' is established in Northern Iraq for the protection of the Kurdish population after the bombing of northern towns by Saddam's air force. It includes a 'no-fly' zone, which Iraqi planes are not allowed to enter, north of the 36th parallel.

1992 **26 August** A 'no-fly' zone is set up in southern Iraq, south of the 32nd parallel, to protect Shias who had rebelled against Baghdad.

1993 **27 June** The US conducts air strikes against the headquarters of the Iraqi Intelligence Service in Baghdad, in retaliation for the attempted assassination of former president George Bush in Kuwait in April.
10 November The Iraqi National Assembly recognizes Kuwait's borders and its independence.

1995 **14 April** UN Security Council Resolution 986 allows the partial resumption of Iraq's oil exports to buy food and medicine – the 'oil-for-food' programme. It is not accepted by Iraq until May 1996 and is not implemented until December that year.
8 August Two of Saddam Hussein's sons-in-law, Lt-Gen. Hussein Kamel al-Majid (chief of Iraq's secret weapons procurement programme), his brother Lt-Col. Saddam Kamel al-Majid, and their families, leave Iraq and are granted asylum in Jordan. When they return the following February, having been promised a pardon, the two men are killed.

1996 **March–June** UN inspection teams from UNSCOM are denied access to disputed weapons sites.
3 September The US extends the northern limit of the southern 'no-fly' zone to the 33rd parallel, just south of Baghdad.
12 December Saddam Hussein's elder son, Uday, is seriously wounded in an assassination attempt.

1997 **29 October** Iraq declares that Americans on the UN inspection teams must leave, after the Security Council passes a resolution threatening to stop Iraqi officials from travelling abroad.
31 October Iraq reiterates that it is ready, if necessary, to face US military action over its decision to expel the weapons inspectors.
20 November Russian Foreign Minister Yevgeny Primakov brokers a compromise in the crisis. When UN inspectors return, they find they are barred from presidential sites.

1998 **23 January** Chief weapons inspector Richard Butler addresses the UN Security Council and presents a bleak report: Iraq will provide no new information.
23 February UN Secretary-General Kofi Annan announces a deal on unrestricted access for weapons inspectors after talks in Baghdad.
2 March The UN Security Council passes a resolution warning Iraq of the 'severest consequences' if it fails to honour the agreement and comply with previous resolutions.
17 April UN inspectors say they have made no progress in verifying whether Iraq has destroyed its weapons of mass destruction.
1 May In an open letter to the Security Council, Iraq warns of 'grave consequences' if UN sanctions against it are not lifted.
27 October Richard Butler says tests carried out by international scientists confirm that Iraq filled missile warheads with the deadly nerve agent VX before the 1991 Gulf War.
31 October Iraq ends all co-operation with UNSCOM.
11 November The UN withdraws all non-essential personnel from Iraq.
14 November Iraq offers to allow inspections to resume.
16 December UN inspectors are withdrawn after Richard Butler reports that the Iraqis are still not co-operating. Hours later, Operation Desert Fox is launched – four days of US and British air strikes aimed at destroying Iraq's nuclear, chemical and biological weapons programmes.

1999 **17 December** The UN Security Council passes Resolution 1284, replacing the existing UNSCOM with UMOVIC, the 'monitoring, verification and inspection commission'. Iraq rejects the resolution.

2000 **Late September** The beginning of the Palestinian uprising, or intifada, in Gaza and the West Bank.

7 November Americans vote in the US presidential election. The result is disputed, starting five weeks of complex, bitterly partisan legal wrangling.
13 December The Democratic candidate, Vice President Al Gore, concedes defeat.

2001 **20 January** George W Bush is inaugurated as 43rd president of the United States.
15 February The US and Britain bomb Iraq's air defence network.
11 September Aircraft hijacked by al-Qaida terrorists plunge into the World Trade Center in New York and the Pentagon in Washington. A fourth plane crashes in Pennsylvania. A total of 3023 people die in the attacks.
13 September US Secretary of State Colin Powell confirms that al-Qaida leader Osama bin Laden, believed to be in Afghanistan, is a suspect.
20 September Washington demands that the Taliban hand over bin Laden. President Bush addresses both houses of the US Congress, watched by British Prime Minister Tony Blair. Bush tells the world: 'Either you are with us, or you are with the terrorists.'
After talks with the US president, Blair says Britain will support a fight against international terrorism for 'as long as it takes'.
7 October The US and Britain begin air and missile strikes against the Taliban and al-Qaida in Afghanistan.
13 November Northern Alliance fighters enter the Afghan capital, Kabul.

2002 **30 January** In his State of the Union address, President Bush links Iraq, North Korea and Iran and their 'terrorist allies' in an 'axis of evil'.
April Baghdad suspends oil exports to protest against Israeli incursions into Palestinian territories. Exports resume after 30 days.
5 July Talks in Vienna between the United Nations and Iraq break down without agreement.
27 August US Vice President Dick Cheney says a policy of containment is no longer an option with Saddam Hussein because doing nothing would be riskier than acting against the Iraqi leader.
7 September Tony Blair has urgent talks at Camp David with President Bush, persuading him to 'take the UN route'.
9 September President Jacques Chirac suggests his plan for two UN resolutions, the first strengthening the weapons inspectors' mandate, the second approving military action if required.
12 September President Bush addresses the UN General Assembly and says leaders must confront the 'grave and gathering danger' presented by Iraq or stand aside while the US acts.
16 September Iraq accepts the 'unconditional' return of UN inspectors.
19 September Iraqi Foreign Minister Naji Sabri al-Hadithi gives a speech to the UN General Assembly declaring that Iraq is 'totally clear of all nuclear, chemical and biological weapons'.
24 September Britain publishes a 50-page dossier saying Iraq could produce a nuclear weapon within one or two years, if it obtains fissile material and other components from abroad.
Parliament is recalled for an emergency debate on the growing crisis. Fifty-six Labour MPs rebel against the government.
30 September UN and Iraqi negotiators meet in Vienna to agree terms for resuming weapons inspections, but the US rejects the inspectors' return without a new Security Council resolution.
10 October Both houses of the US Congress give President Bush the authority to use force against Iraq – if he believes diplomatic or other peaceful methods have failed.

16 October Iraq renews its offer to UN weapons inspectors, after a referendum gives Saddam Hussein another seven-year term as president with 100 per cent of the vote.
8 November The UN Security Council passes Resolution 1441, threatening 'serious consequences' if Iraq does not comply with giving up all weapons of mass destruction.
18 November UN weapons inspectors arrive in Baghdad for the first time since 1998.
3 December Iraqi officials co-operate fully with UN inspectors when a surprise search is carried out on a presidential palace.
7 December Iraq presents the UN with a 12,000-page dossier, claiming it is a complete disclosure of all of its chemical, biological, nuclear and missile programmes. But the US and Britain say it is incomplete and that Iraq is in 'material breach' of Resolution 1441.

2003 **6 January** Saddam Hussein says he is ready for war and accuses UN inspectors of being spies.
9 January After briefing the Security Council the chief UN weapons inspector, Dr Hans Blix, tells reporters that 'in the course of these inspections we have not found any smoking gun'.
11 January A British naval task force leaves for the Gulf, headed by the aircraft carrier HMS *Ark Royal*.
The US announces it is sending up to 35,000 reinforcements, bringing the total number of American military personnel in the region to more than 120,000.
13 January Tony Blair says that weapons of mass destruction will reach terrorists and that Britain could act with the US against Iraq without a second UN resolution.
14 January Chancellor Schröder and President Chirac say they want more time for weapons inspections.
23 January US Defense Secretary Donald Rumsfeld says the positions adopted by France and Germany come from 'old Europe'.
28 January President Bush's State of the Union address alleges a link between Saddam Hussein and al-Qaida.
31 January Bush and Blair meet at the White House and agree on a timetable for military action.
3 February Downing Street issues a new dossier of evidence against Iraq. It turns out to be partly based on a PhD thesis.
5 February Colin Powell makes a presentation to the UN in which he outlines US evidence against Iraq.
10 February France, Germany and Russia issue a joint declaration calling for reinforcement of the inspections regime.
15 February Massive anti-war demonstrations are held around the world.
16 February NATO agrees to measures to support Turkey in the event of a war in Iraq.
18 February President Chirac criticizes east European countries bidding to join the EU for their pro-US stance, calling them 'childish'.
24 February Britain tables a new resolution on Iraq to the Security Council, co-signed by the US and Spain. It states that 'Iraq has failed to take the final opportunity afforded to it in Resolution 1441'. Germany and Russia publish a rival memorandum calling for inspectors to be given more time.
26 February The House of Commons debates Iraq. A total of 121 Labour MPs vote against the government.

1 March Turkey's parliament rejects a government motion allowing US forces to over-fly, or be stationed in, Turkey.

7 March The Turkish army masses troops on the border with Northern Iraq.

9 March International Development Secretary Clare Short discloses deep divisions within the cabinet over possible war with Iraq, describes Blair's actions as 'reckless' and threatens to resign.

10 March Russia indicates it would vote against the UK–US–Spanish draft resolution as it stands.

President Chirac says France would veto the resolution 'no matter what the circumstances'.

16 March A summit in the Azores is attended by the British and Spanish prime ministers and President Bush. The three leaders say 17 March is the last day for Security Council negotiations.

17 March The British Ambassador to the UN says the diplomatic process on Iraq has ended.

The UN Secretary-General orders the evacuation of weapons inspectors from Iraq.

President Bush gives Saddam Hussein and his sons 48 hours to leave Iraq or face war.

Robin Cook resigns as Leader of the House of Commons over the government's stance on Iraq.

18 March MPs vote in favour of military action, despite a rebellion by 138 Labour backbenchers.

President Bush says: 'Intelligence gathered ... leaves no doubt that the Iraq regime continues to possess and conceal some of the most lethal weapons ever devised.'

20 March The war begins, with limited air strikes on Baghdad. In the following days US and British ground troops enter Iraq from the south. The Turkish parliament approves the use of its airspace by coalition aircraft.

21 March The United States fires 1000 cruise missiles on hundreds of targets in Baghdad and elsewhere.

23 March US air raids pound Baghdad, the northern city of Mosul and positions held by Ansar al-Islam, a largely Kurdish Islamist group allegedly linked to al-Qaida.

24 March Iraq's northern oil capital of Kirkuk is rocked by 24 hours of bombardment.

25 March British and US forces take control of the port town of Umm Qasr.

31 March US forces report their first serious battle with the Republican Guard, south of Baghdad.

3 April US troops reach Baghdad airport, 20 kilometres from the city centre.

7 April US forces move into Baghdad and seize several presidential palaces.

8 April President Bush and Tony Blair meet at Hillsborough Castle outside Belfast to discuss the shape of post-war Iraq.

9 April US forces advance into central Baghdad. Amid scenes of jubilation, marines help Iraqis pull down a huge statue of Saddam. In the days that follow, Kurdish fighters and US forces take control of the northern cities of Kirkuk and Mosul. There is widespread looting in the capital and other cities.

13 April US troops enter Saddam's home town of Tikrit.

President Bush accuses Syria of having chemical weapons.

14 April US forces take control of Tikrit, effectively ending the military campaign.

Iraqi police, escorted by US soldiers, begin joint patrols in Baghdad.

15 April Washington threatens Syria with diplomatic and economic sanctions amid reports that Damascus has given refuge to fleeing Iraqi officials.

18 April Thousands of Iraqis stage anti-US protests.

21 April Retired general Jay Garner, the US administrator for Iraq, arrives in Baghdad; he vows to restore water and power as soon as possible. Hundreds of thousands of Shia Muslims gather in the holy city of Karbala for a pilgrimage suppressed under Saddam.

23 April US Secretary of State Colin Powell says France will face consequences for opposing the war.

24 April The US announces oil is again flowing from wells but only for Iraqi use.

28 April At a US-chaired conference, Iraqis from across the political spectrum agree to try to form an interim government within a month. The US military says it is moving its combined air command centre from Saudi Arabia to neighbouring Qatar.

29 April US Deputy Defense Secretary Paul Wolfowitz says the toppling of Saddam has had a 'shaming effect' on the Arab world and he hopes it will encourage other dictatorial rulers to make reforms.

30 April The US formally publishes its 'road map' to peace in the Middle East – a step-by-step process leading to the creation of a Palestinian state by 2005.
US Defense Secretary Donald Rumsfeld arrives in Baghdad and says Iraq is rid of Saddam's 'truly brutal, vicious regime'.
An Arabic newspaper publishes what it says is a handwritten letter signed by Saddam urging Iraqis to rise up against US occupation.

1 May President Bush visits the aircraft carrier USS *Abraham Lincoln* and in a victory speech says: 'The battle of Iraq is one victory in a war on terror that began on September 11, 2001, and still goes on.'
Britain announces it is re-establishing its diplomatic presence in Iraq after a 12-year break.
US and UK air patrols over the 'no-fly' zones are formally brought to an end.

2 May During a visit to London, Donald Rumsfeld says that US-led forces in Iraq 'anticipate' finding Saddam Hussein's weapons of mass destruction, but it will take time.

7 May The *Sydney Morning Herald* publishes details of an audiotape of Saddam Hussein, given to their reporters in Baghdad, urging Iraqis to fight the US-led 'invasion'.

11 May The US administrator for Iraq, Jay Garner, is replaced by career diplomat Paul Bremer.

12 May A series of suicide bomb attacks in the Saudi capital Riyadh targets luxury compounds housing foreign nationals. Al-Qaida is blamed.
Clare Short resigns, accusing Tony Blair of 'rule by diktat'.

14 May A mass grave is uncovered at al-Mahawil, south of Baghdad, containing the remains of at least 3000 people killed during the Shia uprising in southern Iraq in 1991.

22 May The UN Security Council approves a landmark resolution giving US and British forces interim control of Iraq and lifting sanctions. The only Arab member of the council, Syria, is not present.

15

FOREWORD

16   Since William Howard Russell, the first 'embedded' journalist, reported on the Crimean War for *The Times* in 1854, the job of war correspondents has been to bear witness to events on the battlefield and to recount what they see. To cover the war in Iraq the BBC had to be with the armed forces, but also anywhere else that we could provide first-hand eyewitness reporting. As a result, we had teams in Baghdad, in Northern Iraq and in surrounding countries, providing a range of viewpoints. But we knew that these teams could only give us snapshots. The job of the editors in London was to put together these different views, like a jigsaw, in an attempt to see the bigger picture. In the fog of war, that's never easy. We also had to ask questions of political and military leaders on behalf of our audiences, and to reflect their concerns. If a war is justified, what's to be feared from scrutiny?

It was the most reported war in history, with nearly a thousand journalists 'embedded' with the armed forces and twice as many working independently in Kuwait, Qatar, Northern Iraq and Baghdad. It began with live pictures of missiles exploding in Baghdad and coalition forces advancing into Iraq, and ended three weeks later with the symbolism of Saddam Hussein's statue being pulled down in central Baghdad by American troops and Iraqi civilians.

By any standards, the war was a remarkable military achievement. But it was also controversial, dividing Europe, the United Nations and world opinion. The British public were split from the start. The Prime Minister, Tony Blair, faced a huge rebellion from MPs of his own party in parliament, and more than a million people joined an anti-war march through London. There were similar demonstrations in other countries. Yet for US President George Bush and British Prime Minister Tony Blair the threat of weapons of mass destruction and the history of repression in Iraq provided a moral case for military action.

The question for the BBC was not simply how to cover the fighting in Iraq, but also how to reflect the range of opinion about the conflict in a fair and objective way. With strong feelings and divided views, that could never be straightforward. Predictably, for some viewers and listeners we were 'too sceptical', for others 'unquestioning'. We were accused of abandoning impartiality *and* of sticking to it too rigorously, of rushing to judgement *and* of being too cautious. Some of our audience felt there was too much 'live' coverage from the front line for them really to understand what was happening. Others, that we should have shown more graphic images of casualties to illustrate the reality of conflict.

There's not a news organization in the world that can claim to get everything right, all of the time; but when BBC editors and correspondents discuss what to broadcast to our viewers, listeners and online users around the world, they remain committed to accurate and fair reporting, to encouraging a wide range of voices and views, and to being ruthlessly independent.

As well as requiring careful editorial judgement, the Iraq War called for physical courage from our news teams in the field. There was a heavy toll of media casualties. Land mines in Northern Iraq killed an outstanding BBC cameraman, Kaveh Golestan, and injured one of our producers, Stuart Hughes. A BBC translator, Kamaran Muhamed, was also killed when an American shell exploded next to John Simpson's team in a 'friendly fire' incident. All those journalists who lost their lives, and the many others who took risks to report what they saw, were there because they believed in the importance of war reporting and bearing witness to events. They recognized that this war in Iraq was going to be a decisive conflict for the Middle East and beyond.

In the Crimean War, William Howard Russell had to send his dispatches back to London by horse and steamer. Nowadays our correspondents use mobile satellite dishes, laptop editing in the field, and satellite phones not much bigger than a man's hand.

They work under tremendous pressure, as they go live on air or meet ever-tighter deadlines. There's not much opportunity under these circumstances to write at length, or for posterity. This book is their chance to do so. Above all, I hope it will help readers to gain a greater understanding of the war in Iraq – why it happened, what it was like, and its consequences.

Richard Sambrook, Director of BBC News, 30 May 2003

18

John Simpson reporting live from Iraq after a 'friendly fire' incident.

FRONT-LINE STORIES

A key feature of the media's coverage of this war was the 'embedding' of news teams with the military. The BBC had more than a dozen such teams with British and American units. Here, some of the correspondents provide dramatic accounts of their individual experiences of the campaign.

AL-FAW PENINSULA – SECURING THE OIL FIELDS

Clive Myrie

Clive Myrie is Asia Correspondent, based in Singapore. Along with cameraman Darren Conway, he was embedded with 40 Commando, Royal Marines, who were among the first troops to see action in Iraq.

No one on board spoke a word. Chinook helicopters make a lot of noise, their blades slicing through the air like buzz saws through wood, but a few hundred times louder. And yet I cannot really remember hearing the din in the early hours of 20 March. I was too preoccupied.

We were silent for the 20-minute journey flying through the darkness into southern Iraq, alone with our thoughts. I'd noticed the previous day that some of the marines had written letters to loved ones back home in the UK which were only to be posted if they didn't return. I'm a little superstitious and decided not to tempt fate.

On board the Chinook I remember thinking, 'What the hell

am I doing here? Have I gone crazy? We're flying low in order to sneak beneath Iraqi radar, making us sitting ducks for anyone with a decent rifle. And we're going to land right on top of our intended target, the main southern Iraqi oil installation on the al-Faw peninsula. We're not landing a few kilometres away so we can then advance towards it, we're actually going to land right on top of it! I must be crazy; we're all crazy!'

Military manuals call it a 'vertical envelopment manoeuvre', but it's very high-risk. OK, so it's the last thing the Iraqis or any army would expect – you've seized the element of surprise. The Iraqis had little night-vision capability and so wouldn't see us descending vertically until it was too late. But surely they'd hear all those buzz saws? Surely Iraqi anti-aircraft artillery gunners would aim towards the heavens as soon as they heard the din?

On that flight I was praying, along with everyone else, that US special forces had done their job. Navy Seals had flown in less than an hour before us. They had to identify Iraqi troop positions and guide in coalition artillery fire and aerial bombardments, to make our landing a little less rocky. As it turned out for the Chinook just ahead of us, it was a less than smooth touchdown. As soon as it landed it came under attack.

Our own vertical descent was delayed for 10, maybe 15 minutes. We had to hover while Royal Marines beneath us were in the middle of a firefight. This was the beginning of the ground war. Royal Marines from 40 Commando were the first regular coalition troops on Iraqi soil and I had a ringside seat.

Within minutes of our landing on the al-Faw peninsula, night turned to day and we could see what the Royal Marines were risking their necks for. It didn't look like much: a huge industrial plant spread over many acres, with rusting pipework and oil tanks but still in working order; at its heart, the Metering and Manifold Station, or MMS. This was the main terminal through which oil from the Rumaila field to the north flowed south to reach tankers for shipment abroad. It was through the MMS that limited amounts of Iraqi crude were sold as part of the UN's 'oil-for-food' programme. The al-Faw peninsula was also the most fought-over piece of territory during the eight-year Iran–Iraq War.

Securing this area was seen as a crucial first stage in the

campaign. The aim was first to prevent the Iraqis from blowing up the oil infrastructure, thereby destroying the country's wealth, and second to prevent the starting of oil fires, which could slow the advance of coalition forces and cause a possible ecological disaster.

By early morning Royal Marines had fanned out across the area and had encountered more resistance. Intelligence reports suggested there were around 1300 Iraqi troops on al-Faw, up against 900 or so British commandos. Usually generals like an advantage of three to one when going to war. Here, the marines were outnumbered, but it quickly became clear that the Iraqis were poorly trained and badly equipped and their superior numbers meant nothing.

The leader of 40 Commando, Lt-Col. Gordon Messenger, wanted his embeds to get as close to the action as possible. So it was that we went on foot patrol with some of his marines just a couple of hours after landing in hostile territory. As sporadic gunfire rang out all around us, we came across an Iraqi bunker position no more than 30 metres away from where we'd landed in our Chinook. It had been shot to pieces and a dead Iraqi soldier lay nearby in a pool of blood. The bunker was next to a tiny observation post. Inside, the lights were still on and there was a cup of coffee on a table next to some food. The vertical envelopment manoeuvre had worked: the Iraqis had no idea what had hit them.

Other Iraqi bunker positions were being spotted all the time. 'Psy Ops', or psychological operations, were then called in. A marine carrying a heavy backpack with a loud speaker attached would flip the 'on' switch of a tape recorder and the words 'You're surrounded, surrender, you won't be harmed' would boom out in Arabic.

On one occasion we watched from a distance as this scenario was played out. The Iraqis in their bunker didn't budge. In fact they fired back. The British called in a mortar attack and the bunker was mercilessly shelled. When it was deemed safe we went to look at the damage. There were bodies everywhere. I counted six, and one man lay dying on the ground. Royal Marine medics rushed over and tried to save him. His right arm had pretty much been shot off, he had shrapnel wounds to his leg and chest, and I could hear him groaning. The medics tried to stem the bleeding and inserted a drip to keep him hydrated. As a civilian watching all this it was a strange sight because minutes earlier the marines had been trying to kill him. Later I heard that the wounded soldier had died.

Iraqis in other bunker positions knew what was going on and decided it wasn't worth fighting any more. Within three or four hours of the first marines landing on al-Faw, Iraqi troops began to surrender. In their dozens they came out from behind trees in nearby woodland with their hands up, waving white T-shirts, scarves or handkerchiefs tied to sticks. We watched and filmed as some of these first POWs sought safety and shelter, leaving behind fallen comrades in bunkers and dugouts. They shuffled past our camera towards the Royal Marines, in ill-fitting uniforms, some wearing old plimsolls. Each soldier was forced to lie face down on the ground while he was searched, just in case he was a suicide bomber. Then his hands would be tied and he'd be marched out of the area. This was a ragtag army now humiliated.

UMM QASR – ASSAULT ON THE PORT TOWN

Adam Mynott

Adam Mynott is South Asia Correspondent, based in Delhi. He spent the war with Fox Company of the US 15th Marine Expeditionary Unit, which captured the strategically important southern port town of Umm Qasr, encountering considerable resistance from Iraqi troops.

Fox Company crossed the border into Iraq from northern Kuwait at 7.10 a.m., just a few minutes behind schedule. The objective was to capture Umm Qasr, the only deep-water anchorage in Iraq, as quickly as possible. The UN's 'oil-for-food' programme had centred on the port, and before the conflict started coalition forces had made much of securing it early on so that humanitarian aid could start to flow into the country. Iraqi defences in Umm Qasr, I was told, would crumble and the marines would be in the town, in control, in about two hours.

The commander of the 15th MEU had opted for a policy of total disclosure to the journalists embedded with his troops. The conditions he placed on reporters were straightforward: we were to report only events that had happened, not what was planned. Days before the attack took place I had a clear idea of how the 'war plan' should unfold.

I had been living with the marines for a fortnight, sleeping in the open, blasted by sandstorms, devoured by mosquitoes, wondering why I'd agreed to it all. There had been an early sign of what life as an embed would entail. On the second day, we had moved from our dispersal camp to the 'attack position' close to the Iraq border. Lugging all my gear with me, I clambered onto the back of an open truck just as it was beginning to get dark. Thin clouds in the sky and a gentle breeze hinted at what was to come. Half an hour later the breeze had become a gale. Dust and sand were sucked up from the ground and driven with alarming force into every nook and cranny. I covered my head with a scarf, but this presented no obstacle to the probing, grit-laden blasts of wind. My ears, my eyes, my nose, my mouth were clogged with sand.

After six hours of hell we halted and erected a large tent, struggling blindly in the dark, with ropes and sheets of canvas being thrashed around by the tempest. Shortly before dawn we dropped into the sand and fell asleep, to be woken two hours later by shouts from the staff sergeant. I found a scorpion had taken shelter under my sleeping bag, but frankly I was beyond caring. The marines didn't care anyway – they're used to it.

On the morning of 21 March, I was sitting on truck number 7 in a column of 20 vehicles. Alongside me, 25 marines aged between 19 and 24. The most nervous were senior NCOs, who'd seen fighting before; the novices, their young faces daubed with camouflage paint, were excited, eager to fight.

We lumbered forward through a gap cut by British engineers in the sand barricade that runs along the Iraq–Kuwait border. Before the lead vehicles were more than 150 metres into Iraq they came under fire. I was already broadcasting on my mobile phone on BBC radio and television, describing what I could see and hear. We clambered down to take cover and I crouched behind a low bank of sand, my phone pressed to my ear. Ahead, I could see marines firing machine guns and missiles at a ridge in front of us. I was told there was return mortar fire from Iraqi forces but I couldn't see where it was coming from. Minutes later artillery shells started bursting in the sand. 'Get back!' someone screamed and we scrambled and weaved and stumbled our way back the way we'd come.

I was reporting as I ran, talking to Nicky Campbell on BBC Radio Five Live. I'm a lifelong coward, but in this alien environment, running away from artillery shells that were shaking the ground under my feet, I was more concerned about losing the phone signal than about any risk to my own skin. Nicky suggested I ought to stop reporting and look after myself, but by now I had jumped into the relative safety of a ditch and I continued to describe what was going on. I looked at my watch. It was a quarter to nine. We were supposed to be almost in Umm Qasr by now, but Fox Company were no more than a few metres inside Iraq.

Those marines who'd been closest to the artillery explosions were shocked and pale. One young officer leaned on the back of his vehicle, breathing heavily. 'Boy!' he said, 'that was fucking close.' The firing had now stopped and, remarkably, no one had been injured. Rather than push on, the commanding officer, Captain Rick Crevier, radioed for tanks to come to his aid. His men sat in an exposed position for another three quarters of an hour waiting for two American battle tanks to arrive. As the M1 Abrams rumbled up over the ridge there was no sign of any Iraqi troops, but a few hundred metres further on two groups of men, maybe totalling 50 altogether, surrendered.

The column was now advancing down the main road into the town. I was still broadcasting on the phone to as many BBC programmes as I could. I could hear shooting ahead of me, intermittent bursts from machine guns and automatic weapons. Two dead civilians, killed by American fire, lay on the road. One body was badly scorched, slumped alongside a burning truck. The other, a middle-aged man, was lying face down on the tarmac, a deep red stain on his white shirt, just like in the movies. I was told later that as many as 60 Iraqi soldiers died in the attack, but I never saw any of these bodies and this figure was impossible to confirm. One US marine was killed.

The new port was all but deserted when we arrived outside the main gate. Some marines ripped a large portrait of Saddam Hussein from its frame; others went to clear the buildings. The gunfire had largely stopped but US forces had encountered much stiffer resistance than expected and, though the new port had been seized, other parts of Umm Qasr were not in US hands.

I was astonished to hear on my radio later in the afternoon senior coalition commanders saying that Umm Qasr had been 'secured'. I called the news desk in London repeating that the town was far from secure, and that fighting was still going on. My words were reinforced by the sound of gunfire in the background. Later, in Washington, US Defense Secretary Donald Rumsfeld added his voice to claims that it was firmly under US control; I spent much of the following morning denying it had been captured. There was no chance of Umm Qasr being retaken by Iraqis, but pockets of resistance held out for several days.

25

NASIRIYA – BATTLE FOR THE BRIDGES

Andrew North

When the 7000 US marines of Task Force Tarawa were sent to the southern city of Nasiriya in the early stages of the war to secure a supply route over the River Euphrates, they weren't expecting serious opposition. But they ended up in the longest battle of the war. Andrew North, a reporter with BBC Radio 4's The World At One, *was with them from the beginning.*

Looking out past the two marine gunners, I could see distinctive puffs of black smoke appearing on either side of the helicopter. It looked like anti-aircraft fire. It *was* anti-aircraft fire, coming from Iraqi units below in the city of Nasiriya. The Vietnam-era Huey shuddered under the strain as the pilots turned to avoid the attack. Through the open doors, I was staring almost straight down into houses and narrow streets. Moments later, I saw a Cobra helicopter gunship, hovering nearby, open up on Iraqi positions behind me.

It was two days since the fighting had started in Nasiriya, but this wasn't quite what I'd expected when Task Force Tarawa's operations chief had offered me the helicopter ride. Yes, as Colonel Ron Johnson had assured me, hundreds of armoured vehicles from the 1st Marine Division were crossing two key bridges and pushing through on their way to Baghdad. I'd just flown over them, minutes before. But it was clear that this city of some 300,000 people was still far from secure – and not just because of my own mid-air experience. The marines moving along the road were facing persistent Iraqi sniper attacks. And it was one thing getting hardened combat troops through, quite another to try to use the route for supply convoys – the original plan.

Yet when the marines first approached the city's eastern bridge over the Euphrates in the early hours of 23 March, they were expecting little more than token resistance. 'Dinner in Nasiriya tomorrow night,' one senior officer promised me that morning. Because the US Army's 3rd Infantry Division had swept past Nasiriya on its way to Baghdad, some were saying the city had already fallen.

The squawk and crackle on the radios soon told a very different tale: three marines dead, then nine, scores injured. Senior officers looked worried. Along the road between the two bridges, 1st Battalion, 2nd Marines had been caught in heavy Iraqi fire in what became known as 'Ambush Alley'. There were also reports of a 'blue-on-blue', or friendly fire incident, when US aircraft providing air support mistakenly attacked a marine unit. By the end of that day, 18 marines had been killed in the fierce fighting – all from Charlie Company. (The full toll only became clear weeks later, after the remains inside the marines' armoured vehicles had been identified.)

The suspected friendly fire incident wasn't the only mishap on the first day. Strewn across a road in Nasiriya's southern outskirts were the mangled and burnt-out vehicles of a US Army support unit. The soldiers had got lost and strayed into an Iraqi ambush. Nine soldiers were killed and another six captured. Several were later paraded on Iraqi television – to the fury, but also alarm, of the White House. This small city on the edge of the southern marshlands was becoming a serious headache. But some marine officers were equally angry – at the White House, accusing it of giving the American public the impression that taking Iraq would be a walkover, that US troops would be welcomed as liberators. 'What crap; we knew it wouldn't be easy,' snarled one commander. Around the camp there was a sombre mood, as the full scale of the casualties started to sink in and as marines realized how tough this battle was going to be.

Back in 1991, the post-Gulf War uprising in the south collapsed when President Bush Senior first encouraged a rebellion but then allowed Saddam Hussein to crush it; in Shia-dominated places like Nasiriya, his retribution was particularly vicious. 'We did let them down in '91,' Captain Peter Tabash, an Arabic-speaker with the marines' civil affairs unit, admitted. 'This time we have to prove ourselves.'

A few days in, and a concerned-looking General Jim Conway, in charge of the entire marine force in Iraq, suddenly appeared at the front line. 'We're seeing a different kind of Iraqi resistance from what we anticipated,' the General admitted. In particular, he mentioned the 'asymmetric threat' from Fedayeen militia fighters – military-speak for the unconventional, guerrilla-style tactics they had adopted. As he spoke, US artillery batteries were opening up every few minutes, while Cobra gunships circled overhead.

An indignant Colonel Johnson accused the Iraqis of 'breaking the rules of war'. 'Sometimes,' he said, 'they wave white flags to make us think they're surrendering, then they open fire.' Marines said they'd also been coming under attack from Iraqis in civilian buildings and vehicles.

On day three of the fighting, I was shown some of their evidence. A marine unit had just taken control of a hospital near the Euphrates, after coming under constant fire from inside it. Scattered around the now bullet-scarred complex, there were hundreds of AK-47 assault rifles, cases of ammunition and chemical warfare protection suits. In one room, we saw the bodies of three Iraqis in army uniform, pools of fresh blood around them. Twenty more Iraqis had surrendered, but it appeared that a hard core of Fedayeen had simply melted away into the date palm thicket behind the complex.

27

There was no doubt, these were unconventional, guerrilla-style tactics. 'What did you expect the Iraqis to do?' I asked one marine commander. 'Fight in a predictable, conventional way and thereby make themselves easy targets for US forces?' He seemed surprised by the question, saying only that to US troops the idea of using civilian buildings and vehicles was 'inconceivable'.

Late the following evening, I was at one of the marines' main positions on the city's southern outskirts, on a fly-infested rubbish dump. Suddenly, there was a screeching sound and four bright dots in the sky – Iraqi rockets heading our way. 'Get down!' someone shouted and everyone scattered, looking desperately for cover. Machine guns opened up as more rockets landed. When it was over, 30 marines had been injured, many in friendly fire because of the confusion. The Iraqis had used the cover of a sandstorm to get in close and mount another surprise assault.

Yet this proved to be one of the last significant Iraqi attacks. Reinforcements had been brought in, including teams of US special forces. Bit by bit, the Iraqis were being pushed back. But the marines had been forced to move deep into Nasiriya – not the original plan. And by the time they had taken the city, 22 marines had been killed and 57 injured. What's more, the city had been subjected to round-the-clock bombardment. Officers insisted that only military and government-related targets had been hit, but, as I discovered at the city's main hospital a few days later, so too had many civilians.

Almost every ward in the Saddam Hospital was full of people injured by US strikes – mostly women and children. One of the doctors was furious: 'The Americans say they come to free us, but why do they bomb civilians?' He said more than 250 had died of their injuries, showing me the death registration books. Like the rest of the city, the hospital had been without electricity or running water since the start of the war.

Earlier that day, US special forces had found 19-year-old Private Jessica Lynch in this same hospital. She was part of the unfortunate army support unit that had been ambushed. Another doctor showed me the room where she'd been and was keen to point out that the hospital had been treating her 'better than the Iraqi patients'. He hoped US forces would repay the staff by at least ensuring the hospital was secure, particularly as serious looting had by now broken out across the city. But when I returned the next day, not only had the marine guards gone, but inside it was pandemonium.

A group of armed thugs had burst in, threatened staff and then stolen equipment, before torching hospital vehicles. As I tried to piece together what had occurred, I heard wailing and shouting at the front entrance. A man was being brought in, drenched in blood. He'd been shot several times after refusing to hand over his vehicle to thieves. There was nothing doctors could do – he died at the scene.

By coincidence, Brigadier-General Richard Natonski, the com- 29 mander of Task Force Tarawa, had just arrived at the hospital for a visit, along with Colonel Johnson. It was a spin-doctor's nightmare. Surrounded by an angry crowd, the two men promised to restore a marine guard. But such assurances sounded hollow after what had just happened.

It was not a good omen. And unfortunately the near-anarchy in Nasiriya proved to be an early warning of what would happen later in Baghdad – a warning that wasn't heeded.

BASRA – THE SECOND CITY FALLS

Ben Brown

Ben Brown is a Special Correspondent for the Ten O'Clock News *on BBC1. He was previously Moscow Correspondent and has covered many conflicts in the world's most dangerous places. With cameraman Rob Magee and camerawoman Julie Ritson he entered Basra with the Desert Rats – the 7th Armoured Brigade, the Irish Guards.*

It's not every day someone tries to kill you, and not every day you see them being killed instead. It happened to me on a sunny Sunday afternoon in Basra on 6 April, the day the city fell to the British, and it made for the strangest concoction of feelings: part shock, part terror of course, and also – I hesitate to write it – part elation.

I'd been travelling in one of the Warrior armoured cars of the famous Desert Rats. My host for the day was Captain Niall Brennan of the Irish Guards, a dashing young officer with matinée-idol good looks, who would have looked the part in any British conflict down the ages – the Crimea perhaps, or maybe Waterloo. But here he was, waging 21st-century warfare on those Iraqi fighters who were still holding out in Basra, the second city of Iraq.

Captain Brennan told us to meet him at dawn at his headquarters, but when we turned up, he had just staggered out of his sleeping bag. He hadn't had much sleep the night before – he'd been busy attacking Iraqi positions. Now he sat and shared with us a 'wet', a cup of army tea; and with some fellow soldiers he grumbled about the pay-slips they'd just received. The Ministry of Defence had managed to get most of their wages wrong, under-paying them significantly, even as they were about to go and fight, and possibly die, in the name of their country.

The next few hours would bring the final push for Basra, after a two-week siege. An initial assault on Iraqi positions that morning had met with far less resistance than the British had been anticipating. They had found they were pushing at a 'half-open door', they said, so now they pushed it harder and blasted their way through the city in a kind of instant blitzkrieg.

'Jump in the back,' Captain Brennan said, and with that we were hurtling off into battle, the Warrior rocking from side to side as it raced across rough terrain and towards a compound where some of the most hardened of Saddam's Fedayeen militia were making their last stand. Inside the Warrior, the heat was stifling and my shirt was drenched in sweat within the first few seconds. As the noise of machine-gun and tank fire resonated around us, and Cobra attack helicopters hovered overhead, I tightened the strap of my helmet and fastened up my flak jacket. We were about to enter the epicentre of the fighting.

'De-bus, forward right!' ordered Captain Brennan when we got there. In the British army, 'de-bussing' means they're putting you out at a battlefield (rather than a bus stop), and when the doors open you step out of your cosy, armoured cocoon with some trepidation. At first, things seemed to have quietened down a little. There were just sporadic bursts of fire. Then, suddenly, something much louder and right next to us: bullets raking a low wall, no more than a few feet away.

'What the hell was that?' I shouted. It turned out to be another Warrior opening fire. There was panic and confusion; mostly, it transpired, my own. Was this a case of the dreaded friendly fire, one of the military's notorious 'blue-on-blues'? Actually, no. It was a British gunner in the process of saving our lives. Unbeknown to us, an Iraqi militiaman had popped up and tried to fire a rocket-propelled grenade (RPG) at us. While we were inside the Warrior, it would probably have bounced off the armour plating harmlessly, but hanging around outside – well, we were easy prey.

31

'He was playing dead,' Captain Brennan shouted down casually from his turret, as though this sort of thing happened all the time. 'Then he just jumped up and tried to have a go. 2–1 killed him.' 2–1 was the call sign of the neighbouring Warrior, whose gunner had been so watchful and alert. The Iraqi – clever, artful and also suicidally brave – was now lying in a ditch with a large hole in his chest and smoke coming from it, his RPG launcher lying uselessly next to him. I noticed he was wearing slightly gaudy, bright blue trousers and that he had a beard. I guessed he was probably in his late twenties and wondered for a moment whether perhaps he was not an Iraqi at all, but one of the 'foreign' fighters who were reported to have come in to reinforce the ranks of Saddam's faltering militia.

Normally I feel rather revolted if I see bodies on a battlefield; I flinch from looking at them too closely. They are the ultimate reminders of the naked brutality of war, which most of our audience, including our politicians, never get to see because they're usually too horrific to broadcast. But on this occasion I caught myself experiencing a nasty sense of triumph. The man who wanted me dead, was now dead instead. And as the old saying goes, there's nothing more exhilarating than being shot at without result.

When we got back to the Irish Guards' base, a technical college they'd taken over a few days earlier, I shook hands with the gunner from 2–1 who had saved me. I almost wanted to give him a high-five and embrace him, as though he'd scored a goal. It was a natural reaction I suppose, but later I was rather disgusted with my delight. Reporters are supposed to be observers of the battle-field, not participants. I wondered if, by being so close to the British troops, I had somehow crossed an invisible line.

The next day when I went back to see the Irish Guards again, they were in despair. A couple of their soldiers had been killed during the night. Another opportunist Iraqi had apparently shot the pair with a machine gun. I was told they had also stepped out-side their Warrior, very close to where the man with the RPG had been about to fire at us. Britain's death toll in the battle for Basra had not been high, but the Irish Guards told me, miserably, that they had not suffered casualties like this since fighting in Aden in 1967. It made me feel even luckier to be alive.

The worst part for the surviving Irish Guards was knowing that their loved ones back home would have heard on the news that two men were dead, and would naturally be out of their minds with worry. The soldiers converged around the satellite telephone in our armoured car and begged to use it, so they could put their families out of their misery and tell them they were safe and well. One soldier, an especially big, gruff chap from Belfast who looked every bit the hardened sergeant-major, eventually got through to his wife. She broke down with relief the moment she heard his voice, and when he came off the phone, he in turn burst into tears, holding his head in his hands and staggering away from us. It was as extraordinary a sight as I saw in all my time in Iraq.

BAGHDAD – ENTERING THE CAPITAL

Gavin Hewitt

Gavin Hewitt was a correspondent with the BBC's current affairs pro-gramme Panorama *before joining the* Ten O'Clock News *as a Special Correspondent. He and cameraman Peter Gigliotti were embedded with Barbarian Company, Task Force 130, US 3rd Infantry Division as their column of vehicles pushed in from the west along the main highway into the heart of Baghdad.*

'This is it,' shouted Lieutenant Brandon Kelley as he drove his Bradley fighting vehicle up the ramp and onto the highway with the signs pointing to Baghdad city centre. It was Sunday 6 April. For the men of Barbarian Company the war had already lasted much longer than expected but spirits were high. The sooner Baghdad fell the sooner they got to go home.

Under the first flyover bridge there was a partly destroyed Iraqi T72 tank. A dead Iraqi soldier lay spread-eagled in the road, his leg, still in its boot, 30 metres away. On the other side of the highway were 15 civilian vehicles that had been caught up in the fighting. Some had driven into the central reservation, some were half off the road, others had just stopped, as if frozen in a moment of terror. All had their doors open and beside the cars were the bodies. Groups of young Iraqi men were going from car to car. They had no mercy in mind. These were looters of the dead.

The American soldiers fell silent. They kept their thoughts to themselves but they saw everything. Until now they had been fighting a war from a distance. This was death, up close and unavoidable. The company continued towards the Abu Ghuraib turnoff. Beside the road there were another eight or nine charred Iraqi tanks. Some had their turrets blown off, some were upside down. Other American units had been there before us, but on this day we were to go further into the city.

We were still on the highway when the first artillery round landed. The sound was different. There was a sharper crack to the explosion. The company stopped. 'What the hell was that?' shouted Rick, the 20-year-old Humvee driver from Michigan, but you could see from his face that he knew the answer.

The company edged forward again. Another loud explosion. About a hundred metres to the right, dark smoke rose from where the shell had landed. Throughout the war the Iraqis had hardly used their artillery, but here on the outskirts of the capital they did. Several of the Bradleys opened fire but it was unclear what they were firing at.

Minutes seemed to last for ever. One of the American soldiers said, 'They're bracketing the highway. We gotta get off this damn road.' Another betrayed the fear we were all feeling: 'While we just sit here they are walking these fucking rounds right into us.'

33

All around, the faces were tense. Even tanks, let alone the soft-skinned Humvees behind us, are vulnerable to artillery.

The next explosion was followed by a sound like rain as the metal fragments tore through the palm trees. The American soldiers wanted to know what had happened to their counter-batteries. 'Why the hell aren't we firing back?' shouted the driver of the 88, the tank recovery vehicle.

At last the company turned left off the highway into Baghdad's outer suburbs. There were warehouses, small factories and residential housing, but also canals with high banks and deep trenches. The Iraqis had prepared their defences well. Later the Americans admitted they had missed one whole Republican Guard battalion.

The tanks ahead began firing, and dense, black, oily smoke rose above the houses. All around there was machine-gun fire. It was not clear to what extent the Iraqis were returning fire. Iraqi tanks and personnel carriers were burning. There were frequent explosions, some of them caused by ammunition 'cooking off'.

Beside the road were discarded Iraqi uniforms, thrown away in a last desperate act of survival. Other Iraqi soldiers lay dead, burned beyond recognition. One badly injured man was lying on his back beside the road. We all noticed that he was still breathing. In war the column moves on and we were left with the hope that the medics travelling behind might find him.

Along the dusty track that ran beside one canal were six or seven civilian vehicles. All had bullet holes in them. In one, eggs, unbroken, lay on the back seat but the driver and the woman beside him were dead. Close by we saw a man half-submerged in the canal, his hands raised. Everywhere people were cowering under white flags or trying to reach safety.

Two days later, the company moved closer to downtown Baghdad. Beside a residential neighbourhood they found Iraqi military trucks loaded with ammunition but there were no Iraqi soldiers here. The Americans opened fire on the trucks, setting off a series of loud explosions.

Men with guns were seen in the area and the machine guns on top of the American tanks fired down the alleyways. The company stopped. Lt Brandon Kelley and Capt. Darin Nunn had seen a Scud missile on its launcher but it was on the other side of the canal. Everywhere were boxes of RPGs. No one knew whether the Republican Guard had fled at the last moment or whether this was a deliberate tactic: dumping ammunition in the neighbourhoods to support what the Iraqi regime hoped would be street-by-street resistance.

The tanks rejoined the main highway. There was no other traffic but we saw Iraqi cars darting across a bridge. Then the shooting started. Long bursts of automatic fire. We dropped down inside the tank recovery vehicle and closed the back turret. The shooting seemed to be coming from a rooftop but the Iraqi fighters were invisible. The Americans were tense. One of the M16s jammed. 'Can someone give me a weapon that fucking works?' shouted Sanders, the driver. The Americans poured fire into the surrounding buildings.

We entered what looked like an unfinished housing project. It was in the Shula neighbourhood, close to a large mosque. Thirty to forty trucks were piled high with ammunition. It was everywhere. On the ground. On the floors of houses.

There was a 'whoosh' and an RPG flew just over the tank. The Americans opened fire and four men trying to unload rockets were killed. The mood was tense. Baghdad had become a city of ambushes. While the tanks formed a defensive ring, a blue truck was spotted about a hundred metres away. Men again appeared to be unloading weapons. The Americans opened fire with tracer bullets. They bounced off nearby buildings before hitting the truck, and there were huge explosions as the rockets inside the truck caught fire. That evening everyone was on edge. Captain Nunn said: 'These guys are like the Vietcong. They're coming from everywhere.'

For a brief period this was the city the Americans had always feared fighting in. There did not seem to be any organization behind the Iraqi attacks. That made it all the more frightening. The Americans faced bands of men, out of uniform, who jumped from buildings or vehicles, firing wildly.

The next day Barbarian Company pushed forward again. We were hearing reports from the eastern side of the city that the Iraqi government had fled. A giant statue of Saddam had been pulled down. But on the western side of the city the fighting continued.

That afternoon 30 to 40 RPGs were fired at the company. One hit the captain's tank just below where he was standing. 'We've been hit, we've been hit,' he shouted into the radio. The language changed. These were young men in battle who had to kill or be killed. 'Smoke the motherfuckers,' yelled one commander. 'Light 'em up.' Bullets flew down the narrow streets.

What American soldiers feared in Baghdad was a repeat of Mogadishu, of *Black Hawk Down*, of being trapped in streets they knew little about. Before the day was out the captain believed they had killed 100 Iraqis in this one small engagement.

Shooting continued all night but by the next day the mood on the streets had changed. There were people clapping, holding up their babies. One man ran beside the tank shouting, 'Thank you Mr Bush, thank you Mr Bush. Saddam killed my family.' The tank driver, a 20-year-old from Oklahoma, said, 'This is what we came here for.' They had expected to be treated as liberators but it had been a long time coming.

FIREFIGHT AT THE MOSQUE

David Willis

David Willis spent six years in south-east Asia for the BBC before moving to Los Angeles in 2000. He has worked extensively in both North and South America. He and cameraman Mark Hiney spent the war with US marines from Camp Pendleton, California, becoming one of the first embedded teams to reach Baghdad.

'Get some sleep,' the staff sergeant told us, 'you're gonna need it later.' It was a little after 7 a.m. on 10 April on the fringes of a sprawling Baghdad suburb known as Saddam City, and we'd only just woken up; yet rumours were already swirling through the camp that Alpha Company was 'going in'. I ignored the officer's advice, and spent the morning preparing a report for the *One*

O'Clock News. We'd just finished when an agitated corporal approached, waving his arms like a windmill. 'We're leaving – get in the truck!' Behind him, 'Mad Max', the amphibious assault vehicle we were travelling in, was already wheezing into life. A dozen young infantrymen, many of them gung-ho teenagers, sat crammed inside. This was to be the night of their lives.

A few hours later, darkness was gripping the rubbish-strewn streets as Alpha Company's convoy snaked its way through Saddam City. The marines' mission, it emerged, was to seize a mosque where the man who gave this area its name was himself said to be holed up. The young warriors bristled with pride as the nature of their assignment became known: they'd be working alongside special forces and members of the CIA.

37

Gunfire, occasional and distant, bothered no one as we moved through some of the most run-down suburbs of the Iraqi capital. A Shia area, long neglected by Saddam, it was expected to be well-disposed to the invading forces. Crammed in among the marines, their equipment, food and weapons, I gazed up at the stars and drifted into a fitful sleep.

The convoy trundled on its way. Then, all of a sudden: 'Jesus Christ – what was that?' I was not the only one awoken by the huge explosion. Inside the vehicle none of us could see it, but you could feel the impact in the pit of your stomach. Before anyone could peer out, the shooting started – gunfire so heavy, so constant, it sounded like a heavy rain storm. The stars disappeared from view to be replaced by giant flashes of white. The noise was deafening.

To one side of my head the radio exploded into life. The voice at the other end screamed: 'RPG on the left!' Fear suddenly turned to terror. I'd learned before we set off that, unlike other vehicles in the convoy, ours was not equipped to deal with rocket-propelled grenades: it didn't have sufficient armour plating. A well-aimed missile would blow us to pieces.

From dozing one minute, the men of Alpha Company were all of a sudden fighting for their lives. Eyes glazed, their expressions frozen in a maniacal mix of fear and aggression, they opened fire in all directions. I peered gingerly out the top of the vehicle to see an elderly man emerge from an alleyway, dressed in a light grey suit and clutching a rocket launcher. As he fumbled with the trigger, events seemed to unfold in slow motion. I saw one of the marines open fire on him, then another, but the bullets appeared to bounce off his wiry frame. By the time he'd raised the weapon to his shoulder they were raining down, yet by now the old man was indestructible. Hit a dozen times, he continued running towards us. Finally, as he got to within a few yards of the vehicle, his head was thrown back, he sank to his knees and blood spurted from his grey suit. The old man died with his finger still on the trigger.

By now it seemed we were under fire from all sides and, worst of all, the wretched convoy had stalled. 'We're sitting ducks!' screamed one of the marines, feverishly reloading his rifle, as the radio brought us more bad news: 'RPG to the right!' As if to reinforce the danger, word came through that one of the marines had died after being hit in the face, and several others had been airlifted to hospital. Among the injured was 20-year-old Brendan, the handsome, softly spoken son of a Connecticut lawyer and a Brazilian diplomat, who'd ignored his family's advice not to join the marines – by all accounts an uncharacteristic act of defiance that had cost him a bullet in the spine. Bob, his 18-year-old co-driver, a Mormon from Utah, was suffering from severe shock after a bullet entered the side window of their Humvee and smashed the tea mug he had just raised to his mouth.

The battle raged for most of the night, but it seemed like a lifetime. The mosque, it transpired, contained hundreds of Saddam loyalists, but no Saddam. Everyone inside was clearly perfectly willing to die on his behalf, and most of them did. The Americans took only a dozen prisoners of war.

Dawn was breaking as the convoy finally came to rest amid the manicured lawns of a presidential palace on the banks of the Tigris. The desert sun blinded the marines as they spilled from their trucks and tanks, shocked and exhausted. Triage centres were hastily established to deal with the wounded. Buddies embraced, tears were shed, while others disappeared into the presidential grounds to be alone with their thoughts. Relief hung heavy in the morning air. The haunted expressions on their young faces said it all: the men of Alpha Company had come through their first real battle, and everyone present was simply glad to be alive.

CHAPTER ONE
THE ROAD TO WAR
Fergal Keane

Fergal Keane is a BBC Special Correspondent who has covered many con-
flicts during his postings as Northern Ireland, Southern Africa and Asia
Correspondent. In the run-up to war he reported from across the Middle
East, and later from Baghdad and Saddam's Hussein's birthplace, Tikrit.
This chapter traces the origins of the Iraq crisis.

You heard it first on the BBC. It was one of those very rare interviews given by US presidential frontrunners to the foreign media.
The governor of Texas and Republican candidate for the White
House, George W Bush, sat down with the BBC on 18 November
1999 and delivered a sound bite that started pulses racing
across the Middle East. Questioned by the interviewer about Iraq
and what should happen to its president, Saddam Hussein, the
governor replied: 'No one had envisioned Saddam, at least that
point in history, no one envisioned him still standing – it's time to
finish the task.'

But with so much else on the agenda – questions over the US
economy and proposals for tax cuts; the crisis in the Palestinian
territories – the Bush statement didn't dominate the headlines at
home. Several months later George W Bush returned to the
theme of Saddam, this time in his debut presidential debate with
the Democratic contender, Al Gore. The debate moderator asked
how Bush would deal with Saddam's flouting of United Nations
resolutions on weapons of mass destruction.

One observer would later describe Bush as 'belligerent' in his
response. There would be no easing of sanctions, no negotiations,

and the Iraqi opposition would be given all possible assistance. (The assorted opposition groups were fractious and mutually loathing, and had been widely mistrusted by the State Department for years.) And then came one of those rhetorical slips that, in retrospect at least, are very revealing: 'If I found in any way, shape or form that he was developing weapons of mass destruction, I'd take him out – I'm surprised he's still there. I think a lot of other people are as well,' said Bush.

The moderator, American television anchor Brit Hume, was quick to pick up on what seemed like an extraordinary declaration. 'Take him out?' he asked. Was the governor advocating the assassination of a foreign leader, something forbidden under US law? The candidate changed tack immediately. 'Take out the weapons of mass destruction,' he said.

Not for the last time would the line between ridding Iraq of weapons of mass destruction and overthrowing Saddam become blurred, often very deliberately. But there was no mistaking the underlying view of George W Bush and that of many of his senior advisers: the Iraqi leader would not survive to threaten US interests in the Middle East and to taunt another member of the Bush family.

That is not to say that war against Iraq was inevitable with the accession of Bush to the US presidency and the rise of hawkish figures like Defense Secretary Donald Rumsfeld, his deputy Paul Wolfowitz and Vice President Dick Cheney. There may have been a theoretical determination to solve the Iraq issue once and for all, but it was to be the events of September 11 that changed utterly the context in which American foreign policy was conducted and that made a pre-emptive war possible.

* * * * * *

Iraq is often described as the 'cradle of civilization'. The land between the Tigris and Euphrates rivers, known as Mesopotamia, has a recorded history going back over five thousand years. The magnificent civilization of Babylon flourished in the 5th century BC and the Hanging Gardens became a wonder of the ancient world. Arab invaders of the 6th century AD brought with them the most enduring legacy of all: the Islamic faith. And it was in Iraq that the great schism in that faith would erupt into bloody battle. The followers of the Prophet Mohammed's grandson, Hussein, insisted that the faithful should only be led by direct descendants of the Prophet, a stand that directly challenged the rule of the powerful Caliphate and led to the split between orthodox Sunni Islam and the Shia, represented by Hussein. When the Caliphate moved against him, Hussein had only a few hundred warriors to do battle against thousands. On the plains outside Karbala, in what is now central Iraq, Hussein and his followers were defeated and killed. Out of this loss was born the Shia branch of Islam, which in time would become the faith of the majority of Iraq's people and the most potent threat to future rulers, most notably Saddam Hussein.

The seeds of confrontation between the West and Iraq were arguably sown as long ago as 1919 and the Treaty of Versailles; lines drawn on maps of the former Ottoman empire, which had ruled much of the region since the 16th century, stored up no end of trouble for future generations in the Middle East and the Balkans. In the case of Iraq, these lines failed to recognize tribal realities and the aspirations of a nascent Arab nationalist movement. The consequences for the Arabs, Kurds and Turkomans of Mesopotamia would prove disastrous. British colonial rule was by its very nature undemocratic. It would be replaced by a succession of governments, each less committed to democracy and human rights than the one that preceded it, culminating in the Saddam regime. Among the most devastating legacies of the Turkish, and later British, colonial era was the growth and consolidation of a political order that ruled by fear.

At the time of negotiations on the region's future at the end of the First World War, the veteran British traveller and envoy Gertrude Bell wrote home, with extraordinary prescience: 'O my dear they are making such a horrible muddle of the Near East, I confidently anticipate that it will be much worse than before the war ... It's like a nightmare in which you foresee all the horrible things which are going to happen and can't stretch out your hand to prevent them.'

* * * * * *

How far must we go back, then, to find the first footprints on the road to the battle for Iraq? It began, as has so often been the case in history, with the end of a previous war. Most of us will remember the triumphant imagery of allied armour racing across the desert and routing the Iraqis back in 1991. Troops from America, Britain and France, among others, formed an unprecedented coalition to liberate Kuwait. Saddam Hussein looked as if he might well be facing his last days. Yet President George Bush – 'Bush the father' as he is known across the Middle East – demurred from a final strike. Strongly advised by his cautious military chief General Colin Powell, Bush decided that an attack on Baghdad would lead to the breakup of Iraq and wreck the coalition of nations so painstakingly held together during the war. Saddam was out of Kuwait. The declared mission was accomplished.

Instead, the US encouraged Iraqis to overthrow Saddam themselves. So the Kurds and the Shia rose up, but American forces failed to intervene while they were slaughtered. The Iraqi leader stayed in power and his people learned two hard lessons: don't think of rising up again and don't trust anyone who tells you to. Saddam may also have come to the conclusion that the Western powers ultimately preferred a brutal strongman in Iraq to the possibility of a disintegrating state and the rise of Islamist parties.

We recall the tragic humanitarian consequences of the Kurd and Shia uprisings. But much less is remembered of the war's messy political aftermath, and the detail of the negotiations that allowed Saddam to remain in power but that sought to cripple for ever his ability to threaten the peace of the region. He was offered what seemed a straightforward choice: co-operate with UN weapons inspectors and surrender his weapons of mass destruction, or live in perpetuity under punitive economic sanctions. He chose the latter. Well, only up to a point. Thanks to sanctions-busting, Saddam and his elite managed rather well. While they were unable to rebuild Iraq's military machine, they continued to build grand palaces; senior Baath Party officials lived lives of conspicuous luxury and vast sums of money were hidden away. Thus, at its core, the regime did not suffer. Nor did it give the full and unconditional co-operation demanded under the armistice agreement. Within a year of the war's end, Baath Party cadres were threatening and obstructing weapons inspectors in Iraq.

But there was no Gulf War electoral benefit for President

Bush, who lost the next election. A new American president, William Jefferson Clinton, moved into the White House and the US moved on to other foreign policy preoccupations. Ignoring the suffering of his people, Saddam could be forgiven for thinking he had won. He had, after all, survived in power.

Under President Clinton, American foreign policy was focused heavily on the Middle East and Northern Ireland peace processes, on improving relations with Russia and engaging the emerging superpower China. There were other factors at work, too. What started as a humanitarian mission in Somalia ended up as a shooting match on the streets of Mogadishu. The American public recoiled in horror at images of dead American soldiers being dragged through the streets by a cheering mob. President Clinton pulled his forces out of Somalia in March 1994 and America retreated from international military interventions.

Iraq and Saddam continued to slide down the international agenda, and containment became the official doctrine subscribed to by both Washington and London. As one former diplomat put it to me: 'The idea was to make sure he didn't threaten to attack any of his neighbours again, but it ended up being a case of out of sight out of mind. Once he was boxed in, there was no real determination to make sure we located every single item of his weapons.'

Saddam Hussein was quick to detect the new mood, and played a protracted game of cat and mouse with UN inspectors. Promises were made and broken, ultimatums delivered and promises made again. These were mini-crises. But in 1998 a major crisis erupted when the head of UNSCOM – the UN inspection mission – decided that his teams needed to inspect Iraqi presidential palaces. Richard Butler added the palaces to the list of sites to be inspected in the certain knowledge that Saddam Hussein would refuse to accede. When he did refuse, the United States threatened military action.

By August of that year, Saddam had torn up the agreement with the inspectors and banned them from making further searches. America threatened force again and Saddam backed down. But by December he was obstructing the process once more. When UN inspectors were banned from searching the headquarters of the Baath Party in Baghdad, the US threatened force yet again. This time the threats were backed up with air strikes in what was called Operation Desert Fox. The UN inspections were never resumed and a low-level air campaign directed against Iraqi air defences rumbled on into the new millennium. Saddam Hussein remained in power, and the Clinton administration bequeathed a troubling legacy to the man whose father had attacked Saddam a decade before, George W Bush.

Anybody searching for markers as to how the new administration might deal with Saddam Hussein could have looked back to that crucial year 1998 and Operation Desert Fox. An influential group of conservative strategists – nicknamed the 'Vulcans' – wrote an open letter to the Clinton administration advocating regime change in Baghdad. In all, 40 people signed the letter but key among them were Donald Rumsfeld, Paul Wolfowitz and Condoleezza Rice. All three would later occupy pivotal posts in the Bush administration in the run-up to war on Iraq. The letter advocated extensive air strikes, the deployment of US ground forces to the region and the setting up of an Iraqi government in exile.

Like the presidential candidate, this cabal of close advisers believed Saddam represented – in the oft-used phrase of the time – 'a long-term threat to US interests'. As for George W Bush himself, it's difficult to say with certainty when he became intent on overthrowing Saddam, but a study of one of his pre-election interviews makes for very interesting reading. He was speaking to Jim Lehrer on PBS's *McNeil–Lehrer Newshour* programme in February 2000. Asked whether there was a realistic way to deal with weapons of mass destruction when 'you have an evil person in charge', Bush replied: 'Well, I think the most realistic way is to keep them isolated in the world of public opinion and to work with our alliances to keep them isolated. I'm just as frustrated as many Americans are that Saddam Hussein still lives. I think we ought to keep the pressure on him. I will tell you this: if we catch him developing weapons of mass destruction in any way, shape or form, I'll deal with that in a way he won't like.'

The interview can be assessed in a number of ways. I think that Bush was, for the time being, willing to work within the established parameters, i.e. he was willing to continue with the containment of Iraq. The removal of Saddam Hussein was a foreign policy objective, but Bush was shrewd enough to know that winning popular public support for such a campaign would prove difficult. Explaining to families in Idaho and Missouri and New Mexico why their sons and daughters should risk their lives in the Middle East was not a prospect he relished.

Once in office, would Bush move against Iraq? Quite possibly, although he might have postponed a military campaign to a second presidential term and tried to launch it with broader international support. But the dramatic events of September 11, 2001 would change the agenda for ever. The attacks by al-Qaida traumatized the nation and made ordinary Americans acutely sensitive to any threat to national security.

45

The night of September 11, I happened to be in Bogota, Colombia in the company of some American businessmen. We watched the world change live on television. As we sat in horrified awe there was little conversation. One of the men at the bar had tears streaming down his face. Then a tall, powerfully built man walked in and ordered a beer. 'You see that,' he growled. I turned away from the television. 'No, keep on looking buddy. 'Cos that's the result of playing nice guy with these bastards for too long.' He was working in Colombia on the war against drugs, the initiative begun under Bush Senior and now being carried on by his son. 'We are gonna be fighting them for years and we won't stop,' the big man said. 'We won't stop until we beat them all.'

I made frequent visits to New York in the months after September 11. In the early days the city was obviously still in shock. It was so unlike New York, so unlike America, to be this frightened. Had it happened in London I don't doubt we'd all have been just as scared. But London had a history of being attacked. Although nothing on this scale had happened since the Blitz, 30 years of IRA violence had made British society acutely sensitive to the possibility of violent attack. For the Americans, the horror that erupted from a clear blue sky really did seem to come from nowhere. Gone was the Manhattan of brash, outspoken, questing humanity – for a while at least. In its place was a city of great absences, its heart in smouldering ruins, a gash in the skyline.

In the immediate aftermath of September 11 the public tone of the US administration on Iraq was cautious. The Vice President,

Dick Cheney, when asked on television if Saddam Hussein had anything to do with the attacks, replied with a very precise 'no'. But behind the scenes things were rather different. A new, bold and aggressive policy was being conceived. The agenda of the possible had been transformed; it would simply be a question of timing. It had taken the events of September 11 to elevate the wishful thinking of the conservative strategists of the opposition years – the 'Vulcans' – into the governing philosophy of American foreign policy.

America was shocked but energized as well. The humiliations of Mogadishu and the cautious diplomacy of the Clinton era had been buried. Ordinary Americans were now willing to support action against Saddam that they had shied away from several years earlier. They were frightened and they believed, with strong encouragement from the White House, that the Iraqi leader was synonymous with international terrorism, that his weapons of mass destruction would one day find their way into the hands of a group like al-Qaida. The possibility of serious links with al-Qaida would later be described as unproven by senior British intelligence sources, and a good many people in the CIA also regarded the case as less than watertight. But the Bush administration and some in Downing Street were very keen to lump Saddam and America's archenemy Osama bin Laden together. Saddam may not have helped al-Qaida this time, they argued, but some day he might.

By June 2002 President Bush had won a successful military campaign in Afghanistan. The victory had been achieved with minimal casualties among the Americans and their allies. The hand of those who advocated a muscular projection of US power had been immeasurably strengthened. Looking into the future, Condoleezza Rice and others warned of the possibility that poison gas, perhaps even nuclear weaponry, would find its way into the hands of those who hated America. The future threat, they declared, came from the intersection of technology and fundamentalism. Speaking to graduating army officers at West Point on 1 June 2002, President Bush declared: 'If we wait for threats to fully materialize we will have waited too long.' The march along the road to war with Iraq was accelerating.

* * * * * *

All of this was watched from Baghdad with increasing concern. Saddam Hussein, too, realized that it was only a matter of time before Washington turned its attention to an old enemy. With the Taliban gone and al-Qaida on the run, America celebrated victory. Across the Arab world, governments and people were getting nervous. I visited Lebanon around that time. One night over dinner in the Achrafieh district of Beirut, close to where Muslims and Christians once fought across the Green Line dividing the city, I was asked by an Arab friend why America was now talking about attacking Iraq. He was a pragmatist with a very outward-looking view of life and a list of business contacts that stretched from Beirut to Cleveland, Ohio.

'So Saddam is a bastard,' my friend said. I replied that it would be hard on the basis of factual evidence to disagree. 'So he is a bastard and we've known all along he was a bastard.' Certainly his perfidy had been a matter of public record for a considerable period of time, I agreed. 'So why now? Why attack him now? Don't they need people like me as friends here? The USA and the Brits attack Iraq: the people suffer.'

A long discussion followed. Why, I asked, were Arabs willing to put up with Saddam butchering and torturing his people and then complaining when the Americans promised to end the terror? The talking led us back, as it always does in the Middle East, to America's support for Israel. The restaurant where we were eating was situated in a city that had been invaded by Israel 20 years before, a city where Ariel Sharon's air force had inflicted horrific civilian casualties and where he himself had allowed the Phalangist militia to enter the refugee camps of Sabra and Shatila, with horrific consequences. Now the same man was prime minister of Israel, my friend said, and the White House regarded him as an ally.

'Do they think we forget everything that has happened here in this region, that we will turn around and clap them on the back for invading another Arab country the way the Israelis invaded us in 1982?' he said. All of this was spoken in a quiet voice, tinged with exasperation. I asked him what would happen if there was a war. Did he think the Arab world would explode in anger?

'No it won't. There will be protests of course, but the only thing that will cause an explosion is if some lunatic blows up the

47

Muslim holy sites in Palestine. Nothing else will unleash a mass revolt. The secret policemen will make sure none of the despots in this region are threatened. That's not the danger here. The danger is the people you don't see protesting, the guys at home planning terror in their little flats in Cairo and here in Beirut, right across the region, the kind of ones who gave you September 11. They scare me and they should scare America.'

Of course they did scare America. But in those months after September 11 the prescription for dealing with the terrorist threats would include the possibility, as Dick Cheney had warned, of a war that might last longer than a lifetime. The assumption then, as now, is that Arabs would protest but ultimately put up with the war. In the fervid atmosphere of the times the longer-term dangers of having such a sanguine attitude to Arab feelings were generally ignored. I met a British journalist of long acquaintance in a hotel lobby in Amman before the war. 'Oh don't worry about the Arabs,' he said dismissively, 'just feed them and give them money. They're quite servile at the heart of it all.' This was a crude, foolish, racist – and not untypical – characterization.

The neo-conservatives in Washington would not have put it like that. Rather, they spoke of an Arab world that would suffer a cathartic but necessary trauma when Iraq was invaded. A dictator would be overthrown and democracy installed, other dictatorships would collapse and the Middle East could look forward to a bright future. As my Beirut conversation – one of many – showed, this was not how the Arabs saw it. Opinion was more complex than many Westerners understood. Those Arabs I met in Cairo, Amman and Beirut were well capable of understanding that Saddam was a monster, and many also understood that, while the security of America's oil supply was a factor, it was not the issue that gave the pro-war party in Washington a consistent lead in opinion polls. My Beirut friend knew that fear was behind it, but that didn't make him any more likely to accept what America was planning.

* * * * * *

As the case for war was developed, America's strongest ally, the British Prime Minister Tony Blair, made clear his support for the central US demand: Saddam Hussein should give up his weapons

THE ROAD TO WAR

of mass destruction completely or face the threat of military action. He could disarm voluntarily or be disarmed by force. Certainly in Washington, there were few in the White House inner circle who believed Saddam would co-operate. As the presidential spokesman Ari Fleischer put it: 'That is the mother of all hypotheticals.' The idea that the crisis would come to an end with Saddam Hussein still in power, was a non-starter.

At various points, administration figures – even the President himself – wriggled around this issue, declaring that the dismantling of weapons of mass destruction could in itself constitute regime change. But remember the words of George W Bush at the beginning of this chapter: 'It's time to finish the task'. Remember, too, that slip of the tongue about taking out Saddam? Barring a coup d'état within Iraq, Saddam would be attacked and driven from power. Regime change was always the goal. But for political reasons – not least in the Arab world – it was a subject about which Washington and London were both, to different degrees, rather coy until the very final days before the war began. There would follow a long struggle at the United Nations and, for Tony Blair, a battle with public and party opinion at home. But as 2003 dawned, a military build-up was well underway in the Gulf.

It is difficult to know whether Saddam Hussein truly understood the changed nature of the post-September 11 world. If he had, would he have miscalculated so hugely in his dealings with Washington, failing once again to provide the 'immediate and unconditional co-operation' demanded by the United Nations? Those words mattered a great deal if you were determined not to give Washington an excuse for war. What would have happened had Saddam Hussein simply told the unvarnished truth, and delivered up the weapons or materials for which he had previously failed to account? It is one of the great imponderables. Is it at all possible that the march to war and the overthrow of Saddam would have been halted? In the face of full compliance from Saddam, could Washington and London have gone to war anyway? The judgement of the White House might well have been negative, whatever contortions Baghdad performed. The Bush administration was greatly assisted in this by the track record of lies and broken promises that littered the previous decade. Put simply, the administration would probably have said: 'He might be complying in full now but that's no guarantee for the future.' And American public opinion would have been much quicker to accept the verdict of the White House than any words from the chief UN weapons inspector, Dr Hans Blix, or the UN Security Council.

As it was, Saddam Hussein reverted to type. He obfuscated and delayed, and so strengthened the hand of those planning for a war to remove him. Past experience with the UN and the Clinton administration had taught Saddam that threats did not necessarily lead to action. The international opposition to the war almost certainly helped to strengthen his resolve to make only grudging concessions.

I remember an exchange with the Iraqi Ambassador in London several weeks before the war began. We met in the decrepit offices where he sat with a secretary, processing journalists' visas and sending off newspaper cuttings to his masters in Baghdad. Halfway through our conversation – I, too, was after a visa – he was interrupted by a phone call from Baghdad. It was a day or so after the huge London anti-war march in which more than a million people had taken to the streets. The Ambassador was ebullient as he spoke to Baghdad. For my benefit, I suspect, he spoke in English:

'It was truly amazing. I had tears in my eyes. Look you should see the newspapers here this morning. Every page, every page full of photographs.' I could hear laughter from the other end of the telephone line. The conversation finished and the Ambassador turned his attention back to me.

'Do you really think they will go to war now with all this opposition, with the Security Council so divided. Will they attack even if they don't get a second UN resolution?' he asked.

'I am convinced of it,' I told him.

'But suppose they go to Iraq and their soldiers' bodies are coming home in coffins?'

'They will fight and continue to fight until they win,' I replied. 'They will get rid of Saddam Hussein. America has changed. It's not like under Clinton. The country has changed. The American people are afraid after September 11 and they will support this war. Do you really think George W Bush will go into the next election with your president still in power in Baghdad taunting him the way he taunted Bush Senior?'

The Ambassador sat back in his chair and shrugged. Then he asked me the most surprising question. 'So who will take over when Saddam Hussein is driven from power?' It wasn't 'if' Saddam Hussein was driven from power. For all the hopeful talk down the line to Baghdad, he seemed as sure as I was that war was imminent.

In the weeks and days that followed, the military build-up in the Gulf revealed its own truth. In America, *The Washington Post* and *The New York Times* were publishing different versions of General Tommy Franks' war plan, leaked to them by planners in the Pentagon. As the diplomatic battle at the UN intensified, the British Foreign Secretary, Jack Straw, was still maintaining that the chances of war were 60/40 against. I spoke to a lot of diplomats and analysts about that, and not one agreed with him. In Baghdad, Saddam was defiant and threatening to destroy the American invaders. Nobody believed that either. War was coming.

51

CHAPTER TWO

SHOWDOWN AT THE UN

Bridget Kendall

52   *Bridget Kendall is one of the BBC's Diplomatic Correspondents. She was previously Washington Correspondent for four years and before that reported from Moscow. In early 2003, Bridget was in New York covering the negotiations at the UN over Iraq. Here, she considers the attempts, and failure, to resolve the crisis through diplomacy.*

The rows of elderly veterans, bedecked in uniforms and medals, listened patiently as the hot sun beat down on them. On the morning of 26 August 2002, Nashville, Tennessee – better known as the epicentre of American country and western music – was hosting the 103rd National Convention of American War Veterans. And this was the carefully chosen backdrop for a rare public speech by the reclusive American Vice President, Dick Cheney. But Mr Cheney's message was for a far wider audience.

'There is no doubt that Saddam Hussein now has weapons of mass destruction,' he warned. 'He is amassing them to use against our friends – against us.' Efforts to contain him through United Nations inspections, he said, had not worked and it was downright dangerous to suggest that Saddam was somehow 'back in his box'. 'We must take the battle to the enemy,' he insisted. 'The risks of inaction are far greater than the risk of action.' And if there was regime change in Iraq, he predicted that the streets of Basra and Baghdad were 'sure to erupt in joy'.

The speech was a deliberate call to arms. For months the United States had been mulling over whether and how to take on Saddam Hussein. President George W Bush had already endorsed a policy of regime change. He had labelled Iraq one of the three countries in his 'axis of evil', along with Iran and North Korea. In June he outlined a doctrine of pre-emptive military action as the only way to keep the US safe. Dick Cheney had even toured Middle Eastern capitals earlier in the year in a vain quest to sign up Arab leaders.

But throughout the holiday month of August the hotly contested debate on talk shows and in newspapers had centred on the key question that divided hawks and doves in the US administration: should the United States be prepared to go to war against Iraq alone if necessary? A stream of weighty elder statesmen, many of them senior Republicans who had served under George W Bush's father, advised against acting without the support of key allies. Opinion polls suggested most Americans shared that unease.

By the end of August, the chief hawks in the Bush administration were determined to make their case in public. They argued that in a world where terrorists and rogue regimes could strike without warning, America should turn its back on the cumbersome United Nations.

But the final decision belonged to the President. At the start of September, he returned to Washington from his Texas ranch. Immediately he was plunged into a running battle between opposing members of his National Security Council. The hawks continued to warn against getting embroiled in the 'soup' of the United Nations. But the chief dove, Secretary of State Colin Powell, argued the opposite. Consensus building was important, he said, and the President could not just criticize the UN for failing to uphold resolutions that Saddam Hussein had defiantly flouted for 12 years. In the speech the President was due to give to the annual UN General Assembly in New York, he should tell the United Nations it would become irrelevant if it failed to act, but give it a last chance to do so.

That was reinforced by Washington's most important ally, the British Prime Minister Tony Blair. He flew to the US the weekend before the speech to tell the President that the only way to bring the United Nations on board and avoid a damaging rift with allies in Europe was to call for a new resolution.

53

George W Bush was hard to read. Even on the eve of the speech, it was still not clear which way he would go. 'Powell may tell us it's okay, but you never know,' I was told by one senior British official. 'If a new "Rummygram" gets sent to the President, it could change everything.' (Rummygrams were the memos that the Defense Secretary Donald Rumsfeld was prone to fire off, designed to further the aims of the hawks in the administration.)

On 12 September 2002, President Bush stood up in the General Assembly hall and uttered the fateful words, 'We will work with the UN Security Council for the necessary resolutions.' In London nervous British diplomats watching the event live on television heaved a sigh of relief. In fact it was a closer call than many realized. Mr Bush only decided to insert the line at the last minute. But the change was never made to his autocue. When he came to that part of the speech at the podium, the sentence was missing. Luckily, he had the presence of mind to ad-lib the crucial phrase which was to form the basis of six months of diplomatic wrangling.

* * * * * *

President Bush's UN speech may have kept American unilateralist tendencies at bay. But now came the hard part: drafting a resolution tough enough to worry Saddam Hussein, but not so draconian that the UN Security Council would refuse to vote for it. The idea was to get inspectors back into Iraq to search for forbidden weapons, while warning Saddam Hussein that if he deceived or failed to co-operate, he would face serious consequences.

The question was how the 15 votes on the Security Council might line up. Of particular concern were the three other permanent members, besides the US and Britain, who could block any decision by wielding a veto. 'Saddam Hussein hasn't got many fans,' mused one source in the Foreign Office. 'The Chinese won't block a new resolution; the worst they'll do is abstain. The Russians are worried about their economic interests, so probably they can be bought off. And we've got to reassure the French this first resolution won't include an "or else" clause.' The British had another consideration: 'The Americans have laid down a challenge to the UN, so we can't let debate drag on too long. Otherwise they'll pull the plug.'

President Jacques Chirac got in early with the French position. On 9 September, ahead of George Bush's speech, he called for two resolutions: one to send weapons inspectors back into Iraq with a tough new mandate, and a second to endorse military action if that proved necessary. From the outset the French were adamant that there should be no 'automaticity' as they termed it: no automatic trigger that would allow the US to go to war without first coming back to the Security Council for approval.

At this point it was not France but Germany that led the anti-war camp in Europe. Chancellor Gerhard Schröder had embraced a decidedly anti-war stand to secure a narrow re-election victory in September – a move that left him in considerable disfavour in Washington. The French president had left himself a foot in both camps. By not ruling out war as a last resort, he seemed at this stage the better politician.

Russia's position was harder to pin down. One senior Moscow official suggested no new resolution at all was needed. Another proposed sending in inspectors and at the same time gradually lifting sanctions. Russian businessmen in London were confident their president would come on board. 'Iraq owes us billions of dollars, our economic links are too important. Putin will see sense,' one of them told me. But the official Moscow line was that only a peaceful solution to the Iraq crisis, sanctioned by the United Nations, was acceptable. 'We're not in the business of bargaining. This isn't an oriental bazaar,' said President Putin coldly when Tony Blair went to see him in Moscow.

Mr Blair was taking the lead in trying to convince his own sceptical public and the world at large that Saddam Hussein was a menace who threatened regional and global security. He argued that Britain was right to back George W Bush, both to act as a bridge to keep the US and Europe united, and to remind the American president of other sensibilities, such as the Arab view that it was not just Iraq but also the Israeli–Palestinian crisis that needed attention. He insisted that war was not inevitable.

But in Washington the Pentagon was briefing that the troop build-up in the Gulf was being accelerated. And ahead of a vote in Congress to authorize military action, President Bush insisted the American goal was nothing less than ousting the Iraqi government.

55

Meanwhile, as diplomats at the United Nations began the delicate task of negotiations, Saddam Hussein tried to throw the process into confusion. After months of opposing inspections, he suddenly declared that he had changed his mind and UN inspectors could come back to Iraq after all. If his aim was to try to divide the Security Council, it backfired. Now Saddam Hussein was welcoming inspectors back in, why oppose a new UN resolution? The momentum at the Security Council was building.

On 8 November 2002, after weeks of intense diplomacy, the 15 members of the Council gathered for the vote. Resolution 1441 called for tough inspections, driven by a tight timetable and requiring complete Iraqi co-operation. It included the threat that Iraq would face serious consequences if it failed to comply, but only after there had been further Security Council consultations. All 15 ambassadors voted yes, a far better result than American and British diplomats had dared hope for. Even Syria, the Arab representative, who many had assumed would vote no, voted in favour. 'It wasn't just a good result, it was astonishing,' said one diplomat in delighted disbelief.

Why did this first resolution succeed when the second resolution in the months to come was to fail so dismally?

For a start, the diplomats were given time to reach a consensus. Although the original ambition had been to draft, table and vote on the resolution within two weeks, the process took nearly eight. Even the hawks in the Pentagon were prepared to tolerate this: stocks of cruise missiles were still being built up, large numbers of troops were still to be deployed. At this stage, protracted debate at the UN did not upset their timetable.

Secondly, all sides were prepared to be flexible about the wording. The original American draft called for such invasive inspections that some complained it sounded like a cover for military intervention. The US administration agreed to dilute the text. Their private belief was that inspections were bound to lead to war in any case.

In fact there was only the appearance of unity. The resolution was a fudge between two unreconciled positions. France, Russia and others believed they had secured a pledge that a new Security Council vote would be needed before going to war. The

Americans claimed they were only bound to consult the Council, not to seek its permission. The British, aware of the ambiguity, carefully left room to jump ship. The official line in London was that, if it came to war, a second resolution would be preferable but not essential.

But at the United Nations the mood was euphoric. No one was anticipating that they had sown the seeds of subsequent diplomatic disaster. 'We sat on our laurels longer than we should have,' said Britain's Ambassador to the UN, Sir Jeremy Greenstock. 'With hindsight, we should have started negotiating straight after the first resolution in November. Instead we sat back and thought how clever we'd been.'

57

* * * * * *

UN inspectors went back to work in Iraq on 27 November 2002. The head of chemical and biological inspections, Dr Hans Blix, was optimistic that he had the backing of the Americans. 'They did not seem to me to be impatient,' he said of a meeting at the White House in October.

Not yet, maybe. But in fact the Americans were quietly waiting for Saddam Hussein to trip up. They believed that before long a 'smoking gun' would emerge – some clear proof that he was hiding banned weapons; his regime would be caught blatantly and repeatedly obstructing inspectors; or Iraqi scientists, interviewed privately, would reveal hidden warfare programmes, just as Saddam Hussein's son-in-law had done when he defected in the mid-1990s.

But, as days turned into weeks, those expectations were frustrated. The Iraqis made a show of being accommodating, opening up previously out-of-bounds presidential palaces. A few dramatic discoveries – a stack of research documents found at the home of an Iraqi scientist and 11 empty chemical warheads – in the end yielded little. Iraqi scientists seemed reluctant to be questioned in private and, when they were, they all denied knowledge of forbidden weapons programmes. In the view of US and British officials this in itself was incriminating. 'The Iraqis were much better at concealment than we thought they were going to be,' said Sir Jeremy Greenstock. But others, more sceptical of the claim that Iraq was an immediate threat, began to wonder if it meant there were no banned weapons sites to discover.

In American eyes, the most damning event came in December, when Iraq delivered to the United Nations the suitcases of files and computer discs that it claimed contained a full and final declaration of its weapons programmes. Dr Blix ruled it incomplete because it did not deal with all unaccounted-for stocks. He also complained that a list of scientists he had asked for was not comprehensive. The Security Council warned Saddam Hussein that complying passively with the UN's demands was not enough: he needed to show 'pro-active co-operation' to convince them he had nothing to hide. Everyone on the Council wanted to keep Saddam under pressure. But the Americans went further. They formally announced that Iraq was now 'in material breach' of Resolution 1441. Before long the British government was echoing their position.

But that was not the view of the Security Council as a whole. They wanted to hear first from Dr Blix and his counterpart on nuclear weapons, Dr Mohamed El Baradei. Resolution 1441 required them to update the Council at the end of January. Dr Blix said later he thought he had given a balanced picture that suggested much work remained to be done and more Iraqi co-operation was needed to put to rest still-worrying questions. But the American and British governments took heart from his critical tone. 'Hans Blix is our secret weapon,' one British official told journalists afterwards, with what turned out to be misplaced confidence.

* * * * * *

By the start of 2003, strains inside the Security Council were beginning to show, under pressure from several different developments. In the first place, two sceptical countries were scheduled to chair the Council over the next two months – a largely symbolic but still commanding position. France held the chair in January, and in February (because these things are decided alphabetically) it was Germany, which had just been rotated onto the Council for a two-year spell.

Secondly, the next step had to be decided. It was not clear

from Resolution 1441 what should happen after Dr Blix's report at the end of January. Should inspections continue? Or should the Council resolve, as the Bush administration wanted, that the time had come to disarm Iraq by force?

Thirdly, it was becoming clear that a massive build-up of US troops and armour was underway in the Gulf, supplemented by British forces. New announcements from the Pentagon seemed to come almost weekly. Yet the argument that this was a useful way to keep up the pressure on Saddam Hussein – 'the threat of force to back up diplomacy' – rang hollow. However much the British government reassured its own public and European partners that, if Iraq complied, military action could be avoided, the deployments suggested otherwise. And what appeared to be mischievous leaks from Pentagon sources about secret White House meetings on how to run post-war Iraq, made some Security Council members even more suspicious.

On 20 January, simmering tensions erupted into a full-blown row. France, using its prerogative as Chair, called Security Council foreign ministers to a face-to-face meeting in New York. It was ostensibly to discuss terrorism. But the French Foreign Minister, Dominique de Villepin, backed up by his German colleague, Joschka Fischer, confronted Colin Powell about US military intentions. According to American diplomats, Mr Powell was furious.

'Let's put it this way,' said one diplomat, 'The US Secretary of State did not take kindly to being summoned at short notice to New York, forced to break his plans for an important African–American holiday (Martin Luther King Day) in order to be lectured to by the French Foreign Minister.'

To make matters worse, Mr de Villepin then declared to waiting reporters that 'today nothing justifies envisaging military action'. When asked if France would use its veto, he added ominously: 'We will go all the way to the end.'

This 'diplomatic ambush', as one American paper called it, marked an important turning point. 'That meeting changed everything for us,' one French diplomat told me later. 'We realized that the Americans were going to go to war no matter what. They were not listening to us. And it was our moral duty to try and prevent it.' It also changed everything for a highly aggrieved Colin

59

Powell. Up until now he had gone out of his way to argue the European case in Washington. But what was the point of pleading for more time for diplomacy, if the French were ruling out the military option? It meant the UN Security Council could no longer send a single 'strong, powerful message to Saddam Hussein'. As for the British, it was the moment when the French revealed their 'perfidy', as one official put it, by assuming leadership of the anti-war camp. 'It turned out they had been stringing us along all the time,' he told me bitterly. On all sides, trust had broken down.

When the next day President Chirac and Chancellor Schröder presided over a joint session of their two parliaments at Versailles, to celebrate the 40th anniversary of the Franco–German Treaty, the show of unity seemed more than symbolic. From across the Channel, diplomats in London saw a powerful anti-war axis emerging. It could not have been worse. The confrontation was supposed to be with Saddam Hussein. Now it had erupted into a bitter rift that divided not only the Security Council, but the European Union as well.

Desperately trying to stem the tide of anti-war fever, Britain and the US launched a frantic public relations campaign. The centrepiece was on 5 February: a presentation by Colin Powell at the United Nations, to be transmitted live around the globe. It was trailed as the definitive exposé of Iraqi non-compliance, based on classified US intelligence and intercepts. Mr Powell gave his usual polished performance. But it failed to turn the tide of scepticism.

* * * * * *

Worse was to come. What had, until now, been a row inside the UN Security Council suddenly expanded into something far more damaging: a full-blown diplomatic crisis that threatened the entire edifice of transatlantic relations. An apparently routine request for NATO to guarantee military protection for Turkey, should an invasion of Iraq create regional instability, was rejected by France, Germany and Belgium. They argued that to do so now would amount to the endorsement of a war they hoped to avoid if possible. The Bush administration was incensed. And the Washington hawks felt they had been proved right: trying to work through multinational institutions just tied America's hands.

By the time foreign ministers returned to the Security Council on 14 February for a new report from Dr Blix, the stage was set for a showdown. Russia's president, Vladimir Putin, had by now joined the French and German anti-war camp, adding his name to a declaration that insisted inspections should continue.

The US and British were braced for bad news, but it was worse than they feared. This time Dr Blix's report failed to strike the critical note they were hoping for. If anything, he was upbeat. He said Iraq's behaviour had improved, though questions still remained unanswered. Without directly asking for more inspection time, he implied that that was what he wanted. But the real bombshell was his blunt criticism of Colin Powell's presentation of 5 February. He claimed some of the intelligence assumptions were dubious and in one case clearly based on forged documents. His colleague, Dr El Baradei, was even more pointed. 'We have to date found no evidence of nuclear activity in Iraq,' he said, and added that given a few more months he could wrap up his investigation.

Looking slightly shaken, Colin Powell abandoned his notes and made an impassioned, impromptu speech defending American policy. But the mood of the Council was against him. He was met with stony silence. In contrast, the French Foreign Minister's equally heartfelt diatribe against war drew a rare smattering of applause. Diplomats are not supposed to clap in the hallowed chamber of the Security Council. It made the snub even more poignant. Mr Powell's only consolation was a hand-scribbled note slipped to him by the British Foreign Secretary, Jack Straw. 'You made a good speech,' it said. Intended as a private message, it was captured by a photographer's long lens and reprinted in *The New York Times* the next morning.

The significance of the meeting was unmistakable. Far from the US and Britain having won opinion round over the previous two weeks, the reverse had happened. Opposition to war against Iraq had hardened. Instead, support had grown for what was, after all, the status quo: continued inspections.

Meanwhile, in Baghdad, Saddam Hussein delivered a steady stream of carefully timed concessions, providing extra ammunition for those who argued inspections were working. He agreed to allow the destruction of his al-Samoud missiles, whose range

61

exceeded the permitted distance. He allowed inspectors to use aerial reconnaissance. He even signed a presidential decree, outlawing weapons of mass destruction.

On 15 February, a Saturday, massive demonstrations in cities around the world showed the extent of global anti-war feeling. The British government's alarm was palpable. What had been a problem was fast becoming a nightmare. All along, the driving principle had been to preserve a consensus at the Security Council so that there would be no need to decide which ally to side with – Europe or America. But now that a clear split was emerging, Mr Blair was going to face an unenviable choice. To counter the arguments of protestors, he began to make the moral case for removing Saddam Hussein's regime.

At the Foreign Office, an exasperated official admitted the government was no longer sticking to one argument. 'We try to respond to the moment,' he explained. 'So we make a different case each week: weapons of mass destruction, links to terrorists, the moral argument and so on.' It was a telling explanation, born of desperation.

* * * * * *

American patience with the United Nations was wearing thin. Washington wanted to get on with the invasion. There were now a quarter of a million US troops either in the Gulf or en route, and it was nearly summer. Commanders did not want their men to have to fight in the searing heat in heavy chemical protection suits if they could help it.

From the start, administration officials had made it plain they did not think a second resolution was necessary to give a green light for war. 'To be frank, there's only one reason to go back to the UN,' said one American diplomat: 'to help out our friend Tony.'

The trouble was, the arithmetic did not add up. This time the US and Britain were in the minority. Among the five veto-wielders, France, Russia and China all wanted inspections to continue. When it came to the Security Council as a whole, only four out of fifteen were in favour of military action: the US, Britain, Spain and Bulgaria. The anti-war camp could count on five votes: France, Russia and China, joined by Germany and Syria. That left six countries to play for: Angola, Cameroon, Guinea, Pakistan, Mexico and Chile. Even if Britain and the US won them over, any vote could still be blocked by a French or Russian veto.

On 24 February Britain, backed by the US and Spain, tabled a draft second resolution. It was short. It simply said that Iraq had failed to take the final chance that it had been granted. It did not spell out military action. But everyone knew that was its purpose.

Then on 1 March a new crisis broke. Unexpectedly the Turkish parliament voted against giving US forces the right to over-fly, or base themselves on, Turkish territory. Ninety per cent of the Turkish population was against a war and, now that US and British attempts to secure UN cover for the war looked increasingly uncertain, Turkey's new Islamic government decided it was not a risk worth taking.

A similar pattern emerged with several of the Security Council's six undecided nations. Some resented what they regarded as American arrogance that assumed their votes were up for sale. Some feared domestic public reaction. It was the two nations in the United States' own hemisphere that were among the most reluctant to fall in line, acutely sensitive to the notion of American neo-colonialism. In Chile, the left-wing government recalled US covert aid for the coup that deposed Salvadore Allende and brought Augusto Pinochet to power in 1973. In Mexico, President Vincente Fox, facing crucial mid-term elections in the summer, remembered earlier pledges George W Bush had made and failed to keep, and felt disinclined to co-operate.

It was a pattern that also held true for Russia. Vladimir Putin refused to bow to US pressure – an enormously popular move at home but a major blow to Mr Bush and Mr Blair, who had both set great store by their personal relations with the Russian leader. In the end, it may have come down to a lack of finesse in the way Russia was handled. 'The US National Security Advisor, Condoleezza Rice, may have been a Soviet expert, but that doesn't mean she understands Russia,' one senior Moscow official noted.

But it was none of these nations that was cast in the role of chief spoiler. That privilege was accorded to France after President Chirac's interview on prime-time French television on Monday 10 March. 'Regardless of the circumstances, France will vote no,'

63

he said, 'because it considers this evening there are no grounds for waging war.' Even though 'this evening' sounded like a get-out clause, it was a speech deliberately calibrated for maximum effect, to absolve the six undecided countries of the responsibility for deciding which way to vote. If France was going to veto anyway, what was the point?

A similar statement from Russia that it, too, might use its veto made little impact. It was the French who were to blame. By Wednesday, British ministers were openly accusing President Chirac of treachery. But their anger seemed almost theatrical. Already 121 Labour backbenchers had voted against the government and another critical parliamentary debate was looming.

In Paris, French diplomats were unperturbed by the hysterical anti-French headlines in the British tabloids. 'We feel sorry for Tony Blair and we want him to survive,' one senior official at the French Foreign Ministry told me. 'If it helps him to blame us for the failure of his resolution, we will not hold it against him.'

By now it was clear the second resolution was going nowhere. In New York, Sir Jeremy Greenstock took a call from Tony Blair. 'How many votes can you guarantee me?' he asked. 'Four,' said Sir Jeremy. 'Crumbs,' replied the Prime Minister.

That weekend the American president joined the British and Spanish prime ministers for a summit on the windswept Azores in the Atlantic. Officially they were taking stock. Unofficially everyone knew this was a council of war. 'Tomorrow is the moment of truth for the world,' said George W Bush. 'Tomorrow' was the final day for UN negotiations.

The next day in New York, one short announcement confirmed that the UN's role in this part of the saga was over. It fell to Sir Jeremy Greenstock to announce that the US and Britain were giving up the fight and withdrawing their draft resolution. In the UN corridors, shocked diplomats could not conceal their distress. After all the frenzied diplomacy of the past months, the world had come full circle, back to the path proposed by Vice President Cheney the previous August. The United Nations was to be bypassed, regime change imposed on Iraq anyway.

In President Bush's eyes the UN had failed the test. The alternative was to look elsewhere for a 'coalition of the willing'. In the weeks ahead, US military commanders boasted that 50 countries were contributing to the coalition (including tiny Pacific states like Micronesia and the Solomon Islands), but the brutal fact was that, of the 50 'willing', only Britain and Australia contributed ground forces.

The Bush administration's aim was to change the political face of Iraq and the entire Middle East. But the familiar alliances that used to weld together the world's most powerful Western democracies – NATO and the European Union – had been shaken, as had the UN Security Council. The diplomatic damage done on the way to war may yet prove of far greater consequence than the conflict itself.

65

CHAPTER THREE

TOP GUN – BUSH RISES TO THE CHALLENGE

Matt Frei

66 *Matt Frei is Washington Correspondent. Previously he was Southern Europe Correspondent, covering the conflicts in Bosnia and Kosovo, and Asia Correspondent during the economic crisis in the late 1990s and the fall of President Suharto in Indonesia. He reported throughout the war from the US capital, and in this chapter profiles George W Bush and analyses the effect of the war on his presidency.*

In the winter of 2000 George W Bush was hoisted across the finishing line of the disputed presidential election by a Supreme Court that ruled in his favour. 'A coup d'état' one leading Democrat called it. Hillary Clinton, the former First Lady, still refers to George Bush as 'the Resident in the White House, not the President'. The defeated candidate, Al Gore, grew a beard. Grief and indignation jostled with biting humour. Dick Cheney, the new Vice President was older, more experienced – he had served as Defense Secretary under Bush's father – and many thought he was better qualified for the top job. But he was unwell. He had suffered three heart attacks, the first at the age of 36, prompting a nightclub comic to come up with a wicked twist on the old saying about vice presidents. The joke was that 'Bush is only a heartbeat away from the presidency!'

The famous 'Bushisms' – his frequent mangling of the English language – were another rich source of mirth for his critics. It's thought he could be dyslexic, though Bush has denied this. On the campaign trail he had made education and literacy a prime objective – 'because our children isn't learning', he told an audience of disbelieving teachers. What's more, his body language often displayed an alarmingly inappropriate levity. *The New York Times*'s Frank Bruni describes how Bush made goofy expressions at the press corps during a funeral for victims of a church shooting. Bruni believes that the former 'frat boy' from Harvard is slave to a constant desire to please and entertain. This, apparently, stems from the days when George was seven and his mother, the former First Lady Barbara Bush, was grieving the loss of her three-year-old daughter to leukaemia. George was the entertainer, groomed for gregariousness not for greatness. Even his parents once admitted that it was his younger brother Jeb – now the governor of Florida – who was far more likely to end up in the White House.

67

But perhaps the most damning charge made against the newly elected president was his astounding lack of intellectual curiosity. And nowhere was this more obvious than in his ignorance of the world outside America. Although his father had been Ambassador to the UN and Beijing, Director of the CIA and President, George had rarely travelled outside the United States. As a candidate, his knowledge of the most basic foreign affairs was famously patchy. But, as the man himself once put it, inimitably: 'I have always been mis-underestimated!'

Equally surprisingly, perhaps, he displayed a baffling ignorance of popular culture. According to Frank Bruni, Bush had never heard of *Friends* or *Sex and the City* even though they are two of the most widely watched TV programmes in the world. What the President does like to watch is sport on the ESPN network, especially baseball.

But presidents have been misjudged before. Ronald Reagan was widely derided as the handsome but vacant B-movie actor for whom the White House role was too challenging. He is now remembered by many as one of the last century's great presidents and the man who helped to tear down the Berlin Wall and bury Communism. Could greatness, one day, also be George W Bush's epitaph?

Initially, the President was expected by many to follow in his father's clumsy footsteps as 'a one-termer'. He had inherited an economy sliding into recession and had a questionable mandate.

In order to make amends Bush was widely expected to rule with a centrist, bi-partisan agenda that would placate a bitterly divided electorate. Instead he has turned out to be 'not so dumb, not so centrist and not so nice', as one headline put it. His tax cuts harked back to the Reagan era, he has outspent any other predecessor on defence and his much-touted 'compassionate conservatism' – the warm, all-embracing slogan with which Bush hoped to win over millions of disaffected Democrats – was barely mentioned after the inauguration and soon forgotten.

It became obvious that the new president's strategy for staying in power did not involve placating the centre but pleasing the right wing of the Republican Party. George W Bush had clearly learnt from the mistakes committed by his father, who had alienated the conservatives in his own party – most notably by raising taxes – and then watched many of them desert him for the right-wing independent candidate Ross Perot in the 1992 election. The advisers who had planned the election of the younger Bush were determined that history would not repeat itself.

But perhaps the biggest surprise, and the one that has seen the rest of the world scramble for a response, has come from Bush's foreign policy. The man who pledged during a presidential debate with Al Gore that America would rule 'by humble example', is the author of a national security policy which insists that America will *never* be rivalled by any other power. Not only will the United States defend itself with all necessary means, the world's only '*hyperpuissance*' (or 'hyperpower') – a word coined by the French and disliked by the White House – will also ensure that democratic values are imposed, where necessary, on other countries. From having no discernible foreign policy as candidate, George Bush as president has come to approach the rest of the planet with almost evangelical zeal. Furthermore, as everyone – from the Taliban spiritual leader Mullah Omar and Saddam Hussein, to Jacques Chirac and Gerhard Schröder – knows, these are more than empty boasts. President Bush is a rare creature in Washington. The actor and former Republican senator Fred Thompson once joked that 'after two years in this city I long for the realism and sincerity of Hollywood'. George Bush is nothing if not sincere.

Consider the irony. This is a president who came to power pledging to withdraw America from a whole host of foreign policy commitments, not least in the Middle East. George Bush, who was determined to be the opposite of Bill Clinton, declared himself an enemy of 'nation building', which he dismissed as a waste of time and money. But to date the Bush administration has fought two major wars (in Afghanistan and Iraq), deployed troops in the former Soviet republics of Georgia and Uzbekistan, and sent thousands of marines and special forces to the southern Philippines to root out the Abu Sayyaf, a small band of extremist Muslim guerrillas. And the United States is about to spend billions on rebuilding the Iraqi nation. None of this has been done by stealth. These are all declared aims. Once he has made up his mind, this president announces what he will do, and then he actually does it. In that sense at least, this administration should be easy to deal with.

* * * * * *

Three key moments illustrate the extraordinary transformation of George Bush from so-called 'accidental president' to what he is today. The first was on the morning of September 11, 2001 when a stunned President listened as his Chief of Staff, Andrew Card, whispered the news of the second attack on the World Trade Center into his ear. The President was visiting a primary school in Sarasota, Florida. His first public response to a petrified nation was faltering. Minutes later, he was whisked away on Air Force One and was kept from a capital under threat. It was a day of confused and uncertain reaction.

But three days later the same man was standing on top of a pile of rubble at Ground Zero clutching a loudhailer and shouting to the firemen who had assembled in the dust: 'I can hear you. I can hear you. The rest of the world hears you. And the people who knocked these buildings down will hear all of us soon!' Bush had found his voice and risen to the occasion. In the eyes of many Americans, who had been ambivalent about their newly elected leader, this was the moment the long election night of the 2000 campaign ended. President Bush, the wartime leader, had been born. His appearance at Ground Zero was followed up by a robust speech in Congress in which he warned the world that 'you are either with us or you are with the terrorists'. The tone of the administration had been set.

The third moment came on 1 May 2003 when the President flew to the USS *Abraham Lincoln*, a giant aircraft carrier returning from the war after ten months at sea. It was festooned with a banner declaring 'Mission Accomplished'. Bush, the former pilot in the Reserve National Guard, who had spent the Vietnam War flying circles above Texas, stepped from an S3 Viking aircraft clutching his helmet and his harness, grinning from ear to ear. He saluted the service men and women with gusto and spent almost a whole hour posing with them for photographs. The President was in his element. Despite the fact that he, too, had avoided active service, there was none of the embarrassment and awkwardness that Bill Clinton, the ultimate presser of the flesh, used to feel in the presence of the military. In fact the Marines, the Coast Guard and the Air Force do for George Bush what black voters and Hollywood used to do for Bill Clinton: they unite the politician with his people, creating a critical mass of mutual admiration.

'Top Gun', the *New York Post* bellowed on its front page. So potent was this testosterone moment that the Democrats wasted no time in bitching about it. It had wasted taxpayers' money, Senator Robert Byrd, one of the President's most outspoken critics, thundered on Capitol Hill. The Democrats knew immediately that this was the image that could ensure George Bush's re-election. Little, if anything, in this White House is left to chance and the Top Gun photo opportunity had been carefully orchestrated by the White House's political guru Karl Rove. Any clever PR adviser could have done the same. The point is that, two-and-a-half years into the Bush presidency, it also looked plausible.

George Bush has metamorphosed into an effective wartime commander in chief, in tune with the mood of a nation that feels both under attack and unabashed about its strength. Today's America wants to be respected, not loved. It is the combination of vulnerability and military muscle that defines the nation today. The number of post-September 11 Stars and Stripes outside homes in Washington may have diminished, but in Texas, Louisiana or Minnesota the American flag flutters as never before;

roadside billboards hail 'our troops and our Commander in Chief' and red, white and blue bumper stickers boast 'these colours don't run!' George Bush's promises to 'smoke out the terrorists' or to 'hunt them down – dead or alive' may make readers of *The New Yorker* and the *Guardian* cringe but in Main Street America they go down a storm.

A consistent two-thirds of the electorate approve of the way the President is running the country, even though the economy is stuck in a persistent recession and unemployment has climbed above six per cent. One frequent explanation was summed up by a stallholder in the Baltimore Fish Market: 'OK, this guy could spend more time worrying about how to fix the economy. But he's got other things on his mind.'

71

* * * * * *

So much for the evolving images of George Bush; what about the reality?

The 43rd president of the United States is often portrayed as a typical Texan. He spent his early childhood in the small, windswept town of Midland in the oil-fields of western Texas, a place of stifling heat and oppressive religion. There is a black and white photograph of an ash-blond three-year-old George on a pony, his grin disappearing under the broad brim of a stetson. The President clearly has a long-lasting love of Texas and most things Texan. He spends as many weekends as possible on his 16-acre ranch in Crawford, which his staff refer to as 'the Western White House'. Friends and allies such as Tony Blair and Prime Ministers José María Aznar of Spain and John Howard of Australia are invited to huddle round the log fire, eat steaks and hike through the woods.

But for all the Texas hype, there's no getting away from the fact that Bush was born into a very wealthy family, not from the south-west but from the patrician north-east. His father's spiritual home is not Texas but Kennebunkport in Maine, where the family has its summer retreat. Bush Senior combined old money and status – his father Prescott Bush was a senator from Connecticut – with an education at Princeton and an inside knowledge of the world of Washington politics. The first President Bush made money in the oil-fields of Texas but his politics were formed in Washington and New Jersey. His son straddles both worlds with great ease, and his Texan youth may have given him the folksy touch that electrifies crowds.

Every American president benefits from the pomp and circumstance of the office. Air Force One, Marine One, the long motorcades, the Secret Service agents with reflector glasses and crackling ear-pieces and the renditions of 'Hail to the Chief' – these props of power are elaborate and ritualistic. But George W Bush feels far more comfortable with them than his father ever did. He feeds off the aura of the office; his father seemed almost to recoil from it.

72

Confirmation of George Bush's early political potential can be found in the role played by Karl Rove, the baby-faced Political Director of the White House and a man once described as 'Bush's brain'. In Washington, Rove is worshipped as the political genius who has turned the murky business of election and re-election into an art form. Moreover, he prides himself on bestowing his political genius only on candidates he considers worthy. The first time he met the current president was the day before Thanksgiving in 1973. George Bush was taking an MBA at Harvard Business School, after an undergraduate degree at Yale, and was coming to Washington to stay with his parents. Karl Rove, a junior aide to Bush Senior, who was a congressman at the time, was tasked with picking up the eldest son at Union Station and handing him some car keys.

'I can literally remember what he was wearing,' Rove told *The New Yorker*. 'An Air National Guard flight jacket, cowboy boots, blue jeans ... He was exuding more charisma than any one individual should be allowed to have.' Rove realized early on that Bush was good presidential raw material, good clay.

Nevertheless, it would be wrong to assume that George Bush is Karl Rove's creature. In his book *The Right Man*, David Frum, a former Bush speechwriter, confirms that the reality of the White House reflects the formal hierarchy. Vice President Cheney may be more experienced, National Security Advisor Condoleezza Rice more clever and Secretary of State Colin Powell more popular, but, powerful though they are, they have no illusions about who's the boss. Even the outspoken and brash Defense Secretary Donald Rumsfeld – the hawk with the sharpest beak – knows his place. There can be no doubt, in practice as well as in theory, that George Bush is in charge.

This is an important point, especially since there has been a plethora of theories about the power of the neo-conservatives to mould the White House agenda. On the surface, the war in Iraq and the intended transformation of the country into a secular Muslim democracy bear the stamp of the most influential 'neo-con' in the administration, Paul Wolfowitz. A former wrestler and academic who combines some of the broadest shoulders in Washington with one of the biggest brains, Wolfowitz served in the Reagan administration and as Ambassador to Indonesia. He is only the Deputy Secretary of Defense. But rarely has there been such an influential number two.

He was the only deputy to take part in the first war council at Camp David after September 11. Although all minds were focused on Osama bin Laden, al-Qaida and the Taliban, he kept bringing up the issue of Iraq, much to Donald Rumsfeld's annoyance. Before the administration turned it into a mantra, Wolfowitz was already arguing that the nexus between terrorists and rogue states such as Iraq was America's biggest danger. Moreover, he passionately believed in his country's ability and duty to spread democracy, not so much out of a sense of largesse but for reasons of self-preservation and national security. Only by transforming these nations, he argued, could the US prevent a new generation of suicidal terrorists who hated America more than they loved their own lives.

The example that inspired Wolfowitz was the one he knew best. If Indonesia could combine Islam with secular and democratic institutions, why couldn't Iraq or Iran? The neo-cons are unabashed about the use of America's military power to achieve their ends. They also share a distrust of international institutions, from the United Nations to the International Criminal Court, which bind the US. Some, like Richard Perle, an influential Pentagon adviser, believe that after the demise of Communism the US must be the only pole in a 'unipolar' world. Most Americans still shy away from the word 'empire'. The neo-cons

73

may not use the word, but they have less of a problem with the concept.

The pre-emptive war against Iraq was their biggest triumph and clearest vindication. Now they need to make the peace work, and turn their guinea pig into a viable, peaceful country. That part is not so easy. President Bush clearly identifies with much of their agenda. He's sceptical about the United Nations, membership of which he always regarded as a marriage of convenience and not of conviction. When the second UN resolution on Iraq ended in defeat, George Bush quickly sued for divorce, and the war started a few days later.

But the neo-cons have to share their influence over the President with the 'internationalists'. They're an equally powerful lot, starting with Bush's father whose greatest success was to resurrect the United Nations after decades of Cold War sclerosis. Bush Senior, his former Secretary of State James Baker, and Brent Scowcroft, his former National Security Advisor, have consistently urged caution over Iraq. Another counterweight to the neo-cons is, of course, Tony Blair. As the most willing member of the 'coalition of the willing', he's credited with convincing the President to take the UN route. And they all have one particularly powerful ally in the cabinet room: Secretary of State Powell. He's not only America's most popular politician, he also matches his adversaries on the right in tenacity and persuasiveness.

The run-up to the war can be seen as a non-stop tussle between these two camps. In August 2002, while the President was on his ranch in Texas, war clouds were gathering over Washington and Baghdad like a late summer storm. Dick Cheney called Saddam Hussein a 'grave threat' and the UN inspections a 'waste of time'. But a month later George Bush was at the UN pledging to seek one more resolution. The neo-cons grumbled, but held their peace. When Resolution 1441 was passed unanimously in November, they despaired. When the second resolution failed in March 2003, they reacted with a predictable 'we told you so'.

The tussle continued. As soon as US forces had taken control of Baghdad, Donald Rumsfeld turned his sights on Syria, accusing it of harbouring fugitive Iraqi leaders and supporting anti-Israeli groups like Hezbollah. The Syrian chargé d'affaires in Washington told me how, for a week, all lines of communication froze. 'I couldn't get anyone on the phone. Rumsfeld's attack came out of the blue. We thought, "Oh my God. Are we next?"'

The State Department had not been informed about the Pentagon's verbal salvo. When the President was told that Rumsfeld had been shaking his fist at the Syrians, he looked up briefly from his papers and simply said: 'Good!' But three weeks later Colin Powell was visiting Damascus. The Syrians agreed to help find fugitive Iraqis and to withdraw any support from Hezbollah in Southern Lebanon. They were rewarded a few days later with a promise from Ariel Sharon, the hard-line Israeli prime minister, that he would be prepared to hold peace negotiations without conditions. In other words, Colin Powell – who had been savaged by former Speaker of the House and prominent neo-con Newt Gingrich as incompetent ('six months of failed diplomacy followed by one month of successful war') – was back in the saddle.

Richard Norton Smith, a presidential historian, believes that 'George Bush is on the verge of joining a small group of presidents, all now thought of as great, who pitted their top aides against each other, fashioning an agenda from above the fray.' This lofty tradition started as early as 1790, when the cabinet of the new republic was polarized between the pro-French Secretary of State, Thomas Jefferson, and the Anglophile Secretary of the Treasury, Alexander Hamilton. The president then was George Washington. Abraham Lincoln and Dwight Eisenhower encouraged and manipulated equally vicious rifts in their cabinets. A more recent example was Ronald Reagan, whose Secretaries of State and Defense, George Schultz and Caspar Weinberger, fought like cat and dog. At one stage Reagan even joked about the controlled chaos in the White House, saying that 'the right hand didn't know what the *far*-right hand was doing'.

But these cabinet rivalries have been relegated to the footnotes of history. And so far George Bush, too, has been able to play one side off against the other, without feeling diminished by the heavyweights clashing beneath him. He is, after all, a Harvard MBA who specialized in management techniques. This president does not possess the intellect or the verbal dexterity of his Rhodes

Scholar predecessor, but he is extremely self-confident. Two hours before he declared war on Iraq he was playing ball with his two dogs, Barney and Spot, on the South Lawn of the White House. He took a detailed interest in the course of the war without getting involved in the minutiae. It was President Lyndon Johnson who used to call startled field commanders in Vietnam at night, telling them which battalions to deploy where. Bush left that sort of thing to the Pentagon and thus managed to stay aloof from the bruising, albeit short-lived, rows about war strategy.

Throughout the conflict, the White House tried to finesse the image of a commander in chief who kept up-to-date with every development of the war but who did not get bogged down in detail. George Bush made a point of spending the first weekend of the war at Camp David – 'just like his father did during the first weekend of *his* Gulf War,' a senior aide pointed out.

On Saturday 22 March, as we waited for the President to board his helicopter Marine One on the South Lawn, we noticed that he was 15 minutes late – very unusual for a leader obsessed with punctuality. These were the same 15 minutes in which Baghdad was being seriously pounded for the first time.

'Did the President leave late because he was busy watching bombs fall on the Iraqi capital?' Ari Fleischer, his spokesman, was asked later. 'The President doesn't need to watch TV to find out what's going on in the war,' came the rather tart response.

The next day the newspapers were full of insinuations that President Bush was more interested in planning his weekend at Camp David than in following historic events on TV. 'Uncurious George' came the charge yet again. (There is an American fictional children's character called Curious George.) In response, Ari Fleischer rowed back and said that the President did indeed watch the bombing on television, just not excessively. It was a small moment which illustrates just how obsessed this White House is with sending the right message to the public. George Bush may have the Texan touch, and he loves a good off-the-cuff joke, but with his public image nothing is left to chance. Ironically this is encouraged by the news media's smothering attention to every minor detail.

* * * * * *

So what is the source of Bush's confidence? A strong religious belief and the support of his wife, Laura. Charisma and a gregarious nature apart, George W's life was a mess until he was 40. By his own admission, he had a serious drink problem. His Texas oil business had failed and he had yet to make millions as the owner of the highly successful Texas Rangers baseball team, which he managed to buy with a loan underwritten by the now-failed energy giant Enron. Religious rebirth helped him back to sobriety and gave his life a new direction. His wife – a shy, resourceful librarian – coaxed him through the crisis.

Alcohol almost destroyed his life and his victory over it has created a sober culture of self-discipline in the White House. Even today George Bush will only permit himself alcohol-free lager. The former British Ambassador to Washington, Sir Christopher Meyer, once told me what this did to diplomatic dinners at the White House. 'You're in by 7 and out by 9.30. At the latest! It's lights out at 10.' Compare this to President Clinton's marathon sessions, where the staff ordered in pizzas and talked late into the night. Clinton was notoriously unpunctual. Bush is slavishly on time, believing that this is a matter both of courtesy and expediency. 'There is only a finite number of minutes to every presidency,' he once told reporters.

Much has been written about the White House bible classes and prayer breakfasts. Most American presidents are religious. Jimmy Carter was a preacher. Ronald Reagan was devout. Bill Clinton relished the exuberance of the Baptist Church. But this president is a born-again evangelist. He belongs to one of the most conservative, some would say fundamentalist, churches in America – the Southern United Methodists. Bush spices his speeches, including the State of the Union address, with fire and brimstone. The former speechwriter David Frum came up with 'axis of hatred' to describe Iraq, Iran and North Korea. The President changed 'hatred' to 'evil'. Like his fluent Texan, his religion makes many Europeans wince, but it resonates well with a profoundly Christian nation such as the United States.

An important question is how much Bush's politics are influenced by his belief in God. The religious conviction that he was 'doing the right thing' in the wars against the Taliban and Saddam

Hussein made this president less worried about the consequences of failure. This is something that encourages his supporters and scares his detractors.

September 11 was a defining moment for George W Bush. It transformed the direction of his presidency: the conservative with a radical social agenda, an instinctive distrust of foreign institutions and an almost missionary belief in the American way of life, was galvanized into international leadership.

America is not about to acquire an empire in the traditional sense. As the *New York Times* columnist Maureen Dowd quipped recently, 'No self respecting American would want to live in any of the places we invade.' But this president is ready to use the biggest military machine the world has ever seen to impose his will and to keep the enemy at bay, be they terrorists or rogue states. This is the Bush Doctrine. It was born on September 12, 2001.

CHAPTER FOUR

BLAIR'S GAMBLE

Martha Kearney

Martha Kearney is BBC Newsnight's *Political Editor. She is also a well-known presenter of BBC Radio 4's* Today *and* Woman's Hour. *She is based at Westminster, has interviewed the Prime Minister many times and travelled with Mr Blair during the pre-war diplomatic manoeuvring. She reports here on the British prime minister's controversial role as America's key ally in the face of widespread domestic opposition.*

MEMO TO THE PRIME MINISTER

While the government's foreign policy goal must be to encourage the Bush administration onto a multilateral path, it seems prudent to point out possible pitfalls in unconditional support for military action against Iraq.

1 A million people will take to the streets to oppose war. Some will demand regime change in Britain.
2 You will not find a smoking gun before the war begins.
3 Public opinion will demand a second UN resolution as a pre-condition for support. You won't get one.
4 You will provoke the largest parliamentary rebellion in a century.
5 At least one cabinet minister will resign and others in junior ranks will also go.
6 Contrary to Foreign Office predictions, France will join Germany in opposing war. That will damage the UK's position within the EU.

Of course no such memo exists, but it's interesting to consider whether Tony Blair realized just how high the stakes were from the outset. Those close to him reckon there is something in his character that relishes the challenge of being in the minority. Critics call it a kind of machismo: if he believes something strongly enough, he thinks he can persuade the party and Parliament. But this is a sea change for the man once derided as 'Bambi Blair' and 'Phony Tony', in thrall to the focus group. When he first unveiled the plan to scrap Clause Four of the Labour Party's constitution, the party's socialist touchstone, the language in his party conference speech was so coded that members only realized what he'd meant when journalists were briefed afterwards.

80 The build-up to the Iraq War wasn't simply a defining period in Tony Blair's leadership, but also a time when conventional wisdom about British politics was challenged. Parliament is tedious and irrelevant? Debates in the Commons could hardly have been more dramatic. Political apathy? Young people unengaged in politics? Tell that to the million who marched, or millions more who discussed the rights and wrongs of the war round their kitchen tables. The repercussions are likely to be felt for years – in Blair's relationship with his party, the British people, European allies and the wider world.

So was there a single moment when the Prime Minister realized that he was facing the biggest crisis of his career – or did he simply find himself on a conveyor belt from which he couldn't escape? As with so much else, it was the events of September 11 that set the course for the war against Iraq. But this wasn't simply an American determination to pre-empt a further attack. Tony Blair himself had become increasingly convinced of the need to intervene – initially against the threat posed by international terrorism. This was outlined in his party conference speech a month later:

'I believe this is a fight for freedom. And I want to make it a fight for justice too ... The starving, the wretched, the dispossessed, the ignorant, those living in want and squalor from the deserts of Northern Africa to the slums of Gaza, to the mountain ranges of Afghanistan: they too are our cause. This is a moment to seize. The kaleidoscope has been shaken. The pieces are in flux. Soon they will settle again. Before they do, let us re-order this world around us.'

Afghanistan was at the forefront of his mind then, but military action against Iraq would also be embraced by the new foreign policy of liberal interventionism first expounded over Kosovo.

It was clear that Iraq was on the American agenda very soon after September 11. In October 2001 it had already become a pressing political question for British journalists when Tony Blair was touring the Middle East to gain support for the war in Afghanistan. In the sweltering heat of the Omani desert, in a tent that served as the operations centre for the military exercise Operation Swift Sword, I interviewed the Prime Minister for *Newsnight*. At that stage the government hadn't yet committed itself to action against the Taliban, but rumours were already rife about Iraq. I pressed him on the question of whether Saddam Hussein would be next. Tellingly, he refused to rule it out, but he also wanted to be asked about the Middle East peace process. It was an early indication of his price for British support for the US: Bush must in turn engage with Israel and the Palestinians.

That would become a familiar refrain of Blair's, and one that was of immense importance to his backbenchers. While there had been opposition to war in Afghanistan, Iraq would provoke much more widespread resistance both within the Labour Party and in the country. At the end of January 2002 there was widespread concern among Labour MPs over Bush's 'axis of evil' speech, which included Iraq.

Resistance to action against Iraq was growing, with a critical parliamentary Early Day Motion on 4 March signed by many Labour MPs who couldn't be classified as the usual anti-war suspects. It began: 'This House is aware of the deep unease among honourable members on all sides of the House at the prospect that HM Government might support US military action against Iraq.' By the beginning of April, 122 Labour backbenchers had signed the motion.

On 6 April, Tony Blair went to Texas to stay at the Bush ranch. It was there that the PM's senior advisers fully realized what the President was intending. George Bush told a news conference: 'The moment for decision on how to act is not yet with us ... if necessary the action should be military – and again, if necessary and justified, it should involve regime change.'

To many in the Labour Party, 'regime change' smacked of high-handed imperialism. But Tony Blair was starting to stress the

81

moral case for getting rid of Saddam. At a televised news conference on 3 September he promised that a dossier would be published of evidence against the Iraqi leader. He also used a phrase
which would often be repeated – that action would take place
through the UN only if it was a way of dealing with the matter
rather than the means of avoiding it. The get-out clause had been
written in.

Four days later, it was back to Camp David to see President
Bush. After a walk in the Maryland woods, and hours of more
conventional meetings, the President had been convinced to go
down the UN route. But it was also clear that Britain would be a
partner in any military coalition. One senior minister described it
to me like this: 'It was the same pact as with Afghanistan. Go
down the UN route however sceptical you may be about it.
Give Saddam a final opportunity. If he fails to take it, we're
with you.'

But there were to be crucial differences from the Afghan
conflict, which perhaps Downing Street hadn't envisaged. Then,
action was backed by the UN, and after the war a 'coalition of the
willing', an international force of many nations, policed Kabul.
Many Labour MPs who had backed war against al-Qaida and the
Taliban felt very differently about Iraq.

Growing opposition was voiced at the conference of the
Trades Union Congress, which for the second year in a row was
dominated by international affairs. The previous year we'd all
been standing around waiting for Blair's speech on public service
reform, when live TV pictures from the States showed the devas-
tation of September 11. In 2002, trade unionists were debating
America's reaction to that attack – the possibility of war with Iraq.
Typically in the hothouse conference atmosphere, rumours spread
quickly throughout the hall: Blair would face angry protesters,
and be jeered and shouted down. In the end he made a powerfully argued, intense speech that was listened to, if not in agreement, then at least with respect by the majority.

Under sustained pressure from his backbenchers, the Prime
Minister then agreed to a recall of Parliament. A recurrent theme in
trying to build a domestic coalition of the willing for war was the
role of the House of Commons. In theory, a prime minister can

declare war through the use of the Royal prerogative. MPs feared that action would begin before they had had a chance to vote. A debate after British troops had been committed would simply be a rubber stamp. So there were constant calls for Parliament to play a decisive role. On 24 September, MPs were recalled to debate the Iraq crisis, armed with the dossier of evidence against Saddam Hussein, released by Downing Street on the same day. On this occasion there was less talk of regime change. Tony Blair maintained his goal was disarmament, not getting rid of a cruel dictator. During the debate, Labour MP Alan Simpson likened George Bush to a drunk 'who needs to satisfy his thirst for power and oil'. Mr Blair's job as his candid friend, Simpson said, was 'not to pass the bottle' but to restrain him.

83

As I stood on College Green opposite Parliament that night with MPs Michael Ancram and Glenda Jackson for a *Newsnight* special, a small crowd gathered, attracted by the bright TV lights. There was a sense of drama. My producer and I tried to work out just how many Labour MPs had rebelled. The figure was 56 – a substantial revolt – but many MPs were keeping their powder dry, feeling it was too early to make a stand. Rebels now believe the government seriously underestimated the size of the potential revolt at that stage.

But growing resistance *was* evident at the Labour Party conference in Blackpool, a world away from the deserts of Mesopotamia. The Prime Minister, still reeling from an interview in which he'd been asked whether he prayed with George Bush, decided to meet head-on the most powerful criticism – that he was under the President's thumb. This was certainly the view outside the conference hall. I talked to several old ladies enjoying the autumn sunshine on the promenade. The phrase 'Bush's poodle' sprang spontaneously to their lips when I asked about Iraq. That anti-Americanism was also reflected in opinion polls, and inside the Winter Gardens conference centre the Labour leader knew he had to tackle it.

'The basic values of America are our values too, British and European, and they are good values. Democracy, freedom, tolerance, justice. It's easy to be anti-American. There's a lot of it about but remember when and where this alliance was forged: here in Europe, in World War II when Britain and America and every decent citizen in Europe joined forces to liberate Europe from the Nazi evil. My vision of Britain is not as the 51st state of anywhere, but I believe in this alliance and I will fight long and hard to maintain it.'

But many delegates weren't convinced, incredulous that Blair could have become so entwined with a right-wing Republican administration. It was time to hark back to a happier special relationship with the arrival of a famous 'FOB' (Friend of Blair) – no less a luminary than Bill Clinton. He 'love-bombed' the conference from his first words: 'Clinton, Bill. Arkansas CLP' (Constituency Labour Party). It was a clever speech, acknowledging Labour doubts over the war. But his central message was clear – support Tony.

As I interviewed delegates later, they were totally enamoured of Clinton. One of the most resolutely anti-war MPs had an almost post-coital glow. But, like many an Arkansas tryst, the morning after, the audience had their doubts. Resistance to the war was very deep-seated. Some, like Glenda Jackson, had supported war before, in Afghanistan. Again and again I talked to politicians who had 'Blair' stamped through their political being like a stick of Blackpool rock, yet who, off the record, were deeply uneasy about their leader's course of action. Some questioned his almost messianic sense of purpose – 'he thinks he can walk on water' was one comment from a New Labour disciple. It was clear that opposition to the war spread far wider than the usual suspects: the Campaign Group and other convinced pacifists. There's a strong vein of anti-Americanism in Labour Party constituencies, and deep suspicion of US foreign policy. But Downing Street officials think the party has seriously underestimated Bush, falling for the cowboy persona rather than the north-eastern aristocratic Ivy Leaguer that he really is.

Tony Blair had to convince his own MPs, and the wider public, that action against Iraq was worth taking for its own sake. Different arguments were deployed at different times, leading to the criticism that the government was unsure of its ground. The 'kaleidoscope' was shifting this way and that: sometimes the dictator's defiance of the UN was cited, at others the threat of weapons of mass destruction to Britain, Saddam's use of gas against his own people, alleged Iraqi links with al-Qaida, or desire for regime change.

84

On 15 October, speaking in the Commons after the Bali bombing, when the world had again been reminded of the threat from international terrorism, Tony Blair made explicit the link between terrorism and weapons of mass destruction. 'Some say that we should fight terrorism alone and that the issues to do with weapons of mass destruction are a distraction. I reject that entirely. Both, though different in means, are the same in nature. Both are the new threats facing the post-Cold War world. Both are threats from people or states who do not care about human life, who have no compunction about killing the innocent. Both represent the extreme replacing the rational, the fanatic driving out moderation ... Can we really be confident that at some point in time these two threats aren't actually going to be separate but will rather come together?'

The unanimous passing of UN Resolution 1441 boosted Downing Street's case that any action would be multilateral. But still the arguments weren't working, and over the Christmas break, to Number Ten's dismay, opposition hardened among the public and among MPs, who had been subjected to intense pressure and threats of deselection by their constituency parties.

At the beginning of 2003, there was increasing frustration at the top. Tony Blair and party chairman John Reid agreed that people weren't listening to their arguments. If only they could speak to every party branch, they could win the case. Reid decided to talk to as many meetings as possible.

Privately they acknowledged how high the stakes were. Apart from the Iraq issue, the party and Downing Street were at odds over domestic politics and old hands knew that every previous Labour government had been brought down by a major schism between the party and the government.

At the Prime Minister's news conference in January, we were struck by how impassioned he'd become on Iraq. Rightly or wrongly, there was no question that he was convinced of the threat.

'I tell you, every single day I am faced as British prime minister with information about how these weapons are proliferating, about how states are trying to acquire nuclear capability – states you would not want to have that capability – how chemical and biological weapons are being freely traded by groups and individuals right across the world. It is a matter of time, unless we act and take a stand, before terrorism and weapons of mass destruction come together.'

It was around now that a senior cabinet minister assured me off the record that the UN inspectors *would* find a smoking gun. Otherwise, he said, how could they possibly justify military action? That strengthens the argument that the government had envisaged a very different scenario for the outbreak of war – clear evidence against Saddam, and UN backing.

The latter was very important for Labour MPs who were demanding more assurances that any action would come under the auspices of the UN. The 'get-out clause' needed to be clarified. For the first time, on 13 January, Tony Blair spelt out the circumstances in which Britain would go to war *without* the UN: if a country wielded an unreasonable veto (the so-called 'Kosovo option', when action was taken without UN sanction because Russia would have vetoed it). At that stage it was assumed he meant Russia or China, not France. The Foreign Office had been briefed by French Foreign Minister Dominique de Villepin that, however unreasonable the initial noises might appear, France would come round in the end. But the real policy was being driven by Chirac, who, it became clear, would not 'come round'.

The idea that France and Germany were opposed to war fuelled unease on the backbenches. There was open contempt after the publication in early February of the so-called 'dodgy dossier' (entitled 'Iraq – Its Infrastructure of Concealment, Deception and Intimidation'), when it emerged that large sections had been lifted from a Californian postgraduate thesis, rather than intelligence briefings.

While relations between Chirac and Blair grew more distant, the Prime Minister grew closer to President Bush – a friendship described by those close to them as 'incredibly warm'. Watching the two men together at Camp David, I could see Bush's admiration for Blair's articulacy. That was later satirized by a cartoon in *The Washington Post*. The bubble above Bush's head said, 'You're darn tootin'. A grey phone, a new hotline, was installed by the Americans in Blair's Downing Street office; the two leaders spoke daily. One adviser even claims the relationship with Bush was easier than with Clinton, who is more inclined to take umbrage.

* * * * * *

By now, the Prime Minister had to face the fact that his campaign to win people over wasn't working. So he stepped it up. Never can a prime minister have been subjected to so many hostile TV audiences, and hostile in so many different ways. No wonder his Government Communications Director, Alastair Campbell, dubbed it 'the masochism strategy'. Some advisers disliked the plan because the overwhelmingly critical audiences gave the impression that the entire country was opposed to war. When Blair appeared before an audience at the Baltic Exchange art gallery in Newcastle upon Tyne, we got the strongest sense yet of how much he needed the UN: 'If there were a second UN resolution, then I think people would be behind me. I think if there is not, then there is a lot of persuading to do.'

There was no persuading one group of anti-war women on a TV programme, whose slow hand-clap was regarded by one very close Blair aide as the turning point when the public realized that he was acting from conviction – willing to suffer the discomfort of these appearances, and putting his career on the line. The Prime Minister told another friend that he would resign, if necessary.

That prospect appeared more likely on the weekend of 15 February, when more than a million people marched through London against the war. It was Britain's largest-ever demonstration. There were politicians and celebrities. Rev. Jesse Jackson came over from the States. But what was most striking was the number of people who had never been on a march before – there because of their deep misgivings about the war.

In the spring of 2002, former Culture Secretary Chris Smith had voiced his concerns about policy towards Iraq. He was called in by Tony Blair for an hour-long meeting but remained unconvinced. Nearly a year later it was Smith's amendment to a Commons motion that proved decisive. On Friday 21 February a pager message went out to all Labour MPs to 'be prepared for a three-line whip on a substantive motion'. The Smith amendment read: 'this House finds the case for military action against Iraq as yet unproven'.

It was 'Through the Looking Glass' politics: when Tony Blair spoke there was often a glacial silence behind him on the Labour benches; in front, Tory MPs cheered and waved their order papers; a tranche of former ministers voiced their opposition; some left-wingers voiced their support; former Tory Chancellor Ken Clarke was an unlikely peacenik. In the end, 122 Labour members supported the Chris Smith amendment, a third of all MPs who voted, and the potential existed for an even greater revolt. Many MPs' support for the government was conditional on getting a second UN resolution.

The Chief Whip warned Downing Street that they could lose half the Parliamentary Labour Party. The Conservative Chief Whip let it be known that he could only guarantee 100 votes in support of the government. One Number Ten official recalls: 'We knew then it would be bloody difficult. There was even the prospect of losing the parliamentary vote, not just the PLP.' Rumours began to circulate of ministers and their aides preparing to resign.

On Sunday 9 March, International Development Secretary Clare Short asked to appear on BBC Radio 4's *Westminster Hour*. Her attack on the Prime Minister was extraordinary, calling his behaviour 'reckless'. This was stretching the bounds of collective cabinet responsibility to breaking point. The following day, Health Secretary Alan Milburn expressed surprise at Ms Short's comments, in a rare example of one cabinet colleague publicly criticizing another: 'I was particularly surprised because of the huge effort that is going into securing a second resolution and all members of the government should really be behind it.'

But then a huge effort was also put into securing her loyalty – by Tony Blair and her cabinet ally, Chancellor of the Exchequer Gordon Brown. It was felt that her resignation at that stage would have given the rebellion new momentum.

The government was clearly so worried that Defence Secretary Geoff Hoon felt obliged to warn the Americans of the possibility that Britain might not turn up for the war after all. That led to US Defense Secretary Donald Rumsfeld's unhelpful statement: 'To the extent that they [the British] are able to participate, in the event that the President decides to use force, that would obviously be welcomed. To the extent they are not, there are work-arounds and they would not be involved, at least in that phase of it.'

Urgent diplomatic representations followed from London, and a 'clarification' was issued. Meanwhile, at the UN, frenetic efforts were being put into winning a second resolution. But while French opposition to the war proved a disaster for diplomacy in New York, it became, paradoxically, a valuable weapon in domestic politics. As one senior Downing Street official said wryly: 'The French came through for us. They were fantastic.' Tony Blair could invoke his 'get-out clause' – this could be characterized as an unreasonable veto.

The government machine set to work to blame the perfidious French. On 12 March an internal Labour Party briefing paper said they were continuing to work flat out for a second resolution, but admitted that Chirac's statement 'makes the diplomatic task very difficult'. This argument was used to good effect with wavering MPs who could go back to their constituency parties with a reason for backing the government. But stirring up anti-French feeling wasn't without a potential long-term downside. How much more difficult would it make Tony Blair's case for adopting the euro?

The government's argument was also helped by a tactical blunder, when the hard-left Campaign Group dramatically upped the ante, in a statement on 11 March, by claiming that Tony Blair's leadership was at stake: 'It is time for the Prime Minister to consider his position in the interests not just of the country and his party but in the interests of maintaining the framework of world order ... If the Prime Minister is not prepared to stand up to George Bush and call for a peaceful resolution to this crisis, he must make way for those who will.'

For many MPs, however much they distrusted Blair, this was staring into the abyss. Were they really prepared to lose a leader who had been so electorally successful? The US administration was advised informally that they could be dealing with a new prime minister in the autumn if they were not more forthcoming on the Middle East peace process, a key consideration for many Labour MPs in the run-up to the last crucial parliamentary vote.

Further gloomy news came on 13 March when the Leader of the House, Robin Cook, made clear at cabinet that he would resign if the government failed to gain a second resolution. It

89

was a tense weekend. As Tony Blair flew to the Azores for the eve-of-war meeting with George Bush, MPs were talking to their constituency parties about which way they'd vote.

On Monday 17 March we stood outside Downing Street playing that old game of shouting questions at cabinet ministers in the full knowledge that they'll never reply. BBC Political Editor Andrew Marr to Gordon Brown: 'Do you care if Robin Cook resigns?' No reply. 'So you don't care!' Even the sketch writers were out in force, egging us on. Then the news – Cook had left by the back door. He was resigning. As for Clare Short, still no one knew. She couldn't really be staying on after all she'd said, could she?

Back in the Commons the arm twisting was in full swing, ahead of the final vote the following day. The whips gave ministers lists of wavering MPs to be won over. Some were even told that a general election could be declared that night if the vote were lost. Tony Blair was meeting groups himself. According to a later interview with the *Sun*, he'd warned his family that he could lose his job and civil servants were dusting off the procedures for the resignation of a prime minister. The atmosphere in the corridors was highly charged as everyone made a guess at the size of the revolt. Many had swung back to the leadership, persuaded by the 'perfidious French' argument. Others had decided to rebel because of the lack of a second resolution. Then news came through that Cook was to make a personal statement. His words were devastating.

'Tonight the international partnerships most important to us are weakened: the European Union is divided; the Security Council is in stalemate. Those are heavy casualties of a war in which a shot has yet to be fired … On Iraq, I believe that the prevailing mood of the British people is sound. They do not doubt that Saddam is a brutal dictator, but they are not persuaded that he is a clear and present danger to Britain. They want inspections to be given a chance, and they suspect that they are being pushed too quickly into conflict by a US administration with an agenda of its own. Above all, they are uneasy at Britain going out on a limb on a military adventure without a broader international coalition and against the hostility of many of our traditional allies.'

He received an unprecedented standing ovation. Some think that if he'd spoken during the main debate on the Tuesday, more

MPs would have been tempted to rebel. As it was, they were making their minds up right until the last minute. Tony Blair and his senior cabinet ministers were still seeing people up until 8 o'clock on the night of the vote. Despite the pressure, 139 Labour MPs voted against the government, a third of the parliamentary Labour Party. This was serious but still lower than many in the government had feared.

* * * * * *

Where has all this left the Prime Minister? He has now deployed British troops – the hardest decision for any leader – in Kosovo, Sierra Leone, Afghanistan and Iraq. The stress has etched itself on his face and hairline. There had been no certainty of success. One senior official said at times it felt as though they were being swept through a narrow channel, never knowing if they'd end up on the rocks. Perhaps that course was even more difficult to steer now. A major international realignment seemed to be taking place, making it harder than ever for Tony Blair to be the self-professed bridge between Europe and America.

As for Blair's standing back home, there was at first a 'Baghdad bounce' in the opinion polls, and those close to Blair thought there would be an important long-term benefit. Before the war there had been a serious lack of trust in the government, so even when there were improvements in public services, no one believed it. But now they thought that voters would be more inclined to trust the Prime Minister.

But for Blair himself, the experience of war leadership may encourage a bunker mentality in peace time – reliance on a few trusted advisers. That was one of Clare Short's criticisms when she finally resigned on 12 May, accusing Tony Blair of rule by diktat. She is not alone. There are many in the Labour Party who'll never forgive him, and the rebels on Iraq are now prepared to defy him again on the domestic front. Voters who admired his steadfastness against Saddam now want to know what he'll do for their public services. It was something George Bush's father learned the hard way after the first Gulf War. To adapt the reminder on the wall of Bill Clinton's campaign headquarters – 'It's the Health Service, stupid.'

CHAPTER FIVE

THE DISUNITED STATES OF EUROPE

Stephen Sackur

92   *Stephen Sackur is Europe Correspondent, based in Brussels. His former posts include Cairo, Jerusalem and Washington. He reported the first Gulf War for the BBC from British army headquarters in Kuwait and southern Iraq. He describes how the European institutions fell into disarray as the leading nations took opposing positions over the Iraq crisis.*

It was one of the most disturbing images of the war and it came from a tranquil place thousands of kilometres from the crucible of violence and human misery in Iraq. It was a stark message addressed to 'Les Rosbeefs' (sic) – the derisive French term for the British – daubed onto the stone memorial overlooking the vast Commonwealth military cemetery in Etaples, northern France. All it took was a can of paint and a heart filled with hate.

'Dig up your trash, it is contaminating our soil.' The words taunted the memory of the 11,000 British soldiers buried in Etaples, men who had died defending France in the First World War. 'Saddam will win – he will spill more of your blood.' These crude graffiti, written by an unknown hand, appeared one week after the war in Iraq began. Within hours they'd been seen, and photographed, by a party of British visitors. A couple of days later the desecration of the cemetery was front-page news.

By the time I arrived in Etaples a team from the Commonwealth War Graves Commission had cleansed the grey stone memorial of its poisonous words. Under scudding rain clouds the countless lines of graves bore silent witness to the unfathomable pain of war, past and present. The manicured pathways were deserted.

I had come to this melancholy place to meet Jean Nelson, the regional maintenance chief of the War Graves Commission. When we talked he had tears in his eyes. 'I'm hurt, so hurt and ashamed by what has happened here,' he said. Jean's grandfather served with the British army in the Great War, fought on the Western Front and, when the slaughter was over, worked as a gardener at the Etaples military cemetery. Jean's father served in the Second World War, then continued the family tradition by devoting himself to the upkeep of the war graves. So Jean himself, with a Scottish father and a French mother, is a third-generation guardian of the Commonwealth war dead in northern France.

'I want you to understand one thing,' he told me. 'Of course   93
we have differences over the war in Iraq, but no one in Etaples condones what has happened here. These words were disgusting, crazy – the work of a madman – please don't assume that all of France thinks this way.'

Most French people were indeed appalled by the Etaples desecration. President Jacques Chirac spoke for the vast majority of his compatriots in his remarkable letter of personal apology for the incident addressed to the Queen. 'Madam, I was appalled and deeply shocked to learn of the desecration,' he wrote. 'On behalf of France, and personally, I want to express my most sincere regrets.' He went further: 'I can tell you that at the moment when your soldiers are engaged in combat the thoughts of the French are naturally turning towards them.'

But no amount of politesse could disguise a simple truth: the attack on Iraq had roused deep anger and hostility not just in France but across much of Europe. The determination of George W Bush and Tony Blair to take decisive action against Saddam Hussein left the continent deeply divided – governments at odds with each other; voters alienated from their own leaders. Europe's most important institutions showed signs of the strain. The European Union, NATO, five decades of assumptions about the transatlantic alliance – all were sorely tested by the Iraq crisis and all were found wanting.

* * * * * *

My first insight into the depth of European disquiet over Iraq came six months before the war began. On a balmy evening in early September 2002, I drove to Aachen, in the west of Germany, to assess the mood of German voters just two weeks before their federal elections. Chancellor Gerhard Schröder's campaign bandwagon had rolled into town. A crowd of perhaps 2000 was gathered in the square behind Aachen's magnificent cathedral to see the leader of the ruling Social Democrats in the flesh.

I found little enthusiasm for Mr Schröder – a man with many of the strengths, and weaknesses, of a Teutonic Bill Clinton. Most people grumbled about Germany's flagging economy and a trail of broken promises; one alluded to allegations of an extramarital affair (the Chancellor is already on his fourth wife). In the end, though, many said they would still vote to keep their tarnished leader. And the reason was encapsulated in a single word: Iraq.

Gerhard Schröder is an astute politician. A month before polling day he was ten percentage points behind his stolid conservative opponent, Edmund Stoiber. He knew he would be defeated unless he could find one big issue to resonate with Germany's voters, which is why, after a tepid arrival on the stage in Aachen and some unconvincing rhetoric about economic reform, Schröder turned his attention to the dominant foreign policy issue of the day. 'I promise you this,' he said, his voice suddenly intimate yet powerful, 'if there is a war, not one German soldier will be sent to Iraq.' It was a well-rehearsed line, which prompted the most thunderous applause of the night. He went on: 'And I say this to our American ally. A true friend says the difficult thing that needs saying, even if it is not always welcome.'

Two weeks later Schröder became Germany's very own 'Comeback Kid'; the SPD/Green coalition held on to power by the narrowest of margins. Political commentators agreed that it was the Chancellor's increasingly strident anti-war stance that had saved his political skin.

The Americans were outraged by what they regarded as Schröder's cynicism. In a striking breach of protocol, President Bush refused to call his erstwhile ally to congratulate him on his re-election. But the personal venom directed by Washington at the hapless Chancellor, whose domestic woes were about to

multiply, missed the point. Schröder wasn't leading and manipu-
lating public opinion – he was following it.

Several weeks after the election I went to Cologne to see if
Germans had begun to question the wisdom of their trenchant
opposition to the Iraq War. They had not; if anything, attitudes
had hardened. In a day of exhaustive interviewing I couldn't find
a single person – not one – who was prepared to back the
Bush–Blair strategy. And this in a country defined by its post-1945
strategic partnership with the United States, indeed a country still
prepared to play host to tens of thousands of US troops.

At Cologne's Sports University (imagine a more earnest version of the kids from *Fame*) the class of 2003 was bewildered and
angry. 'Where are these chemical weapons? It's just an excuse –
the Americans want the oil,' one said. Another butted in: 'Look,
I lived for a year in North Carolina. I have no problem with
Americans, but this Bush government is dangerous for all of us.'

In a suburban kindergarten, young mothers were picking up
their toddlers. 'There will be more threats, more terrorists and
suicide bombs after this war,' one woman predicted gloomily. In a
beer hall in the centre of the city a group of pensioners was
settling down for an early dinner; men and women with silver hair
and florid faces, who were children when Cologne was reduced to a
smouldering ruin by Allied bombing at the end of the Second World
War. 'We've seen enough wars, enough bombs,' one man growled.
'We know better than anyone that war brings no good.'

These were voices from the heart of a continent scarred by
a dark 20th-century history. They reflected a deep-seated
European aversion to war and militarism, and a desperate desire
to believe in a benign world community governed by multilateral
institutions.

Robert Kagan, an American commentator on international
relations, put it this way: 'Europeans are from Venus,' he wrote,
'Americans from Mars'. It was a seductive aphorism that gained
common currency in the weeks before the Iraq War. In his fortu-
itously timed book *Of Paradise and Power*, he portrayed a post-
nationalist Europe at once idealistic and hopelessly naïve, 'softened'
by prosperity and open borders, no longer willing or able to project
military power. Kagan's America, on the other hand, remained an

95

aggressively nationalistic military superpower, ready to use force to combat 'threats' overseas, driven by an uncomplicated sense of righteousness. The contrast was neat, and it appeared to offer a plausible explanation for the transatlantic rift caused by the Iraq crisis; but the reality was more complicated than this clash of temperaments between the ancient Gods could ever convey.

France was the key player in Europe's response to the Iraq challenge, and French diplomatic strategy was defined by two men with a grandiose (and none too Venus-like) vision of their country's place in the world.

For President Jacques Chirac the Iraq crisis represented an unmissable opportunity to stamp his mark on global affairs. His political career, though consistently successful, had never quite matched his vaulting ambition. He'd long been dogged by the whiff of scandal. There were allegations of a lavish lifestyle funded by a personal slush fund, and constant whispers about his connections to unsavoury dictators overseas – including Saddam Hussein. In the Elysée Palace, too, Chirac had suffered frustrations. For years he was constrained by 'co-habitation' with a Socialist prime minister – until, that is, the French right secured an overwhelming victory in the parliamentary elections of 2002.

At last Jacques Chirac was free to pursue his own, and what he saw as France's, rightful destiny. One of his first, and most significant, decisions was to promote his long-time confidant and chief of staff Dominique de Villepin to the post of Foreign Minister. 'They're incredibly close ... Chirac is the doting father and de Villepin is his brainy son,' was how one French commentator described them.

De Villepin quickly became a central character in the prolonged diplomatic drama that preceded the war. With his carefully coiffed grey locks, his chiselled features and his penchant for poetry and literary quotation, he cut a dashing figure. Like Chirac, he had a vision of a resurgent France bestriding the world stage, fulfilling her historic role as leader of Europe and counterweight to the United States. In short, de Villepin was, and is, an avid disciple of Charles de Gaulle.

'Today orphaned, uncertain, easily disenchanted, France still burns with a desire for history,' he wrote in a pamphlet entitled

'The Cry of the Gargoyle', which aroused little interest when it was first published but was required reading in the first weeks of 2003. 'France should be,' the gargoyle declared, 'an ardent defender of her rank.'

President Jacques Chirac was not, on the face of it, a knee-jerk anti-American – he had studied in the United States and even claimed a brief stint as a reporter on the New Orleans *Times-Picayune* – but he viewed the Bush administration's stance on Iraq as a provocation, an attempt to set the seal on a unipolar world in which Europe's role was that of loyal lackey. 'Pay no attention to what Chirac might say about his affection for the United States from his student days. This is not the question. His view is something deep, deep within him. For Chirac, the Americans understand nothing.' That was the conclusion of the French writer Guy Sorman, a long-time confidant of the French president.

Indeed, the Iraq crisis tapped into a well-established reservoir of French resentment. Chirac had long suspected the Americans of malign interference in European affairs. For example, Washington was known to be unenthusiastic about EU plans to develop its own military capability; and US officials had been lobbying hard for Brussels to offer the prospect of EU membership to Turkey, as well as to the newly democratic states of eastern Europe. The French leader sensed a blatant effort to shift the balance of power in Europe in a more pro-American direction.

Given this context, it was hardly surprising that George Bush's decision to apply 'pre-emptive force' in Iraq produced one of the most damaging diplomatic confrontations in Europe since the close of the Second World War. Beyond the specific arguments about military intervention in Iraq lay a series of profoundly troubling questions: Who speaks for Europe in the international arena? Is the United States a permanent partner or a potentially dangerous dominatrix? And, to put it crudely, does Europe matter?

Jacques Chirac had answers for all those questions. In no small measure he felt he *was* the answer. After the passage of UN Security Council Resolution 1441 he moved quickly to forge an alliance with Chancellor Schröder, assuming that a joint Franco–German stance against America's 'rush to war' would, in effect, define the EU position.

97

The Chirac–Schröder double act was a wondrous example of political expediency. In years past neither man had been able to disguise his dislike for the other – Chirac had even made plain his preference for Edmund Stoiber in the recent German election. But both leaders recognized a common interest in standing up to the United States. Yes, it was good for their domestic popularity (polls put opposition to the war at roughly 80 per cent in both countries), but more significantly it allowed them to revive the notion of a Franco–German motor, driving the European Union forward. And it sent a clear message to the Americans: don't take Europe for granted. Significantly, after one of their regular bilateral meetings in mid-January 2003, the two men announced not just a joint position on Iraq – more time for weapons inspections, faith in the UN process, tireless efforts to avert war – but also a joint initiative on the constitutional reform of the EU.

An assertive, Gaullist France, dragging an economically straitened Germany in its wake, was making good on the vision sketched out by Dominique de Villepin in 'The Cry of the Gargoyle'. She was 'defending her rank'.

The consequences for the European Union were disastrous. It wasn't just the Blair government in Britain that resented this Paris powerplay. Prime Minister José María Aznar of Spain had carefully cultivated his own close relationship with President George W Bush. It was a part of his broader effort to give Spain more clout in the international arena. Spanish officials deeply resented what they saw as French arrogance, as did the governments in Rome, Lisbon and Copenhagen.

And the Americans, livid with Chirac and Schröder, couldn't resist the opportunity to rub a bagful of salt into the European wound. At the Pentagon, Donald Rumsfeld was asked an artfully loaded question: what did he think of the French and German decision to side with Saddam Hussein rather than George Bush? Rumsfeld gave a wolfish grin and came up with an answer that resonated across Europe like a gunshot. 'France has been a problem,' he acknowledged, 'Germany has been a problem; but I think that's old Europe ... and the centre of gravity in Europe is shifting to the east.'

'Old Europe': with one contemptuous phrase the abrasive

Secretary of Defense appeared to toss France and Germany – pillars of NATO and the European Union – into the dustbin of history. Not only that, he also pointed to a 'New Europe' of vibrant, pro-American democracies in formerly Communist Eastern Europe. It was an exquisite piece of diplomatic mischief-making.

Rumsfeld's comments left officials in Paris, Berlin and EU headquarters in Brussels almost apoplectic with rage. Editorial writers in newspapers across the continent fulminated at America's arrogance, but the truth was that the notion of a Europe divided between Old and New had struck a painful nerve. Within days José María Aznar drew up a letter of support for America's tough stance on Iraq; it was co-signed by the leaders of Britain, Italy, Portugal and Denmark. It also had the backing of leaders from Poland, the Czech Republic and Hungary – leading lights in Mr Rumsfeld's 'New Europe'. And soon after came another pro-American declaration from the so-called 'Vilnius 10' – five more east European countries about to enter the EU, plus a collection of Balkan states keen to reap the rewards of loyalty to Washington.

In the weeks before the war the European Union was, to coin a blunt phrase used by its External Affairs Commissioner, Chris Patten, 'in a bloody mess'. Hastily arranged summit meetings did nothing to paper over the cracks. Tony Blair and Jacques Chirac became the de facto leaders of two opposing camps, divided by a profound difference of strategic vision. The Blairites insisted that Europe must maintain its close partnership with the United States; to do otherwise would hasten irrelevance, if not instability. The French and the Germans demanded a more muscular assertion of a specifically European world view. The EU, they clearly believed, could be a counterweight, an alternative, to the so-called *'hyper-puissance'*.

But of course the EU could hardly be a credible player on the world stage, nor even command the respect of its own citizens, if it remained crippled by division. So Jacques Chirac decided to apply some diplomatic muscle. At an emergency summit in Brussels in mid-February he launched an extraordinary attack on the former Soviet Bloc countries preparing to join the European club. He condemned their support for the United States, dismissed them as 'reckless, childish and badly brought up', and added that they 'had missed an excellent opportunity to shut up'. In case anyone failed to get the point, he concluded that the candidate countries' behaviour threatened to jeopardize their chances of joining the union.

Long after this presidential eruption was over, French officials were trying to put out the diplomatic fires left in its wake. Leaders from the applicant countries were appalled by the tone and content of Chirac's remarks. One privately compared him to Leonid Brezhnev. In public they were more restrained. 'We are too well brought up,' was the jibe from Hungary's prime minister. But if the French believed they could impose their will on the EU newcomers they were sadly mistaken. Having taken orders from Moscow for so many years the citizens of eastern Europe were not going to bow to the master of the Elysée Palace.

The Iraq War left European diplomats morosely surveying extensive collateral damage. At a time when the much-vaunted Convention on the Future of Europe was supposed to be grappling with the big issues facing an enlarged union – how to streamline its leadership, how to move towards a common foreign and security policy – a deep rift had been exposed. The 15 members had failed the Iraq test, had indeed failed to act as a union at all. And there was every prospect of the division over Europe's strategic direction becoming more intractable with the expansion to 25.

* * * * * *

A few kilometres from the centre of Brussels, far removed from the intimacy of the EU *quartier* where bureaucrats and journalists lunch and gossip, you come across one of the most miserable buildings ever erected in this stolid city. It lies next to a busy suburban road; a sprawl of low-rise concrete boxes with all the charm of an East German technical college. This is NATO, the central pillar of America's post-1945 commitment to Europe's security, the collective defence alliance which faced down Soviet Communism and which, even more rapidly than the European Union, embraced the east European countries it once prepared to fight. NATO was a creation of the Cold War. It outlasted the Warsaw Pact, but then found itself with an uncertain role.

In Kosovo it was a useful vehicle for American and European intervention; not so when the US decided to go it alone in Afghanistan.

In the early months of the Iraq crisis NATO was again side-lined, but in February 2003 the alliance, like the EU, was forced to confront the questions raised by the looming war. Turkey, a NATO member and northern neighbour of Iraq, turned to the collective membership for help. The Turks invoked Article Four of the North Atlantic Treaty – the obligation on all members to consult if any one of them feels threatened – in order to discuss plans for the defence of their border with Iraq. The assumption (in Washington as much as Ankara) was that early warning aircraft and Patriot missile batteries would be rapidly deployed.

But three out of NATO's 19 members refused to allow the planning process to begin. France, backed by Germany and Belgium, exercised its right of veto, declaring that the organization should not be seen to undertake military planning while the UN weapons inspections process was still viable. They accused the United States of trying to press-gang the alliance into accepting 'the logic of war'. Once again Jacques Chirac had decided to confront the '*hyperpuissance*' and another piece of Europe's institutional architecture was in danger of collapse.

For the best part of a week, NATO ambassadors camped out in their dreary headquarters trying to overcome the impasse. The atmosphere in the corridors was poisonous. In the midst of one closed-door meeting an official emerged to report with ill-disguised glee, 'My God the French Ambassador is taking a pasting.' The fresh-faced and usually supremely affable American Ambassador, Nick Burns, told me: 'There is a real crisis underway in NATO. Our credibility is being put to the test, and we must deal with it by agreeing tomorrow.'

In the end, it took a week of argument before the Turks got their defensive support. Approval came from 18 members; a procedural gambit was used to allow the French to sit on their hands and maintain their dignity. It was a suitably sorry end to one of the most damaging episodes in NATO's history. The collective principle, the cornerstone of the alliance, had been undermined, and on all sides there were new questions about NATO's relevance. The

Americans talked pointedly about future alliances being 'coalitions of the willing'; the French contemplated the possibility of building a common defence structure with a hard core of allies in the European Union (basically Germany plus the combined military might of Belgium and Luxembourg).

NATO's Secretary-General, Lord Robertson, was left with the unenviable task of picking up the pieces. At the end of the war a reporter asked him if members had resolved their differences. 'I'm always optimistic, but I'm not stupid,' was his cryptic reply. Even more telling was his comment to ambassadors from the seven east European nations about to join the alliance. They were on a formal tour of NATO headquarters at the height of the February impasse. 'Well,' said the Secretary-General with a wan smile, 'do you still want to join?'

Had Lord Robertson visited Burgas on Bulgaria's Black Sea coast he would perhaps have been reassured. For a few days later, in this eastern outpost of Donald Rumsfeld's 'New Europe', I found few doubts about NATO's continued relevance and even fewer doubts about the wisdom of sticking close to the United States. Burgas is not a pretty sight. Grimy tenements sag as if weighed down by decades of disappointment; antiquated factories belch and wheeze like old men on borrowed time; and on the edge of town there is a dilapidated airport, the terminal building deserted except for a mangy cat. To the American military, though, Burgas airport has a seductive asset: one of the longest runways in eastern Europe, which is why the Pentagon requested permission to base six huge refuelling aircraft there in preparation for the air campaign in Iraq. The Bulgarian government was only too happy to oblige.

When I arrived at this unlikely outpost of American military power, local dignitaries and journalists were being given a cockpit tour by Colonel Jim Muscatel of the US Air Force. 'Isn't this something?' he enthused afterwards. 'The local governor here used to be a Communist. Now he's my friend.'

The United States is busy making new best friends right across eastern Europe. Very soon some of the American troops deployed in Germany may be heading to new bases in Poland, Hungary, perhaps even Burgas.

'We want the benefits of NATO, and the EU,' said Evgenii Dainov, a Bulgarian political scientist. 'But if we had to choose, we'd take NATO.' I asked why. 'Because we live in a rough neighbourhood, and we remember our history. In the end the Americans, not the French, will be the best guarantors of our freedom and security.'

* * * * * *

Faced with war in Iraq, Europe was a house hopelessly divided – over the moral and the legal issues, and over the wisdom of the whole enterprise. The governments of the continent were split down the middle. But the prevailing mood of the European public was much more one-sided: they were largely against this American war. Their preoccupation was not the potential threat posed by Saddam Hussein, but profound suspicion of the American superpower.

And the end of the war did not signal an end to that suspicion. Anti-Americanism remains a powerful force across the continent, even in countries such as Spain and Italy that offered official backing for the military campaign. Throughout their governments' strong support for the American action, popular opinion had remained deeply hostile. Already there were new causes, new slogans. US policy towards Syria, Iran and the Palestinians was rousing vehement European opposition. At the first EU summit after the toppling of Saddam Hussein, thousands of furious protestors gathered in Athens. While Europe's leaders sought to overcome their damaging rift, petrol bombs were being lobbed at the British and American embassies.

'You may think I'm crazy,' said a friend of mine in Greece, 'but I truly believe there could be a war between America and Europe in my children's lifetime.' A Greek film director went on a TV chat show and declared: 'The Americans are animals. It is a statistical fact that the American mind stops developing at the age of 13.'

Those kinds of views are no more representative of the European mainstream than the hateful slogans daubed on the cemetery in Etaples. But both Tony Blair and Jacques Chirac – the key protagonists in Europe's showdown over Iraq – know the crisis has landed the continent at an historic crossroads. In one direction lies continued partnership with the globally dominant

United States, an Atlanticist assumption of shared goals and values. The other path involves more risk. It leads to a Europe capable of projecting a muscular, independent presence on the world stage. It also points to a new, difficult relationship with this continent's erstwhile protector, the American superpower. Tony Blair appears intent on heading one way, Jacques Chirac the other. Both men claim to speak for Europe, but only one of them will ultimately be proved right.

104

CHAPTER SIX

'SHOCK AND AWE' – AN INEVITABLE VICTORY

Paul Adams

Paul Adams is Defence Correspondent. He was formerly Belgrade and   105
Middle East Correspondent, covering the Palestinian uprising in 2000. In
the build-up to the war he reported on Ministry of Defence preparations,
and was at US forward headquarters CENTCOM, at the Sayliya base in
Qatar, for the duration of the conflict. In this chapter, he reviews and
analyses the progress of the war as seen by coalition commanders.

'This will be a campaign unlike anything else in history.'
General Tommy Franks, 22 March 2003.

A day after American and British troops entered Iraq, the man
charged with running the war made his first appearance before
journalists assembled in the briefing room at CENTCOM. For
those of us who'd already been there a while, wondering when
the quarter-of-a-million-dollar 'Hollywood set' with its plasma
screens would be used, it was a welcome development. The
British were already briefing all-comers, but had not yet been
allowed to use the elaborate press room. The Americans, who
reserved the right to use it first, were nowhere to be seen. The
war had begun and my American colleagues were beginning to
wring their hands. When was someone going to come out and tell
them something to justify their existence here?

So we fell on Tommy Franks with a kind of guilty gratitude.
And he didn't disappoint. For someone reportedly shy of the
media, his performance was commanding. He listed eight campaign objectives, from the removal of Saddam Hussein to the

elimination of Iraq's weapons of mass destruction. And he made bold claims for what was to follow. Operation Iraqi Freedom, he said, would be 'characterized by shock, by surprise, by flexibility, by the employment of precise munitions on a scale never seen before, and by the application of overwhelming force'.

We'd already had a foretaste. The previous evening, 20 minutes of devastating pyrotechnics were beamed live from Baghdad. Twenty minutes of explosions, fireballs and mushroom clouds that looked for all the world like the beginning of the 'shock and awe' tactics we'd all been reading about for months. It ended abruptly, just as US Defense Secretary Donald Rumsfeld and Richard Myers, the Chairman of the US Joint Chiefs of Staff, entered the Pentagon briefing room – 11,000 kilometres away – to announce that the air war had begun. Washington was keen, as ever, to keep military and media cycles synchronized.

But what was this 'shock and awe' that we were watching? The phrase sounded brutal and had already served to heighten fears among the war's many opponents that Iraq was about to be pulverized. Britain's top commander at CENTCOM, Air Marshal Brian Burridge, pointedly refused to use it, preferring instead the suitably academic-sounding 'effects-based warfare'. The two phrases seemed to match the two commanders. The tall, imposing, jug-eared Texan seemed just the man to inflict a dose of shock and awe on Iraq, while his shorter, bespectacled British counterpart appeared to embody something a little more nuanced.

But while it was tempting to draw distinctions between the two major coalition partners, 'shock and awe' and 'effects-based warfare' were essentially the same thing. There was never any intention to lay waste to Baghdad or to target Iraq's infrastructure. 'Our role was to shock the regime, not the good people of Baghdad,' Burridge told me as the campaign drew to a close. 'The whole point … is to get inside their minds and say "we know what you do and where you do it, and we've destroyed it. Now, what do you think of that?"'

Closer examination of those awe-inspiring 20 minutes on 21 March showed what he meant. Among the targets featured on the coalition's voluminous Master Target List (perhaps the most comprehensive account of a country's key facilities ever compiled before a war and the result of years of systematic aerial monitoring) was Baghdad's famous Rashid Hotel. Underneath was a huge, reinforced command and control bunker. But 200 metres away was a less well-protected communications switch, connecting the bunker with the outside world. There were still foreign journalists staying in the hotel. To attack the Rashid would certainly have resulted in scores of civilian casualties. And so, amid all the fire and the fury of that night, the communications switch was struck instead. The effect was the same: the bunker could no longer function.

Of all the effects coalition planners were looking to achieve, this was one of the most important: disrupting the Iraqi regime's ability to exercise control over its armed forces, leaving key commanders wondering what on earth was going on. There's ample evidence that it worked. The very first attack on Baghdad, at dawn on 20 March, may have had the most dramatic effect of all. At the Sayliya base on the edge of Doha, it took almost everyone by surprise. Standing in front of a camera, in the middle of a long series of live interviews, I felt my knees wobble as a colleague handed me a scribbled note informing me that Saddam Hussein had been among the targets. Perhaps the war would be over before it had even begun? In Kuwait, a US spokesman, Major Chris Hughes, called the attack by a pair of F-117 Night Hawk stealth fighters a 'decapitation' attempt against the regime. A British official, with surprising understatement, called it 'a shot across Iraq's bows'.

Weeks later, it was still not clear whether the Iraqi leadership had been decapitated or not. Suspicions generated by Saddam Hussein's well-documented use of doubles, and the possibility of pre-recording, meant that a series of televised speeches and 'public' appearances were generally considered inconclusive. But one fact soon became clear to the staff at CENTCOM as they strained, through every sophisticated eavesdropping method at their disposal, to hear the radio traffic in and out of Baghdad: Saddam Hussein had simply disappeared. Whatever else he was doing after that night, he did not appear to be issuing orders. It was to be three weeks before US marines pulled down his statue in Firdos (Paradise) Square, but the man who had so dominated Iraq for three decades ceased to be militarily relevant on the very first night.

107

American and British bombing continued to target command and control facilities, breaking up the Iraqi military and security organizations into a series of fragmented, rudderless vessels, adrift in a sea of powerful currents controlled from hundreds of kilometres away. By early April, the eerily impassive chief American spokesman, Brigadier General Vince Brooks, told reporters: 'We can't tell who's in charge. I don't think the Iraqi people can tell who's in charge either. And we have indications that the Iraqi forces don't know who's in charge.'

Relentless information operations served to confuse the Iraqi leadership even further. 'We had to make the regime fracture by believing they were losing,' Burridge told me, 'if necessary by more than they actually were.' This, more than the pyrotechnics, was what shock and awe was all about. Despite the obvious disparity in simple brute force between the two sides, it was information – Iraq's lack or it and the coalition's super-abundance – that guaranteed a quick and, for the coalition at least, relatively painless victory. 'There are other ways of doing shock and awe than by breaking things,' Burridge said.

108

A second 'decapitation' attempt, on 7 April, demonstrated that speed was another of the advantages that came with information superiority. According to Lt-Col. Frank Swan, weapons system officer aboard the B-1B Lancer tasked with hitting a restaurant in the Mansur district of Baghdad, it didn't take long to switch from the bomber's original mission when word came that senior leaders, possibly Saddam Hussein and his sons, might be meeting there. 'We had another target area that we were planned to go to,' Swan said. 'And … from the time we got the co-ordinates, it took 12 minutes to get the bombs on target. So that's how quick the system can work.'

Southern Iraq was littered with evidence that the coalition's high-speed strategy was working and that Iraq's battle plan was never really implemented. Oil installations rigged for destruction survived intact. Key bridges over the Tigris and Euphrates were never demolished, despite signs that this should have happened. And, most significant to coalition commanders, the key Republican Guard divisions guarding the southern approaches to Baghdad never moved into sensible defensive positions. It seems perfectly possible that they didn't really know where the advancing US 3rd

Infantry Division and 1st Marine Expeditionary Force were. A senior Iraqi officer, captured on the day US forces first entered Baghdad, is said to have been astonished to find the enemy so close. He believed what Iraq's irrepressible Information Minister had repeatedly said: that American troops were still far from the capital. Other Iraqi officers, interviewed after the fighting ended, said that their orders had become increasingly confused and, towards the end, had petered out altogether.

Of course, this was always going to be an extraordinarily uneven contest, between an unrivalled military superpower, flexing new, high-tech muscles, and the demoralized remnants of Iraq's once substantial armed forces. On paper, Saddam Hussein had an estimated 390,000 military personnel at his disposal (not including more than 600,000 reservists), in excess of 2500 tanks and around 300 combat aircraft. The coalition, on the other hand, deployed a total of no more than 250,000 personnel, with around 450 main battle tanks and more than 600 combat aircraft. But the figures are misleading: a lot of Iraqi equipment was old, poorly serviced, and in some cases entirely unusable. Discretion, for some members of Iraq's armed forces, was clearly the better part of valour. Not a single Iraqi fixed-wing aircraft took to the skies during the war. Perhaps the pilots were heeding the blunt warnings from Qatar. In the words of an American official at CENTCOM: 'If they fly, they die'.

But nor do the simple figures do justice to the nature of the contest. How, for example, do you measure the impact of more than 40 million leaflets dropped on Iraq before the war even began, covering everything from simple instructions to military units on how to surrender, to dire warnings of the consequences for anyone thinking of using chemical or biological weapons? Or the coalition's ability to send text messages to the mobile phones of individual Iraqi commanders, exhorting them not to fight? As military teams set about analysing the campaign, these were some of the calculations they needed to make.

They would also examine the role played by an extraordinarily high number of American, British and Australian special forces. In Qatar, we were shown tantalizing footage, shot by the military themselves, illustrating this largely secret world: an

109

assault on a presidential palace, complete with the sound of foot-steps echoing in the empty corridors; the rescue of Private Jessica Lynch from a hospital in Nasiriya; or the seizing of a dam to pre-vent it from being blown up. These were carefully selected and edited highlights of a hugely influential, and generally invisible, aspect of the campaign.

* * * * * *

A thousand kilometres from Baghdad, amid the serried ranks of unprepossessing warehouses that make up the Sayliya base, it wasn't always easy to keep pace with rapidly unfolding events far to the north. With few exceptions, the daily briefings were mostly anodyne, aimed not at the journalists – who pitched up, more in hope than expectation, every afternoon – but at breakfast rooms across America. Away from the briefing room, the pickings were even slimmer. Reporters desperate for facts swarmed every time a clean-cut, polite American military spokesman ventured into the crowded corridors. But the constraints imposed by 'operational security' or, just as often, a reluctance to speak out of turn, meant we always came away disappointed. The White House media rela-tions hotshot appointed as Tommy Frank's chief spokesman (and granted the temporary rank of two-star general) was affable when you were lucky enough to run into him but was generally con-spicuous by his absence. On really bad days, some journalists resorted to interviewing each other – always a sure sign that things are not going well.

A small team of British media handlers worked hard to fill the void. With sun-tanned features and unwavering stance – feet apart, thumbs tucked into belt loops at the back of his camouflage trousers – Group Captain Al Lockwood appeared before the cameras day after day, in one live interview after another, answering questions with a natural equanimity. But the British also realized that sound bites alone would not be enough. And so, for a sense of what was really happening, I found a scrap of shade in the courtyard outside the press centre each morning, to be briefed by the one man on the base who seemed to have a licence to talk. Beyond noting the fact that he appeared to exist on a diet of coffee and chain-smoked cigarettes, I'll respect his desire to remain anonymous. But he, more than anyone, was willing to shed light on the rapid pace of events in Iraq, often explaining what was happening, saying who was where and alerting me to developments that had yet to unfold, trusting me not to reveal them until reports from the field suggested they were already underway.

It was an adult way of doing things, and one that the Americans could not, or would not, emulate. I quickly realized that being a long way from the action, however odd it sometimes felt, did not need to be an impediment to understanding. With vivid accounts from embedded journalists pouring onto the newswires, usually with a speed that the military's own public information chain could not match, and the opportunity to hear what my own BBC colleagues were saying, I felt there was more than enough detail to process. Those private courtyard briefings enabled me to pull strands together and interpret what was going on: the very reason for being at CENTCOM in the first place. It wasn't just the military whose technological advances made this a very different conflict from the first Gulf War, a dozen years earlier. With the internet, mobile phones and satellite dishes able to broadcast on the move, the media have taken their own great strides. Somewhere in the welter of information it was possible to detect the outlines, and sometimes the detail, of the campaign.

The impact of the embeds was enormous. Walking into the BBC's cramped cubby-hole of an office on the morning of 21 March, I was immediately transfixed by the sight of American tanks racing across the featureless deserts of southern Iraq. The ground war had begun and for the first time in history, here was a full-scale invasion, live on TV. The images were fuzzy, sometimes barely discernible, but the spectacle was riveting. Two days later, all heads in the press centre turned to watch a bank of monitors showing live pictures of a gun battle in Umm Qasr. Again, the images were arresting, and network commentators were wondering how well the campaign could really be going if such drama was still being played out so close to the Kuwaiti border. But in strategic terms, the skirmish at Umm Qasr was almost insignificant. The real story had already shifted about 250 kilometres to the north-west, where American troops were preparing to cross the Euphrates for the first time.

If the presence of the embeds occasionally gave rise to misunderstandings, they were sometimes able to contradict the military's own misleading statements. The most graphic, and troubling, example came on 31 March, when soldiers from the 3rd Infantry Division fired on a civilian vehicle approaching a checkpoint near Najaf, killing ten civilians, including women and children. CENTCOM's statement claimed the vehicle failed to stop 'even after warning shots were fired'.

But a *Washington Post* report by William Branigin, who witnessed the incident, told a very different story. He said soldiers manning the checkpoint had failed, in the confusion, to respond to repeated orders to fire warning shots. Branigin heard the furious response of Capt. Ronny Johnson: 'You just fucking killed a family because you didn't fire a warning shot soon enough!' An initial investigation found that soldiers 'responded in accordance with the rules of engagement to protect themselves'.

When things went wrong, cracks appeared in the smooth veneer of the CENTCOM media operation, providing a rare frisson of raw excitement in this otherwise bloodless place. On 8 April, when American tank fire hit the offices of al-Jazeera and Reuters in Baghdad, killing three journalists, a sense of panic gripped the press centre. Reporters, galvanized by the news, demanded explanations for events already witnessed on live TV. Squadrons of camera crews attempted to ambush CENTCOM officials. Faced with seemingly incontrovertible evidence, the military spokesmen were outgunned and attempted to beat a hasty retreat.

'We must make this go away!' one pleaded with another as both took cover. It was the nearest thing to combat either of them had seen since the war began. The following day, US marines arrived at the Palestine Hotel, where the tank round had hit the Reuters office just 24 hours earlier. 'Liberating' the hotel was perhaps a way of saying sorry for what had happened. Their arrival was certainly welcome. With the Iraqi authorities no longer in evidence and the whiff of anarchy already in the air, the journalists staying there were understandably nervous. That morning, I received a message from my BBC colleague, Paul Wood. 'Will US troops want to come to the Palestine Hotel soon?' he asked. 'We're hoping so. Things are unravelling here.' For once, I was able to elicit a response from General Franks' spokesman. 'Tell them it won't be long.' It was a message I was happy to relay.

There were, of course, other ways in which this one-sided war didn't always go completely to plan. For the British in particular, it got off to a difficult start. For three days, Brian Burridge and his staff were buffeted by news of disasters involving mainly British personnel. After helicopter accidents that claimed 19 lives, and the accidental downing of an RAF Tornado by an American Patriot missile, the British were left wondering just what mishap they would suffer next. 'The first three days were dreadful,' Burridge told me later. 'When it's three accidents on the trot. That was hard. Very hard.'

In fact, the following days brought other incidents of 'friendly fire', a reminder that, for all the emphasis on what military people are fond of calling 'situational awareness', the speed and intensity of this kind of warfare mean that accidents are almost bound to happen. Sometimes this is because systems fail. More often, human error of some kind is to blame. But the relatively high number of deaths attributable to friendly fire (around a dozen) raised immediate questions about the kind of IFF (Identification Friend or Foe) systems being used and whether enough had been done since the 1991 Gulf War to prevent such episodes. For Burridge, an aviator himself, the downing of the Tornado came at the worst possible time. The fallout from the campaign's first friendly fire episode was bad enough, but the British commander had other things on his mind that day.

'That was the point when we realized that these bastards were going to slow us down in Basra,' he said, referring to the sudden appearance of small pockets of determined paramilitary groups in towns and cities across the south. Already mourning the loss of the Tornado's two crew members, this was a sombre realization. 'If ever gloom descended, that was it,' he admitted.

Britain's contribution to the campaign, codenamed Operation Telic (a computer-generated name, unlike its more portentous American equivalent), in conventional ground terms at least, focused on the south. British warplanes flew missions across the country and special forces were active almost everywhere, but

113

securing the south, including Basra, was the task handed to 26,000 troops, including three fighting brigades: 7th Armoured (the 'Desert Rats'), 16 Air Assault and 3 Commando. While American troops raced towards Baghdad, bypassing towns wherever they could, the British were involved in a rather more conventional effort to take and hold ground. Some rash politicians had predicted that it would all be over in a matter of days and some of the same impatience could be sensed at CENTCOM. Officials announced that an 'uprising' had occurred in Basra, and clung to the story long after it became apparent that nothing much had happened. An intelligence source told me later that nothing had ever been reported from inside the city to support such a bold contention. But while critics wondered what was taking so long, the British settled into a patient strategy, screening the movement of civilians in and out of Basra, hitting fighters loyal to Saddam Hussein whenever intelligence or surveillance made this possible, and slowly pushing Iraq's second-largest city towards what some called 'the tipping point'. Brian Burridge made use of a wide range of tactical intelligence, gathered from SAS units inserted into the city at an early stage, and from a number of key human sources. It did take longer than most planners had expected, but it was subtle and, in the end, highly successful. When the city finally fell, on 7 April, the men of 3 Para walked into the centre without firing a shot.

There were holdups for the Americans too. Burridge's 'bastards' were causing problems everywhere. A motley, but determined, mixture of Baath Party paramilitaries, the so-called Saddam Fedayeen and members of the Special Security Organization, were harrying the long American supply lines. General Franks did his best to sound positive, dismissing them as 'dead-enders', but acknowledging there had been some 'terrific fire-fights'. A gruff, burly, menacing-looking special forces general had another way of putting it. 'If this was easy,' he told us one day, 'they'd call it golf.'

But while American and British planners had always worked on the assumption that Saddam Hussein's forces would try to slow down the coalition's advance on Baghdad, they later admitted they hadn't quite anticipated *how*. Two things in particular surprised

114

them: the number of Arab fighters, many of them Syrians, who arrived on the scene eager to fight; and the willingness of forces loyal to Saddam Hussein to use terror to achieve results.

At first, it sounded like coalition propaganda, but as reports of intimidation and coercion mounted, from the military and from embedded reporters, they became hard to ignore: in Basra, reluctant soldiers forced at gunpoint to mount suicidal attacks on British soldiers; in Nasiriya and elsewhere, civilians used as human shields by non-uniformed fighters; at Safwan, people who dared to celebrate the arrival of coalition troops later gunned down by Baath Party militiamen. For anyone familiar with the human rights record of Saddam Hussein's regime, this was hardly uncharacteristic behaviour, but as one official put it to me: 'It's one thing to read about this stuff in books; it's another to see it with your own eyes.'

As they made their way north, the Americans found it hard to distinguish between combatants and civilians. Reports from journalists on the spot suggested that frustrated American troops were shooting at anyone who got in their way. Civilians were being killed, by both sides.

By 27 March, the US army's senior ground commander in Iraq, Lt-Gen. William Wallace, was feeling exasperated. He joined a chorus of revulsion against the desperate tactics being used against his men, but speaking to two American reporters he went further, uttering one of the most widely quoted lines of the entire campaign: 'The enemy we're fighting is different from the one we'd war-gamed against.'

It was, in retrospect, not such a remarkable revelation, but it was seized upon by sceptics as evidence that the campaign, just seven days old, was not going well and, worse, that it had been ill-prepared. With apocalyptic dust storms raging across southern Iraq and the lead elements of the American advance pausing to consolidate positions and supply lines before pushing on to Baghdad, this was the start of a classic 'wobble' – the moment when a lack of discernible momentum causes everyone to wonder what's wrong.

Before long, the term 'operational pause' surfaced in reports from embedded journalists, some of whom were, after the headlong dash of the past week, now sitting still. Back at CENTCOM there were jitters. 'The Americans are getting a bit tense,' my British source confided as we braved our own modest sandstorm. Amid criticisms that the American ground forces lacked firepower, there was even talk of sending British Challenger 2 tanks to help out. But the Desert Rats were busy dealing with Basra, and in London defence chiefs were themselves very nervous of getting over-extended.

The fate of the stranded American 4th Infantry Division heightened the sense of things not going quite to plan. Most of its equipment was still on the high seas, redeployed to the Gulf from the eastern Mediterranean after the Turkish parliament drove a coach and horses through the war plan by refusing to allow the most technologically advanced heavy armour in the world to enter Northern Iraq from Turkish soil. The unit's soldiers were still at home in Texas, wondering if they would ever play the leading role they'd been promised. The loss of a substantial northern front was a real blow which, for understandable reasons, senior commanders were reluctant to acknowledge. They'd kept Baghdad's attention at least partially focused on the north through the use of large numbers of special forces and a well-publicized parachute drop by members of the 173rd Airborne Brigade. But Turkey's unexpected rebuff meant that the armoured advance on Baghdad would only come from the south. And if the 4th Infantry Division was needed to guarantee success, the generals would simply have to wait for it to arrive.

The wobble quickly gathered momentum. The veteran American investigative journalist Seymour Hersh, writing in *The New Yorker*, accused Donald Rumsfeld of failing to anticipate the real nature of the conflict, and of being so impressed by 'shock and awe' that he overruled military chiefs who had wanted to send a much bigger force to invade Iraq. As the dust swirled, the troops waited and the critics sniped, it began to look like a crisis.

But the moment passed. Perhaps not surprisingly, it fell to Tommy Franks, in his third and last CENTCOM news conference, to put the record straight. Returning to the Hollywood set, he delivered a bravura performance. He dismissed talk of disagreements in Washington. To those who speculated that the size of the invasion force was being hastily revised, he pointed out that there had been no new deployment orders issued since the start of the war. As for the 4th Infantry Division, he argued that it had been 'quite important, strategically and operationally, to have that very heavy force precisely where it was until the day it moved'. He trumped his earlier rhetorical flourish, listing not eight, but *nine* reasons why the campaign was 'on plan'. Among them: oil fields were secure; airfields had been seized and were now being put to use; a terrorist camp in Northern Iraq had been destroyed; humanitarian aid was flowing; coalition aircraft were working '24 hours a day across every square foot of Iraq'.

The reference to air power was key, and pointed to another aspect of the campaign that few of us really saw. Talk of an operational pause simply failed to take account of the utterly relentless bombardment of three hapless Republican Guard divisions given the unenviable task of defending Baghdad. Troops may indeed have been taking stock, but the air war never let up. Sandstorms prevented Apache attack helicopters and A-10 Tankbusters from flying, but other jets carried on regardless.

A huge increase in the number of satellite-guided precision weapons used, compared with earlier campaigns, meant that the bombing was extremely effective, far more so than some had expected. The much-vaunted satellite-guided 'smart bombs' (Joint Direct-Attack Munitions – JDAMs – and Britain's Enhanced Paveway) did what they were supposed to do, enabling British and American pilots to hit targets by day and night in all but the worst weather. Coalition aircraft dropped less than ten per cent of the ordnance used during the first Gulf War, but the much higher proportion of precision-guided weaponry meant more was achieved with less.

Commanders also benefited from a torrent of imagery, much of it in real time, from satellites, spy planes and unmanned aerial vehicles, which allowed decisions to be made quickly and on the basis of accurate information. Burridge said he was never in any doubt that air power would be vindicated – hardly surprising, given his senior position within the RAF – but even though it would be many weeks before any kind of comprehensive battle damage assessment was completed, he was still impressed. 'Figures will show that the amount of armour that was written

117

down from the air in this campaign is staggering,' he said.

Advancing American troops found themselves passing the twisted wreckage that was all that was left behind of the Medina, Baghdad and al-Nida divisions. At CENTCOM, officials estimated that as much as 50 per cent of each division had been destroyed. But, as they moved towards Baghdad, some wondered if they weren't walking into a trap. They were now well into the 'red zone', an imaginary ring around the capital where it was thought that Saddam Hussein's forces, realizing the game was up, might finally resort to the use of chemical weapons. We'd heard inconclusive reports that suggested the Iraqis might be preparing chemical munitions. Surely this was the moment?

But it never happened. Like setting fire to the oil fields and blowing the bridges, perhaps this had once been part of the plan. Perhaps the orders never got through. Officials at the base continued to issue warnings, during and after the fall of Baghdad. After months of talking up Iraq's non-conventional capability, it was almost as if the military men sought some sort of gruesome vindication. But, having come to Iraq and seen plenty of other disagreeable things, most had long since switched their priorities. Never mind weapons of mass destruction, they seemed to be saying, look how this regime treats its own people.

And so to the climax of the campaign: the capture of Baghdad, and one of the most bizarre episodes of the war. On the morning of 5 April, American officers at Doha's Joint Operations Centre were hunched over their computer screens as usual. There was already a mood of excitement. Elements of the 3rd Infantry Division (3ID) were now at the gates of the city. The end of the war was in sight, but who really knew what the vast, sprawling capital would hold?

As the high-tech 'blue force tracker' scrolled onto wall-mounted plasma screens, there was a sharp intake of breath. The tracker enables commanders to follow individual units as they move across a battle space hundreds, even thousands, of kilometres away. And now it showed a series of dots heading straight for the centre of the city. A column of American armoured vehicles was ploughing into Baghdad from the south. Not only that, but the soldiers on board were not crack combat troops but some of

3ID's supporting elements, driving what a senior British officer at the base described as 'the equivalent of a three-ton truck with the regimental silver'.

It was a mistake. The convoy, which should have skirted the city, had taken a wrong turn. It could have proved a costly disaster. But according to one official at CENTCOM, the order was given to plough on. After reaching the Qadisiya district, on the western bank of the Tigris, it turned west and headed for the safety of the airport, secured only the day before. On a day of confusing and sometimes contradictory accounts, a column of M1 tanks and M2 Bradley fighting vehicles took the same route, on a so-called 'thunder run', spraying gunfire as they went and killing an unknown number of Iraqis in the process. Some US officials put the death toll as high as 2000.

In media briefings later that day, American spokesmen described what had happened as 'armoured reconnaissance'. No one admitted that part of it shouldn't have happened. But as a piece of 'effects-based warfare', it was highly effective. The spectacle of American armour moving into Baghdad, apparently at will, shocked the city's inhabitants and what was left of its defences. Emboldened, American troops arrived in the centre two days later, this time to stay, having once again encountered little organized resistance. The British were impressed. Burridge praised the 'audacity and sheer brilliance' of the US advance on Baghdad. It was, he told us, 'something that military historians and academics will pore over in great detail for decades to come'.

But it had its dark side too. How many Iraqi civilians died the day the Americans rolled into their capital? Some of the pictures broadcast that day appeared to show an almost indiscriminate use of firepower. The impact on Arab viewers worried some of those in Doha. 'There's already deep suspicion throughout the Arab world about why the Americans are doing this,' one British official admitted to me. 'The worry is you'll feed every anti-American suspicion by going in and breaking all the china.'

The campaign ended, with more of a whimper than a bang, in Tikrit. Moral and political doubts remained in many quarters. The coalition's perceived inability to unearth Iraq's legendary weapons of mass destruction in the war's immediate aftermath caused some to wonder if the very reason it had been waged in the first place wasn't a cover for other, less honourable, intentions. Perhaps this was a warning to less vulnerable countries in the region and further afield not to dabble in dirty weapons. 'Sure, it's about weapons of mass destruction,' a Western intelligence source said as the war was drawing to a close. 'Just not *Iraqi* weapons of mass destruction.'

But Operation Iraqi Freedom confounded its military critics almost entirely. It had taken less than four weeks and achieved most of its objectives. It showed that a campaign waged not with overwhelming numbers, or even brand new equipment, but with an unparalleled mastery of information, could achieve dramatic results. The B-52 bomber might be an ancient airframe in service since the early 1950s, but equipped with precision-guided munitions and operating in close co-ordination with other parts of the military machine, it could do things its Cold War pilots would not have dreamed of, including hitting multiple targets on a single sortie. Supply lines might become extended and vulnerable and there might not be as much heavy armour as the text books recommend, but, if you were faster and more agile than your opponent, you'd probably win.

Iraq was, of course, a paper tiger. It had obsolete equipment and, apart from small numbers of paramilitaries, little real desire to fight. And a new way of war did not necessarily prevent some old ways of making mistakes: once again, cluster munitions killed and maimed civilians. Human rights groups challenged the Pentagon's assertion that only one civilian was killed by a cluster bomb, saying the true figure was over 200. In the weeks immediately after the war, it was hard to be sure how many innocent bystanders had died.

After two quick successes, in Afghanistan and Iraq, the US is feeling more powerful than ever. Future conflicts won't always be so easy. For Washington's coalition partners, they may not even be possible. Britain's armed forces performed well in Iraq, but they were now dangerously overstretched. The outgoing Chief of Defence Staff, Admiral Sir Michael Boyce, warned that his forces could not fight another war for two years without 'serious pain'. Another officer put it more bluntly: 'Don't ask us to do anything for 18–24 months,' he told me. 'We can't.'

CHAPTER SEVEN

A BAGHDAD DIARY

Rageh Omaar

Rageh Omaar is Africa Correspondent, based in Johannesburg. Before   121
that he reported from Amman and then returned to London as Developing
World Correspondent. He has frequently been on assignment in Iraq and
remained in Baghdad throughout the coalition bombardment. This is his
personal account of the last days of Saddam's regime.

Most Iraqis had never known anything other than the cruel and
enclosed world that Saddam Hussein built and ruled for nearly a
quarter of a century. Every day during those long and dark years,
the Iraqi leader's image watched over his people. In the mornings,
he was there on the front page of every newspaper. As Iraqis of all
ages, faiths and circumstances went to their factories, schools and
offices they would pass the hundreds of thousands of statues and
pictures of Saddam erected all over the country. At their places of
work, or at the restaurants in which they socialized, the portrait of
Saddam Hussein was everywhere. At the foot of these icons were
inscribed the various slogans dreamt up by the technocrats of the
regime as they tried to portray the great man in ever loftier guises:
'Saddam Hussein – the leader blessed with victory by God' and
'Saddam Hussein – an immaculate leader for an immaculate
people'. And each night, as they watched Iraqi television (the only
kind they had access to), he would be there again on the news,
regardless of the relevance or importance of what he had done
that day. There was more to this than a dictator's vanity. It was a
careful and conscious political strategy to provide the Iraqi leader
with such a sense of permanence in the eyes of his people that

any alternative would seem unthinkable. It was the very essence of totalitarianism.

I've been reporting for the BBC from inside Iraq on and off for seven years and I've spent most of that time in Baghdad. It was a period that encompassed much. A decade of war and economic destruction caused by sanctions had not just taken a physical and human toll, it had also left a trail of psychological damage throughout Iraqi society. And yet this world that Saddam Hussein had built came crashing down in 22 dramatic days.

I stayed in Baghdad throughout the war and watched this unique chapter of Iraqi history come to an end with seven BBC colleagues – correspondents Paul Wood and Andrew Gilligan; cameramen Andrew Kilrain; Duncan Stone and Malek Kenaan; TV engineer Mustafa al-Salman; and bureau chief Paul Danahar, who held the whole operation together. From our vantage point in the Palestine Hotel on the eastern bank of the River Tigris, we saw and chronicled the violent destruction of the regime. We travelled across the entire city and witnessed at first hand how Saddam's oppressive grip over Baghdad and its people was broken. At night, we looked out from our hotel rooms to the opposite bank of the Tigris, a few hundred metres away, where nearly all of the Iraqi dictator's main government buildings and presidential palaces were located. And we saw these monuments to false grandeur smashed to bits by a hail of missiles and bombs.

With Paul Danahar and Andrew Kilrain, I spent exactly a year watching Baghdad slide towards war. We visited Iraq many times from March 2002 – only weeks after President Bush's State of the Union speech in which he described Iraq as being part of an 'axis of evil' – until March 2003. We recorded every twist and turn of the crisis. We watched the weapons inspectors return to Iraq to pursue their fruitless search for prohibited weapons, while the US and Britain built up their invasion force in the Gulf. Throughout this period nobody we met in Iraq, whether in Saddam Hussein's government or among ordinary people, ever doubted that President Bush and Prime Minister Blair would eventually invade the country.

At the end of the 1991 Gulf War, Saddam Hussein stood on the very brink of destruction. Fourteen of Iraq's eighteen provinces had been lost to rebel forces. His army, after fleeing from Kuwait, deserted him and many joined in the rebellions. Yet the uprising was, in the minds of ordinary Iraqis, betrayed by the unwillingness of Britain and the United States to support the revolt fully and to go all the way to Baghdad. Thousands paid with their lives.

Since those tumultuous and briefly hopeful days of March and April 1991, ordinary Iraqis had been devastated by the impact of sanctions. No aspect of normal life had been spared the ravages of 'the embargo', as they referred to it. Meanwhile, the political elite, the very people sanctions were supposed to undermine, grew rich beyond their wildest dreams. For these people, UN sanctions had effectively turned the whole of Iraq into an economic monopoly of which they were the prime beneficiaries. It had been handed to them on a plate. The importation of everything, from medical equipment to rice and flour, was a licence to print money. But worse still for ordinary Iraqis, sanctions had allowed the regime to become not just a dictatorship of fear, but also one of need. Food rations were administered by the UN, but distributed through the Iraqi Ministry of Trade. Every family would go to an official distribution centre each month, show their ration cards and collect their food. In effect, it meant that the people of Iraq now relied on Saddam Hussein's state apparatus to feed their families. Little wonder then that by 2003, after 12 years of this – and after they'd seen Saddam throw out with impunity the first UN weapons inspectors – Iraqis would not believe anything about regime change until they were certain that British and American armour was in Iraq and heading for the capital.

123

* * * * * *

The people of Baghdad had been sleepwalking. Now they were awake, stirred into action by an unexpected shock: George W Bush and Tony Blair had at last set Saddam Hussein and his two sons a definitive 48-hour deadline to leave the country. Until now, the threat of war had not seemed so imminent.

In January we had driven in from Jordan, over the flat plains of the desert to the checkpoint at Abu Ghuraib outside Baghdad. It was a huge telecommunications and army base, but the few soldiers at the checkpoint cursorily examined the civilian cars thronging the junction and just waved us through. In the heart of Baghdad, there were equally few obvious signs that the city was getting ready for war: no tanks or armoured vehicles moving through the streets; no mobile air-defence units being relocated.

The colourful central Shorja market had stubbornly remained its usual busy self for months. The main concerns of shoppers had been finding the best prices for things such as tomato purée and cola from stallholders in the narrow alleyways. But suddenly, with the ultimatum to Saddam Hussein and his sons, it was transformed into a mosaic of desperate faces as people tried to buy up the last remaining oil lamps, masking tape and boards to protect windows from being blown in. Frantic crowds gathered around the stalls looking for matches, candles, dried produce and plastic buckets for storing water. For me, Shorja market was a very good indicator of the public mood in the city. And I had never seen it like this before.

Adnan Mustapha Hamid, a young restaurant manager, was typical of the many who thronged the market that day. 'I know the British and Americans say they will spare civilian targets,' he told me, 'but few of us believe them. I think they're going to bomb everything, and most of us are just going to stay at home.'

The next day, 19 March, marked the moment that Baghdad stopped being the bustling city we had known. It became a ghost town, waiting to be besieged and bombed. In the early hours of that morning, before the city awoke, the UN weapons inspectors slipped out of Baghdad. Their mission was at an end. It had been replaced by Washington's desire to confront Saddam Hussein. Diplomats, too, began packing their bags. That morning the French, who'd frustrated the attempts by Britain and the United States to get a second UN resolution, finally departed. Some of the French diplomats tried to keep a brave face, hugging and consoling their local Iraqi staff who were in tears, fearful of what would become of them and their families.

I walked down Saadoun Street on the final night of peace. Here was one of the busiest commercial and shopping streets of Baghdad, yet almost nobody was about. It was eerie. There were just eight hours before the deadline for war expired. Every single shop, restaurant and property had been locked and boarded up. The last few cars sped quickly along the empty streets.

Then, just before a clear and beautiful dawn, a dreadful and spine-chilling wail of air-raid sirens resounded across Baghdad. Seconds later, on the western edge of the city, tracer fire from anti-aircraft positions arced across the sky. The orange and pink glow of the tracers seemed to hang in the sky like tiny stars, before finally burning out. Soon afterwards, the batteries positioned across the River Tigris from our hotel joined in. It wasn't the enormous bombardment that had been threatened, but turned out to be a strike aimed at assassinating Saddam Hussein and his senior officials. For the Iraqi capital, the agonizing wait for war was finally over.

125

The Iraqi government wasted no time in trying to show that it was still in control. Less than three hours after the first attack, the man at the centre of it all appeared on television. Saddam was in the olive-green military uniform and black beret he had started to wear a few days before the war. But, unusually, he was wearing a large pair of black-rimmed reading glasses, fuelling suspicion that it might have been a double. Certainly, I had never seen him wear these glasses in public before. Noting the exact moment the first shots in the war had been fired, he told his people: 'With the dawn prayers of this day the criminal Bush Junior, together with his allies, launched the crime that they'd been promising against Iraq.' He urged every man in Iraq to fight back: 'Draw your swords,' he said, his voice rising to emphasize the command. 'Attack these criminals … Long live Iraq! Long live Iraq!'

Shabab Television, controlled by his elder son, Uday, began a round-the-clock diet of militaristic and patriotic songs. By mid-morning, the Minister of Information, Mohammed Saeed al-Sahhaf, appeared before those Western journalists still remaining in Baghdad. He started as he meant to go on throughout the war. Distrustful of the media, and with his own parallel version of reality, he said of the Anglo–American coalition: 'I am sure that they are stupid, and they will never succeed … At the same time, this is a good testimony, a good proof that they are killers, they are criminals and they believe in assassination.'

In the first days of the war, there was an almost palpable sense of relief among the Iraqi leadership and one of consternation among ordinary Iraqis. For months, Western media reports had filtered back, predicting a massive initial onslaught, especially on Baghdad, aimed at overwhelming the Iraqi regime and rendering any response hopeless. It was thought that the first 48 hours would see the use of more than 3000 cruise missiles. These reports had reached officials and ordinary people alike. But the reality was different. You could almost hear officials saying to themselves, 'Is this it?'

Ordinary Iraqis who'd prayed the war would finish off the regime in a matter of days, now had misgivings. On the second day, Information Minister Sahhaf crowed that 'In 1991 we saw a much larger scale of military action than we have seen now. We can absorb all military threats ... this is no problem for us.' Could he be right?

But that same night Mr Sahhaf and the rest of Baghdad got a taste of the 'shock and awe' threatened by the US; it was the moment the war began to have a devastating impact on the city and its people. The attack can't have lasted for more than an hour and a half, but it destroyed nearly a quarter of a century of the dictator's symbols. It came so fast that many of the air-raid sirens were never sounded. The bombardment tore into the heart of Saddam Hussein's most cherished and forbidding compounds.

From the balcony of our hotel room on the 13th floor, my BBC colleagues and I gazed out at many of the buildings from which Saddam Hussein and his ministers had exercised power. We saw them disappear in cauldrons of fire and ash. At times it was hard to find the language to convey the other-worldly nature of this onslaught: its sheer violence, the thunderous noise which reverberated through every street and avenue of the city, and the terrifying sight of plumes of debris being hurled at least 100 metres into the air. And all of this was taking place only a few hundred metres from where we were. Ministry buildings, presidential compounds, intelligence and security installations – all of them smashed apart and left ablaze. Such was the ferocity that in one five-minute period I estimated there must have been at least 30 or 40 strikes. Each time I saw an explosion, I would wait a split-second for the blast waves to arrive. The windows of our hotel rooms, though reinforced with blast-proofing material, would shudder and the whole hotel would gently sway. It was a terrible experience which made us feel small and vulnerable. But the targeting seemed to owe as much to political factors as military considerations. Many of the buildings had almost certainly been evacuated. But Washington and London were trying to humiliate Saddam Hussein. It was a demonstration to ordinary people of the ease with which the government's key buildings, built at such great expense and with such vainglory, could be destroyed, in little over an hour. The television footage filmed by Andrew Kilrain, Duncan Stone and Malek Kenaan is breathtaking. Looking back at it, weeks after the end of the war, the images and sounds of that night still shock me.

127

In the very heart of the capital, close to some of the key government buildings, were houses and apartment blocks in which ordinary Iraqis lived and sheltered with their loved ones. They huddled indoors as their neighbourhoods were torn apart. Their main concern was just to survive. And it got worse. Soon the city was surrounded by a choking black haze from fires aimed at trying to confuse the coalition war planes. We could hear them flying overhead. So *this* was what it was like to be on the wrong end of the world's only superpower.

Extraordinarily powerful munitions were used in the air attacks on Baghdad and, even with all the care in the world, there were bound to be civilian casualties. It was difficult to come to an accurate number. The International Committee of the Red Cross and Médecins sans Frontières remained in the city during the war, working with medical teams at the main hospitals, which were already dilapidated and short of supplies. Just about everything, from painkillers to sterilizing fluid, was needed because of the years of sanctions. Exhausted staff battled to cope, despite fears about their own families and about what lay ahead.

We were expecting the Iraqi authorities to make outlandish claims. But the briefings by the Minister of Information contained figures that, though hard to corroborate, were not unbelievable. When the Iraqis said cluster bombs had been used in the town of Hilla, it turned out to be true. What proved to be utterly false were the regular assertions by Mr Sahhaf that British and

American forces were making no advances towards Baghdad.

And then there were the bombings that seemed to go wrong. The first one came on 26 March, in the Sha'ab working-class district in the north of Baghdad. The entire city had been engulfed in the worst sandstorms in living memory, creating a blood-red haze that turned the day into perpetual dusk. When we arrived at the scene, we emerged from our car to the wail of ambulance sirens and the sight of hundreds of people looking dazed amid the carnage. Eyewitnesses and emergency teams said that at least 17 civilians had died (the figure was later revised to 14) and dozens had been wounded when two large explosions hit the area, the result of incoming missiles or bombs. The cause of the explosions was later disputed by US military spokesmen, but the fact of the matter was that virtually everyone that foreign reporters spoke to at the scene *believed* they were caused by the coalition

'We are just trying to make a living in our shops,' one man told me. 'What do they want from us, why are they doing this? Our homes are gone and our livelihoods are gone.'

* * * * * *

On 30 March, the Ministry of Information, where all Western journalists had to base their offices, was bombed. Directly across the road from it was a large compound of public apartment blocks. The next day, Paul Danahar, Duncan Stone and I went to visit the Abdallah family there. They were middle-class, educated and well-travelled, and sceptical about the political motives for the war. We found them clearing up broken glass and damaged furniture in their home. From the kitchen window, we were able to look across to the roof of the Ministry. We could see the remains of the BBC television position where our satellite dish for transmitting our reports back to London had been. 'Tony Blair is wrong to think that Iraqis will welcome his soldiers with open arms,' said Najda Abdallah. 'People around here look on the foreign soldiers as robbers trying to break into their homes.'

Meanwhile, the obstinate and shrill defiance of Iraqi ministers began to speak volumes about the real priorities of the regime. They would describe how even ordinary peasants, armed with nothing more than their ancient rifles and muskets, would come out of their dwellings at the sound of British and American planes and fire up at the sky. It was evidence, the ministers said, of their undying fealty to Saddam.

The Minister of Defence, General Sultan Hashim Ahmed, told a news conference on 27 March that the Iraqi leadership fully expected Baghdad to be encircled within five to ten days (he wasn't far wrong) but that this would only be the beginning: 'In the end, the invaders will have to enter [the city]. Baghdad is the capital of civilization,' he said. 'We inherited it from our fore-fathers and history shall see how we defend it.'

Thus did the regime see itself in its dying moments. Its leaders believed utterly in the idea that they had an anointed role as defenders of Arab and Islamic honour against the modern crusaders. Worse still, the regime believed that, even after all the cruelty of Saddam's rule, the fact that British and American soldiers were only 50 kilometres from Baghdad would somehow be enough to persuade the Iraqi army and people to fight and die for their cause. It wasn't, and the city's vaunted defenders, the tens of thousands of Republican Guards who had been pulled back to the environs of Baghdad, simply evaporated.

129

And yet, each day, to the increasing consternation and bemusement of the gathered journalists, senior Iraqi officials would proclaim how American forces advancing on Baghdad were on the verge of comprehensive defeat. We would then all sit and watch television footage from journalists embedded with those units clearly showing their steady and certain advance. One such moment came on 4 April when US forces were reported as being on the outskirts of Saddam International Airport, 12 kilo-metres from the heart of Baghdad. The inimitable Minister of Information was in typical form. The airport, he said, would be 'their graveyard'. Besides, he added, 'we've decided to allow the invading forces there so we can nail them down'.

The truth was that it was all coming to an end. Three days later, on 7 April, at around 7 a.m. Baghdad time, Paul Danahar called me in my hotel room. 'Take a look outside your window at the other side of the river,' he said. 'It's incredible.' There, barely 500 metres away, were two American armoured personnel carri-ers beside the Republican Presidential Palace. To the sound of small-arms fire and explosions, troops from the 3rd Infantry Division were storming the compound. As they were doing so, stunned and terrified Iraqi guards fled for their lives. Some of them were still in their underwear as they ran along the river bank. This is how Saddam Hussein's regime ended – not in the blaze of glory it had predicted for itself, but abandoned by its own people and even by the very guards supposed to protect the palaces of the leader himself. Gone was the fear and terror on which Saddam's rule had been built.

The symbolic end to Saddam Hussein's tyranny came on a still and sunny afternoon in Baghdad on 9 April. It was heralded by the roar of American tanks and armoured personnel carriers, driven by young marines who hadn't even been born when the Iraqi dictator came to power. They came up the road towards our hotel, the world's TV cameras beaming the pictures live as they drove into Paradise Square to help several hundred Iraqis tear down a 10-metre cast iron statue of the dictator. The Iraqis had been using a sledgehammer. Now, it seemed, they were going to get some help. There was delirium all around.

The marines placed a cable around the statue and shouted instructions to each other. The armoured personnel carrier reversed. It was about to happen – Saddam, and his 25-year rule of terror, were going to come crashing down. People threw stones and chanted 'Death to Saddam'. For an agonizing moment the statue teetered on its pedestal. But the marines revved the engine of the APC. That was it. The statue tipped and fell. Iraqis scrambled past the marines to begin attacking it, jumping on it, smashing it to pieces. Some were chanting, others were in floods of tears. This was the moment President Bush and Prime Minister Blair had dreamed about – the image of joyous liberation.

It didn't last long. Liberation brought chaos, wholesale looting and violence in its wake, the most powerful military in the world seemingly unable or unwilling to do anything about it. The National Museum of Iraq was ransacked; treasures stolen, ancient statues decapitated. Parts of the National Library, which contained some 5000 of the earliest known manuscripts, were torched. Even hospitals did not escape the looting frenzy, as conditions continued to deteriorate and medical staff were stretched to the limit.

It was clear that humanitarian aid was urgently needed. People were frantic to know who was going to fill the political vacuum left by Saddam's demise. The Americans would have to make contact with city administrators and get them back to work, to re-establish water and electricity supplies. They might be part of the old regime, but they were needed.

One afternoon I went to pick my way through the ruins of Iraq's Central Bank. We filmed two young men who'd walked off the street with a hammer in the vain hope of breaking open its vaults. Another young man, better dressed and clearly from a more prosperous background, came into the derelict building, having heard the noisy banging. He was slightly bewildered by what was happening. We talked about the agonies and uncertainties that now faced his country. 'Iraq is free, but ruined,' he told me. 'Who will now put this country back together again, and in whose image?'

131

* * * * * *

We eventually left Baghdad on 13 April. By then US forces had occupied most of the city. Those of us who'd remained in the Iraqi capital throughout the war were leaving a place that had been utterly transformed, by the physical destruction from weeks of bombardment and the looting that followed. The day we left, we drove across the Sinak Bridge over the River Tigris past four burnt-out vehicles, two mangled bodies still lying in their seats. Down the road, the Ministry of Information was still burning from the looting of the previous day. At the junction opposite the Foreign Ministry, we had to slow down as we tried to get past the unexploded mortar shells, broken glass and bullet casings. All of us felt we were leaving a city that had also undergone an enormous psychological and emotional shock from which it would take a long time to recover. A system of government, which for decades had controlled the Iraqi people's view of the world, their contact with foreigners and their basic aspirations, had been brought down in a matter of weeks – and it was hard to see what would be put in its place. Just before I left, one of my closest Iraqi friends said: 'It's as though the lid that kept this country's competing tensions in place has suddenly been lifted.'

Just after midday I reached the border and drove across the two kilometres of no-man's land into Jordan. This was the moment I closed the chapter on seven years in which I'd chronicled Iraq's lurch from economic destruction to diplomatic crisis, and finally into war and an uncertain peace.

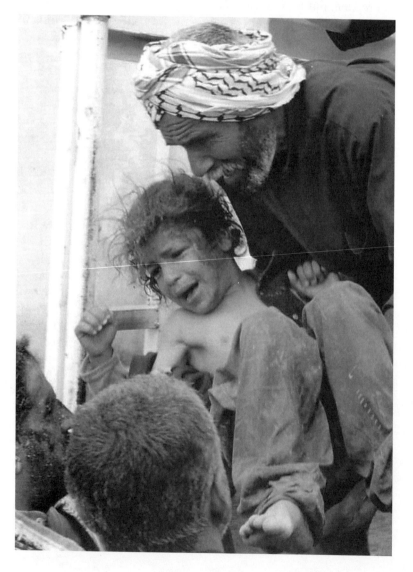

CHAPTER EIGHT

SADDAM – A DICTATOR OF MASS DESTRUCTION

John Simpson

John Simpson is World Affairs Editor. In his long career he has reported 133
from well over 100 countries, interviewing many of the world's most promi-
nent leaders and witnessing key events in recent history. He spent most of the
first Gulf War in Baghdad. This time, John was in the Kurdish-controlled
north of Iraq before moving to the capital. He was travelling in a convoy
that was mistakenly attacked by a US plane; a number of people, including
the BBC translator Kamaran Muhamed, were killed, and John and other
members of his team were among the injured. Here, drawing on his long
experience of Iraq, he looks at Saddam Hussein's history and character.

For 13 years, since the invasion of Kuwait, there have been few
more familiar names and faces on earth. Everywhere there was a
radio set, people had heard of Saddam Hussein; everywhere there
was a television, those jowly features, that bristling moustache,
those dark, watchful eyes were immediately recognizable. This,
perhaps, was why people found the notion of Saddam's doubles
so irresistibly fascinating. Was it really possible that the features
we had come to know so well could have been successfully
duplicated?

His personality counted, too, in a way that has begun to die
out in the modern world. Most presidents and prime ministers are
so constrained in what they do that it scarcely matters whether, in
private, they have ungovernable tempers or a ferocious need to
assert themselves. There were remarkably few constraints on
Saddam Hussein. If he wanted to do something, he did it. The
chief function of his ministers and advisers was to make it happen.

Yet Saddam was never the crazed dictator of Western imaginings. He was rational, highly intelligent and thoroughly well-informed. His favourite listening was the BBC's Arabic Service; his favourite viewing was al-Jazeera, the 24-hour Arabic news service, and BBC World. He apparently never watched Iraqi television, whose programmes were almost exclusively about him.

Anyone who receives such terrified adulation is bound to have a fairly warped view of themselves and their capacities. Saddam never cultivated the foreign friendships that some other Arab leaders have enjoyed, and his foreign visitors were mostly yes-men. But, like his hero Joseph Stalin, Saddam retained a basic shrewdness which endured despite all the worship; and he was a good deal shrewder than most of his enemies. His actions when he was strong, such as the war against Iran and the invasion of Kuwait, were often foolhardy, but he played a weak hand superbly well, outmanoeuvring the Americans and British brilliantly.

In power he was hard-working and surprisingly austere for a man who created so many monuments to himself and his glory. His main personal expenditure was on suits and shoes – perhaps because during his poverty-stricken childhood he had had to go around barefoot – and he bought up every book and document relating to Stalin. He would frequently read official documents throughout the night and would then sleep in for a few hours, in a narrow bed with a hard mattress.

Having ordered the poisoning of a good many of his enemies, he was always frightened that someone might poison him. Thallium, which is impossible to trace outside a laboratory, was his preferred instrument and the substance he feared the most. As a result he would have different meals prepared for him every day in each of his 18 palaces; he would arrive without warning, and one of his closest aides would select dishes at random for him.

He suffered for many years from a slipped disc, and swam a great deal in the swimming pools that were a feature of every palace. The palaces themselves were a show of ostentation and power, which is why he built the majority of them at the height of the UN sanctions after the first Gulf War. They were his way of telling the Iraqi people that in spite of the privations they were suffering, he was there to stay. Privately, Saddam talked more and more about his days on the run, before the Baath Party came to power, and like most conspirators he hankered after the old days of simple living and uncertainty.

At moments of international tension, when it seemed the Americans would target him personally, Saddam would drive around in an American Winnebago, parking under bridges at night. As an alternative, his men would simply commandeer a house for the night in a suburb or village, and Saddam would stay there until morning. During the first Gulf War he used a Passat car with just one bodyguard sitting beside him, and would meet his cabinet colleagues in some prearranged village outside Baghdad.

Still, we know remarkably little about what Saddam Hussein was like in private during the days of his power. The great majority of those who met him saw only the official face: measured, stern, unyielding, or sometimes jovial in a menacing kind of way. 'In case you are wondering whether this is really Saddam Hussein,' he told some foreign visitors a few days after the BBC had broadcast a documentary that revealed the extent to which he used doubles to relieve the burden of public appearances, 'I promise you this is the real one'. He pinched his cheek and shook his jowls, and laughed – as did the visitors, when it was obviously safe to do so.

Yet as with Joseph Stalin, whom he regarded as his mentor in the art of government, there was a human side to Saddam Hussein that lay below the ferocious calculation and the official cruelty. 'You should have seen him on his hands and knees on the carpet, giving his grandchildren a ride on his back,' a family hanger-on once said. 'He would laugh and play with them, and they loved him. It was good to be around him at times like that.'

And yet, of course, Saddam later gave orders that the fathers of those grandchildren should be killed, after they had defected to Jordan. As for his own sons, the violent, raucous Uday and the quieter and more intelligent Qusay, he sent them (according to Uday himself) on regular visits during their early teens to torture chambers and execution yards, in order to toughen them for the life ahead.

The history of modern Iraq, of the Middle East, and to some extent of modern Britain, Europe and the United States, has been dictated by the personality of Saddam Hussein. If he had been a cautious figure, like Hafez al-Assad of Syria or Hosni Mubarak of Egypt, there would have been no confrontation with the Western powers and no invasion of neighbouring countries. If he had been less ferocious towards his own people, he might have been over-thrown as soon as he began to take risky and controversial decisions.

It was Saddam's character that dictated what he did and what became of him and his country. Everything else – the deaths of a million people in the war he launched against Iran in 1980, the reckless invasion of Kuwait, his resistance to the determination of President George W Bush to find a way of overthrowing him – derives from this. He was encouraged from birth to see himself as a fighter. His parents were poor and humble people, who were strong nationalists: 'Saddam' means 'confronter', while his younger sister was called 'Siham' – 'spear'.

There have been attempts in the West to emphasize similarities between Saddam's childhood and those of Hitler and Stalin, both of whom had vicious, drunken fathers and worshipping mothers. Yet the circumstances were very different. Saddam's parents were second cousins, from the dreary and poverty-stricken village of al-Ouja, beside the River Tigris, eight kilometres south of Tikrit. His natural father, Hussein al-Majid, disappeared while Saddam and Siham were very young; their mother, Subha Tulfah, married her first cousin Hassan al-Ibrahim, a former school care-taker. Saddam was wanted neither by his natural father, nor by his mother's second husband.

It is not clear whether he was born in wedlock (an angry jibe about mothers who were prostitutes, which the Kuwaiti delega-tion made during the tense negotiations in July 1990, seems to have been the final straw that led directly to his decision to invade Kuwait). His very date of birth is uncertain; officially, it was 29 April 1937, a national holiday during his years of power. According to his birth certificate, however, it was 1 July 1939, and this is more likely to be correct; during his years as an aspiring Baath Party leader Saddam probably wanted to pretend he was older than he really was.

Saddam told one of his official biographers: 'My birth was not a joyful occasion; there were no roses or aromatic plants around my cradle.' There are much-repeated stories that Hassan al-Ibrahim

136

beat him savagely and called him 'the son of a dog'. Yet Saddam kept on the best of terms with his stepbrothers Barzan, Sabawi and Watban, and promoted them to high office. He never lost his links with al-Ouja or Tikrit, where he built a particularly sumptuous palace, and he always retained his harsh central-Iraqi accent, though it was dangerous for anyone to make fun of it or imitate it. For the rest of his life he carried the three blueish dots of a Tikriti tribal tattoo on the back of his left hand.

Saddam's rise from obscurity was made possible through his uncle, Khairallah Tulfah, an army officer and fierce nationalist who sympathized with the Nazis and wanted an end to British domination over Iraq. Saddam joined the Baath ('Renaissance') Party in 1957, and quickly progressed thanks to his uncle's friendship with Ahmad Hassan al-Bakr, a leading figure in the party. The Baathists rejected both British control over Iraq and the Communists' desire to make the country dependent on Moscow. For them, wider Arab union was what mattered. So from the very start of his political career Saddam, the confronter, condemned foreign control and wanted to make Iraq and the Arab world truly independent of external forces.

Much of the story of his career has become familiar: how, in October 1959, Saddam was chosen to be part of the assassination team that attacked President Abdul Karim Qassem, only a year after Qassem had led the successful coup against the young British-supported king, Faisal II. Qassem escaped with his life, and Saddam may not have played such a heroic part in the attempt as the later hagiographies made out; but he escaped and spent the next three years as an exile in Damascus and Cairo.

In Egypt he married the formidable Sajida, whose reaction to his extramarital affairs would later make his life increasingly difficult. During his exile in Cairo, Saddam also established another long-term relationship: he made contact with the CIA. The nature of his links with the United States at this point has never been entirely clear, but the Americans much preferred the Baathists to the Qassem regime because Qassem was coming increasingly under Soviet influence, and the CIA began helping the Baathists to overthrow him.

This duly happened in February 1963, and Saddam's mentor

General Ahmad Hassan al-Bakr became prime minister in the new government. The United States was delighted: al-Bakr was a notable anti-Communist, and that was all that mattered. Saddam, though he was only 24, was starting to become a serious force behind the scenes: the following year he helped to create Jehaz Haneen, the Baathist security system. But the Baathists were a difficult, violent group and were soon kicked out of the government. Some members, including Saddam Hussein, were arrested; but whereas most of them were tortured and kept in terrible conditions, Saddam himself thrived. He escaped in 1966. Not surprisingly the rumours started to go round that the CIA had looked after its own; and indeed soon after Saddam escaped Robert Anderson of the CIA had a meeting with him.

138

The result, perhaps, was the successful coup two years later, which was headed by al-Bakr and a number of leading Tikritis. Saddam was made deputy chairman of the Baath Party's Revolutionary Command Council but this was kept secret at the time, perhaps because he was still so young, or because he was essentially an underground figure.

Slowly, Saddam came to dominate the party. His long interest in Stalin now began to pay off. Like the Soviet leader, he introduced commissars into the army to provide political control over the often restless officer class, and he started wiping out his rivals and enemies within the Baath Party. It was a heady time for a man still in his early thirties. He became a familiar and rather dreaded figure at the Nadi al-Said Club in Baghdad, smoking his Cuban cigars and drinking Johnny Walker Black Label and Mateus rosé. No one who was invited to play tennis with him wanted to win a point, and when he dived into the pool the other swimmers used to get out and leave it to him and his cronies.

His influence was always strongly secular. He brought back horse-racing, which President Qassem had banned, and he introduced a number of modernizing measures which gave him a popularity that never entirely faded, especially among women: linking remote villages to the national electricity grid, giving women equal pay, allowing them to choose their own husbands and if necessary divorce them, providing free television sets and refrigerators to the poor.

It was all made possible because of oil. In the 1970s Iraq was able to produce around three million barrels of oil a day. In early 1972 Saddam negotiated a wide-ranging friendship treaty with the Soviet Union, under the terms of which Moscow agreed not to join any international boycott against Iraq. A matter of weeks later, on 1 June 1972, Saddam announced the nationalization of the Iraq Petroleum Company. It was a brilliant success. Saddam had done all the things that the CIA had backed him only a few years earlier in order to prevent.

An orgy of military spending followed, especially after Saddam's cousin (and also, thanks to the intricacies of Tikriti family life, his brother-in-law) Adnan Khairullah became Defence Minister in 1977. Iraq's military spending increased ninefold, and Soviet tanks, helicopters, aircraft and artillery, and French helicopters and fighters were bought by the hundred. Saddam Hussein was probably not clear at this stage whom he wanted to fight, but he wanted to be able to fight someone. He was demonstrating his own strength; and after six years in which he pretended in public to be the junior partner to President al-Bakr, it was time to show who the real power in the land was. In July 1979 he forced al-Bakr to resign, and took the title of president. He was 40 years old – or, at most, 42.

The enormous levels of credit that Saddam Hussein could now call on, thanks to oil nationalization, allowed his imagination free rein and he created Iraq in the way he chose. It was not an attractive way, and other countries, which should perhaps have known better, behaved unattractively as well. France agreed to set up Iraq's first laboratory capable of creating bacteriological and biological weapons, the Institut Mérieux.

With help from French, American, Italian, Belgian and German companies, Iraq created laboratories that developed poison-gas capability, though not all these companies may have realized the full implications of what they were being asked to do. By the beginning of the 1980s Iraq was in a position to use mustard gas, Tabun and DX nerve agents, and was well on the way to developing anthrax, typhoid and cholera as weapons of war.

Two decades later, many people questioned whether Saddam's possession of weapons of mass destruction was anything more than a propaganda myth put out by the British and Americans; but it

139

was certainly true before the first Gulf War, and if Saddam destroyed many of his weapons later or sent them out of the country to Egypt and Syria, it was a matter of tactics rather than principle.

In 1975 Saddam Hussein made public his determination to acquire nuclear weapons within ten years. Jacques Chirac, then prime minister of France under President Giscard d'Estaing, invited Saddam to visit the nuclear research centre at Cadaroche and inspect France's new fast-breeder reactor. He must surely have understood, despite Saddam's assurance that he simply wanted to be able to generate power, that this was a major part of Iraq's strategy for developing nuclear weapons. In a deal which at that time was worth $3 billion, France agreed to sell Iraq an Osiris reactor for nuclear research and also a smaller Isis reactor. The Isis was similar to the Dimona research reactor that France had sold to Israel in 1956, and was capable of producing several nuclear weapons. Under the co-operation treaty that governed the sale, France also agreed to train 600 Iraqi nuclear technicians.

There was immense international anger when the terms of the treaty leaked out, and France was obliged to withdraw from some of its obligations. However, plenty of other countries were keen to get their hands on the huge amount of Iraqi money on offer, and Brazil, and possibly India and China, offered their help. In 1979 an Italian company agreed to sell Iraq the laboratories to provide enough plutonium to create an atomic bomb within two years.

In September 1980 Saddam Hussein launched an unprovoked attack on Iran, encouraged by the Reagan administration, which was alarmed by the fall of its key ally, the Shah, and the recent Islamic revolution. Eight months later, on 7 June 1981, Israeli planes bombed Iraq's al-Tuwaitha nuclear plant, only four weeks before it was due to become operational. (Iranian aircraft had attacked it unsuccessfully a week after the war had begun.) After the plant was destroyed, Saddam gave orders that work should concentrate on chemical and biological weapons instead. In this, Iraq had the help of a number of West German companies.

Of the various types of poison gas that Iraq used against Iran during the war, the oldest and most basic type, mustard gas, proved to be the most effective. From the day it was first used, early in 1984, tens of thousands of Iranian soldiers were affected by it, many of them dying miserable deaths long after the war was over. Iran eventually caved in to domestic pressure to deploy mustard gas as well, but gave it up after less than a year: it is a difficult weapon to use effectively, since an unexpected shift in the wind can bring it back on the soldiers who have used it. Thousands of Iraqis were injured by their own gas shells.

The United States, having quietly encouraged Saddam to invade Iran, had to come sharply to his aid as the war dragged on and Iran's strategic abilities and greater manpower began to tell. In December 1983 Donald Rumsfeld, who as US Defense Secretary 20 years later was to be America's leading hawk, paid his first visit to Baghdad as President Reagan's special envoy. He got on well with Saddam, and gave him a special message from the President which apparently assured him that Washington would not allow him to lose the war. After the Iranian success in capturing the al-Faw peninsula from Iraq in February 1986, the Reagan administration began redressing the balance in earnest by giving Saddam satellite intelligence that allowed Iraq to counterattack. Once again the Americans, by helping Saddam, had made it possible for him to survive.

The terrible destruction of the war he had begun seemed to have little effect on Saddam Hussein. Like Stalin, he was impervious to the sufferings of others. An American profiler for the CIA maintains that Saddam displayed all the symptoms of malignant narcissism. This mental condition is very far from the traditional concept of insanity but involves a total absence of sympathy for those who oppose you.

According to some accounts, Saddam shed tears when his son Uday was attacked and seriously injured by a group of assassins; and there were other occasions when he was visibly upset by minor accidents to his children. Yet there was no pity of any kind towards anyone close to him whom he believed showed signs of being about to betray him. 'I can tell simply by looking someone in the eyes whether he is loyal or a traitor,' he told one of his biographers.

Time and again people close to him were arrested and executed. In the ferocious show of power he staged at the al-Khuld conference centre in July 1979, five days after taking power, 60 or more people were bundled out as he watched, smoking his cigar contentedly. Twenty-two of them were executed immediately. One was Adnan Hussein al-Hamdani, whom he had made the head of his private office only a few days before. On the day he was arrested and shot, Hamdani's wife was on a shopping expedition with Saddam's wife in Paris. In March 1982 the Health Minister suggested that Saddam should step down temporarily while a peace settlement with Iran was negotiated; Saddam took him into the next room and shot him.

Twenty-four offences carried the death penalty in Iraq during the 1980s: the highest number for any country. Two thousand people were executed for treason between Saddam's emergence as president and the start of the first Gulf War. The man who eventually became his Foreign Minister, Naji Sabri al-Hadithi, was ordered home from his position as press attaché in London and told that his brother had been arrested for plotting against Saddam's life. Al-Hadithi agreed to write a grovelling letter, which revealed that his brother had always been a cheap and evil character; his reward for this was that he alone of the male members of the family was not obliged to be a member of the firing-squad that executed his brother. An armed security man stood behind each member of the squad, with orders to shoot him dead if there was the slightest suspicion he was aiming to miss. Nevertheless, al-Hadithi's own punishment was not over. For several years he was obliged to serve as a teacher at a village school in a remote part of Iraq; and even when he was rehabilitated and rose to be Saddam's Foreign Minister he never dared to look him in the eye. His gaze was always humbly on the ground in front of him.

Punishment in Saddam's Iraq was exemplary. When, not long before the outbreak of the first Gulf War, Lt-Gen. Omar al-Hazzaa criticized Saddam to a friend, he was overheard and arrested. His tongue was cut out, he was shot in the back of the neck, and his eldest son was executed. His house was knocked down, and no one dared to help his destitute wife for fear of being regarded as a traitor too.

As the Iran–Iraq war came to an end in March 1988, the Kurdish town of Halabjeh surrendered to the advancing Iranian forces, which were then forced to withdraw by an Iraqi counter-attack. For three days Saddam's air force attacked the town, using bombs that contained Tabun gas and a hydrogen cyanide compound developed with the help of German advisers at the chemical weapons plant at Samarra. Five thousand people are thought to have died. It was the town's punishment for its disloyalty to Saddam Hussein.

The same ferocity existed within the presidential family as well. Any hint of disloyalty or disagreement was savagely punished. Adnan Khairullah, Saddam's cousin and the brother of Saddam's wife Sajida, took her side when it became clear that Saddam had been having an affair with the wife of a senior Iraqi Airways executive. In 1989 Adnan was invited to a family party in Mosul which was intended to settle the problem, but the atmosphere was bad and Adnan stormed out. Saddam then instructed his son-in law Hussein Kamel al-Majid to 'sort things out'. Al-Majid confessed later that he put explosives and a timer on board Adnan's helicopter, which blew up shortly afterwards. The official version was that it crashed during a sandstorm. A statue was erected to Adnan in Baghdad.

Like so many of Saddam Hussein's policies, the invasion of Kuwait in August 1990 seemed like an act of great rashness, based on his belief in his own military genius, which was non-existent, and his faith in Iraq's defensive capability. Privately, though, Saddam told the Palestinian leader Yasser Arafat a few weeks later that he had had no alternative: 'Unless they are kept busy, my generals will plot to overthrow me.' Saddam believed, rightly or wrongly, that he could only stay in power if there was a constant state of emergency inside and outside the country.

The United States miscalculated badly too. When the war was over, President George Bush decided to let a weak Saddam survive in power rather than run the risk that Iraq would break into pieces. This played directly into Saddam's hands; it enabled him to crush the Shia and Kurdish uprisings and eventually to re-establish his power as strongly as before. Few suffered more than the so-called Marsh Arabs, who had long been a target of Saddam's hostility. President Clinton tried to keep Saddam pinned down by a combination of UN sanctions, weapons inspections and occasional missile strikes, but this was equally ineffective and the ordinary people of Iraq bore the burden of the suffering.

As a result, there was a string of plots and coup attempts against Saddam. In 1996 a waitress at one of the presidential palaces confessed that she had agreed to bring him food that was poisoned with thallium. She and everyone she named as conspirators were put to death.

Yet it was the stresses breaking out again within Saddam's own family that nearly brought down the entire dynasty and had far-reaching consequences for the country as a whole. It began in 1994 with a growing three-way rivalry between Saddam's elder son Uday, Uday's uncle Watban al-Tikriti (Saddam's half-brother, the Interior Minister), and Hussein Kamel al-Majid, who had married Saddam's favourite daughter, Raghda, and had some reason to regard himself as Saddam's favoured heir.

144

Uday forced Watban to resign, and then broke into a private party that Watban was giving, killed a couple of his friends, and shot him in the leg. Hussein Kamel al-Majid feared that he would be next on Uday's list, and in August 1995 he persuaded his brother Saddam Kamel al-Majid (who had married Saddam Hussein's second daughter, Rana) that they must escape to Jordan, taking their wives with them.

In Amman, Hussein Kamel, who had been Saddam's head of weapons procurement, talked freely to the CIA and British intelligence. Seven years later, the information he gave them was still the basis of their knowledge and understanding of Saddam's arsenal. It was then that he also revealed he had arranged the murder of Saddam's brother-in-law Adnan by blowing up his helicopter. Altogether he provided extraordinary insights into Saddam Hussein's dysfunctional family and his dysfunctional regime. In February 1996, after taking a phone call from Saddam, the brothers decided to go home. They should have known better.

There was a suitably mafia-like conclusion. Saddam, heavily drunk, sent a group of relatives to deal with them. A gun-battle around their villa lasted for more than 12 hours before they ran out of ammunition and were summarily executed. Raghda and Rana were sent to live with their mother, Sajida, both apparently vowing they would never speak to their father again.

The second Gulf War was as unavoidable as the first. Yet whereas the first war may have been caused by Saddam's need to keep his generals occupied, this one was directed mostly by American political considerations. Saddam Hussein understood that nothing he could do, short of giving up power, would save him.

Saddam recruited several retired senior officers who had served in the Russian and Serbian armies to help in Iraq's defence, and although the Iraqis were no more successful in 2003 than they had been in 1991, their planning and tactics were a great deal more coherent than they were 12 years earlier. If the will to resist had been widespread among Iraqi soldiers, the defence might have been a great deal more effective. There were plenty of examples of resistance – more than in 1991 – but, as before, the Iraqi army as a whole had no great desire to fight, and the generals' plans came to nothing.

Saddam Hussein, having survived so many attempts to get rid of him, was finally overthrown in April 2003 when American troops fought their way against relatively light resistance into Baghdad. There were a couple of supposed sightings of him in the streets of the city over the following days, but it seems safe to assume that this was his main double, who had been used for propaganda appearances before. According to a Republican Guard general, Saddam himself went down to southern Baghdad as the Americans were entering the city, and fired off a couple of rocket-propelled grenades at the tanks before making his escape.

That would be consistent with everything we know about him. Saddam Hussein was no quitter. From his hideout he continued to issue handwritten orders to his surviving lieutenants and to the Arab media. His aim was somehow to regain the necessary strength to return to power one day. Extraordinarily, it was an aim supported by many people in Baghdad, Tikrit and Mosul. The legend of Saddam Hussein has fixed itself in the minds of Iraqis and is impossible to kill. Whatever happens to him in reality, he will remain a malign presence in the country for generations to come. So much ferocity, determination, anger and courage cannot easily be dissipated.

CHAPTER NINE

CONFUSION AND BETRAYAL – AN ARAB MOSAIC

Caroline Hawley

146 *Caroline Hawley is Amman Correspondent and has been based in the Middle East for the BBC for the past four years. Before being posted to Jordan she worked in Cairo and Jerusalem, and has reported from most of the other countries in the region. She also set up the BBC bureau in Baghdad before being expelled by the authorities prior to the war. In this chapter she looks at reaction to the Iraq crisis across the Arab world.*

It was the defining moment of the war, but in the Central Café in downtown Amman, Ismail al-Mani could not bring himself to look at the TV screen. He puffed on his water pipe and struggled to concentrate on his hand of cards as the statue of Saddam Hussein, in central Baghdad's Paradise Square, was slowly torn down. In a corner of the café a group of Iraqi exiles cheered. But Ismail told me he felt only a profound sense of defeat. 'It really hurts,' said the retired hotel manager, whose family fled from Jerusalem to Jordan during the 1948 Arab–Israeli war. 'I can't look at it. It's just too painful. We Arabs were once a great nation. We were in Spain for 700 years. And where are we now? We're beaten in our own homes.'

Elsewhere in Amman, Jordanians shook their heads in dismay and bewilderment. They simply didn't want to believe what they were seeing. Saddam Hussein had been, for decades, a symbol of defiance against the West; Baghdad a last bastion of Arab pride. At the news stands, the papers still carried front-page pictures of Iraqi resistance against American and British forces – among them a colour photograph of women carrying Kalashnikovs. A few days earlier, the front page of Jordan's biggest newspaper showed a farmer in his field, who, the Iraqis said, had brought down an American helicopter with a hunting rifle.

Around the Arab world, ordinary people had taken heart from these images of defiance. For them, this was heroism to counter decades of humiliation at the hands of the West and its ally Israel. 'I feel like they're fighting for all of us – for all Arabs,' a beautiful 19-year-old Fine Arts student had told me with gleaming eyes, as battles raged in Basra and Nasiriya. 'I feel proud.'

Arabs may have failed to protect Palestinian land from expro-priation, but across the Middle East they were determined Iraq would not fall to invading forces. After a particularly bad day for the Americans, one Jordanian newspaper, *al-Arab al-Yom*, carried the headline: 'Day of Glorious Losses for American forces'. But the tele-vision screens were filled with Iraqi losses too – hospital wards over-flowing with civilian casualties, who were described as 'martyrs'.

And across the Arab world, protestors took to the streets. If the demonstrations weren't on the scale of those in Western capitals, it was probably because Arabs felt impotent; they didn't believe their voices would count. Still, many braved water-cannons and police batons to demonstrate against the American 'aggression'. It was a war that, Arabs were convinced, was being waged for oil and to redraw the map of the Middle East in Israel's favour.

But the protests were in part against their own undemocratic governments too. They were venting pent-up frustrations over a profound sense of political powerlessness, mixed with disgust at Arab complicity in the war and anger at the West.

In the early days of the war, the tension in central Amman was palpable. In one café, an old man in a chequered headdress exploded in fury when he found out we worked for the BBC. 'British,' he screamed. 'Leave!' In a part of the world famous for its hospitality, it was a sign of the extraordinary resentment that was simmering across the region. An Iraqi exile who voiced his opposition to Saddam Hussein on an Amman street was hounded away by a group of angry Jordanians.

But it was not so much that Arabs were standing *for* Saddam Hussein; rather, they were standing *against* Britain and America. While the Americans were fighting Saddam Hussein, the Iraqi

147

leader – whatever his faults – was for many Arabs 'the enemy of my enemy and therefore my friend'.

And Arab governments friendly to the West had rarely been so edgy. There was little doubt that their powerful security services could keep control of the streets, but at what price? Moderates were worried that the war would strengthen the hand of Islamic militants, and that popular frustration and anger, already running high over events in the Palestinian territories, might be driven underground. 'This war will have negative effects on everyone,' the Jordanian prime minister, Ali Abu Ragheb, warned. 'There will be no winners.'

One man was benefiting, however. His voice blared out across Amman, and shopkeepers couldn't stock enough of his recordings. Shaaban Abdel Rahim was taking the Middle East by storm. The former Egyptian laundryman had shot to fame at the height of the Palestinian uprising with his song 'I Hate Israel'. As the American and British forces invaded Iraq, 'Don't Hit Iraq' became an instant hit. 'Enough,' the lyrics went. 'Chechnya, Afghanistan, Palestine, South Lebanon, the Golan Heights, and now Iraq. This is too much to bear. This is unfair. Enough. Enough. Why don't you turn to Israel and leave Iraq. Enough, enough, enough, enough.'

'It captures our mood,' the tapeseller opposite Amman's Roman amphitheatre told me. 'No one wants to buy love songs in these circumstances. We're all depressed.' In the tiny tape store, Shaaban Abdel Rahim crooned on in the background, singing of September 11 and its aftermath in the Muslim world:

'Since the fall of the towers, we are living in tornadoes,' the song goes on. 'Enough ... enough ... enough. You say, we are going to put an end to terrorism but striking Iraq is not the solution, striking Iraq is not the solution.'

In fact, many Arabs, officials and ordinary people alike, were concerned the war would *increase* terrorism. In Egypt, which spent a decade putting down an Islamic insurgency that began in the late 1980s, President Mubarak warned that an attack on Iraq would have 'horrible repercussions' and that 'instead of having one bin Laden we could face 100 bin Ladens'.

But while Egyptian officials shared Shaaban Abdel Rahim's sentiments about American double standards, they didn't want their home-grown pop sensation on air. State-run radio in Egypt and Jordan wouldn't touch him. Washington's two key US allies, both with peace treaties with Israel, felt they were having enough trouble trying to contain the anti-American fury the invasion of Iraq had unleashed. In March 2003, 15,000 demonstrators took to the streets of Cairo in a peaceful protest, and in Jordan there were reported clashes with police in the capital, Amman, and the southern town of Maan. An opinion poll in the same month showed that only ten per cent of Jordanians held a positive view of the US.

Both President Mubarak and King Abdullah of Jordan appealed to their people to be more 'civilized' in their protests. As unelected leaders, both men were nervous. Both gave nationwide addresses insisting that they were 'at one' with their people and that they shared their pain. But many Jordanians scoffed. The American troops that Jordan was quietly hosting were the talk of the town. 'No to US bases, no to US bases!' Jordanians chanted at demonstration after demonstration.

Officials insisted the troops were only there for 'defensive purposes', and to man Patriot anti-missile batteries to protect Jordanian territory from a possible missile attack by Saddam Hussein. But in the sleepy oasis town of Azraq in the eastern desert, home to a military airbase, local residents believed otherwise. They complained they were being kept up at night by the roar of unmarked military planes, while local Bedouin reported sightings of coalition special forces. 'I'm 70 years old,' one man told me. 'And I haven't seen a foreign army on my soil since the British withdrew from Jordan.' It wasn't lost on the Arab 'street' that the vast military build-up was taking place from Arab land. 'We're walking a tightrope,' one Jordanian official confessed. 'We've got to back the winning horse. But we can't afford to be seen to be doing so.'

Several other Arab countries were in a similarly delicate position. Saudi Arabia was equally adamant that the American troops on its soil were for 'defence' only, not combat operations. There was, of course, Kuwait, but also tiny Qatar – headquarters of the famous al-Jazeera television station – which was playing host to US Central Command. And Bahrain is home to the US Navy's 5th Fleet.

Syria, by contrast, was always stridently opposed to an American attack on Iraq. Of all Arab governments, Damascus probably had the most to fear from a war to remove Iraq's ruling Baath Party. After all, the way Washington was talking, its own rival branch of the Baath, which had also been in power since the 1960s, could be next.

After three decades of icy relations, Syria and Iraq had been steadily improving ties since the late 1990s, and increasing their bilateral trade. At an Arab summit in the Egyptian Red Sea resort of Sharm el-Sheikh at the end of February, Syrian officials pressed for a resolution that would go beyond the ritual hand-wringing of such occasions – and bar the Americans and British from the use of Arab land to launch their invasion.

Syria's young ruler, Bashar al-Assad, sensed political danger ahead. His assumption of power from his father Hafez in 2000 had led to talk of the Arab world's first 'republican dynasty'. Now he warned his fellow Arab leaders, 'We are all targeted. We are all in danger.'

The summit, set against the rugged mountains of Sinai, had been billed as a final effort to come up with a united Arab position to prevent war. But it quickly descended into farce. It was Colonel Gaddafi of Libya, true to form, who provided the entertainment. His towering female bodyguards had already scrapped with Egyptian security officials at the entrance to the Mövenpick Golf Resort where the summit was taking place. Inside, Muammar Gaddafi broke with summit politesse and accused the Saudis of having been willing to 'strike an alliance with the devil' when they invited American troops to protect the kingdom after Iraq invaded Kuwait in 1990. As Gaddafi and Crown Prince Abdullah of Saudi Arabia traded insults, the embarrassed Egyptian hosts quickly cut their live television coverage from inside the Mövenpick and ordinary Arabs shook their heads in despair at the divisions among their leaders. In the end, the assembled Arab leaders agreed on their 'complete rejection of any aggression on Iraq' but stopped short of barring member states from allowing the Americans to use their land. It was a compromise that would, of course, pave the way for war.

And so Arab leaders braced themselves for the consequences.

It was not just public opinion that they worried about. They were also concerned about Iraq breaking up along ethnic and sectarian lines. They believed democracy in Iraq would be a Pandora's box. And, knowing they lacked democratic legitimacy, they were nervous.

'The majority of the Arab leaders feel challenged by the idea of a new Iraq,' the Jordanian political commentator Uraib Rantawi told me from his office in central Amman. 'Iraqi oil will rival Saudi oil on the world markets. A moderate Iraq with strong ties to the West would challenge Egypt's regional role. A democratic Iraq would challenge all Arab countries.'

'Arab leaders don't want to see elections and political parties in Iraq,' Rantawi continued. 'For many of them that would be a nightmare because they know they will be next to be pushed into making reforms.'

151

Ordinary Arabs had different concerns. They thought that the Iraqi people, after more than a decade of sanctions, had suffered enough. And they were deeply suspicious of American motives. From the coffee shops of Cairo to the shopping malls of Saudi Arabia, Arabs were adamant. The war was not about weapons of mass destruction, or about September 11, or about bringing democracy. It was an unjustified aggression that was killing fellow Arabs and deepening a collective feeling of humiliation. And it was about domination.

In Amman's smartest bridal parlour, Abeer and her fiancé, Rashid, showed me the wedding dress they'd decided to put back on the shelf for the moment. The well-off young Jordanian couple had decided that they couldn't go through with their wedding plans while Iraqis were dying. 'Of course I'm sad to put off my marriage,' Abeer told me, 'but it just wouldn't have felt right.'

And hundreds of Arabs were preparing for an even bigger sacrifice. Incensed by what they were seeing on their television screens, they decided to go to Iraq to take up arms to fight. At Iraq's embassy in Damascus, visas were being processed within hours. Like the Arabs who'd fought against the Soviets in Afghanistan in the 1980s – among them Osama bin Laden – they packed their bags to fight jihad against 'infidel invaders'.

Funerals in Jordan and Lebanon for two of those who'd been killed in the war were accompanied by drum-beats of celebration

– they'd died in the service of God. Posters for Thair Othman, a Palestinian refugee from Beirut's Burj el-Barajneh camp, called him a 'martyr of Palestine and Iraq', now the twin causes of the Arab world.

Some Arab fighters were still resisting the American troops when I arrived in Baghdad just after the city fell. In a hospital in the Shia suburb once called Saddam City and now Sadr City, people were terrified by the Arab volunteers who were fighting alongside the Iraqi militia, Saddam's Fedayeen. 'These Arab fighters don't understand,' a young, turbaned sheikh told me, as he toured a ward full of the war-wounded. 'They're backing Saddam against us, and we're Muslims and Arabs too.'

152

Arabs had mobilized in the name of the 'Iraqi people' without knowing what Iraqis really wanted. And who could blame them? Such was Saddam Hussein's grip on power, so solid the wall of fear that he had constructed over decades, that Iraqis inside Iraq never had a voice.

Before I was declared *persona non grata* by the Iraqi authorities in late 2002, the government-appointed imam of a mosque in the Shia holy city Karbala told me that 'everyone loves Saddam Hussein – even his enemies'. It was an example of the sycophancy that the Iraqi leader had always demanded of his officials. But it did contain a kernel of truth. Many ordinary Arabs had turned a deaf ear to reports of his excesses because he was standing up to the West.

So Arab volunteers who went to defend Iraq spoke, on their return home, of their shock and disillusion. They'd gone with high ideals to fight alongside Saddam Hussein's soldiers in order to protect Arab land. A 25-year-old Syrian fighter, Amir, told me how he and his group of friends had been given rifles by their Iraqi guards at the start of the war. They'd then had their radios confiscated so they couldn't listen to the news, and had been informed they would soon be sent out to perform 'martyrdom operations'. Now back in Damascus, he recalled how they were met with hostility when they left their military camp after the fall of Baghdad, and found themselves in a nearby village. 'We never imagined that the Iraqis would turn against us,' he said. 'We never imagined that the Iraqis would actually welcome the Americans.'

Another Lebanese volunteer described how his excitement about fighting for Iraq evaporated when he finally arrived in Baghdad. 'Despite air raids and heavy explosions and rocket firing that could be heard in all parts of the city, and images and news of hundreds of injured or dead civilians, people, in general, were acting normally and seemed uninterested in what was going on around them,' he told Beirut's *Daily Star* on his return home. 'It was my first shock. I expected to see people rushing around, constructing street barricades and digging holes in preparation for defending the capital city of Baghdad against the coming invasion or siege. The general scene was far from that.'

So when Baghdad fell, Arabs around the Middle East were left struggling to comprehend what had happened. For months, they had heard Saddam Hussein vow to fight to the end, to force the Americans to 'commit suicide at the gates of Baghdad'. And then the resistance crumbled, first in Baghdad, and shortly afterwards in Saddam Hussein's home town, Tikrit, where many had expected him to make a final stand. Except in Kuwait – where the memory of Iraq's 1990 invasion is still fresh – there was almost no rejoicing in the Arab world.

As Iraqis experienced their first taste of freedom, fellow Arabs were simply stunned by what had happened. They watched openmouthed as al-Jazeera television showed live footage of a man beating one of Saddam Hussein's ubiquitous portraits, hitting his face with a shoe – the ultimate Arab insult. For Arab leaders, used to inculcating reverence in their people, this was dangerous stuff. And for ordinary Arabs it was troubling too. Many told me it heralded a new age of imperialism.

'Maybe the Americans are forcing them to celebrate,' the owner of a mobile phone shop said, trying to explain away the images he'd just seen. 'It could be that they're doing it under the barrel of a gun.'

In Amman's Central Café, Ismail al-Mani finally glanced up from his game of cards to see Iraqis pulling a rope around the neck of Saddam Hussein's statue. But he dismissed the scenes of Iraqi jubilation. 'They will wake up soon,' he said. 'If the Americans and the British stay in Iraq, they will wake up to see they're being ruled by a foreign power.'

Even the Central Café's ever-cheery waiter was depressed. 'It's the saddest news I've ever heard,' he told me as he prepared a water pipe for a customer. 'It's opened the door to British and American colonialism throughout the region. God protect us from what will come.'

For 23-year-old Zaffar Shami, his 'dream' of pan-Arabism had been 'obliterated' with the fall of Baghdad, ancient capital of the Muslims and 'the jewel of the Arab world'. 'We'd watched the Iraqis with pride and a bit of envy,' the Palestinian–Jordanian student said. 'They were fighting my wars, and my fathers' wars. They were bringing back my rights, and my fathers' rights.' And then it all came tumbling down.

Amid all the despondency, Hisham Kassem, a gentle Egyptian publisher and civil libertarian, felt like a lonely man as he quietly rejoiced at the end of Saddam Hussein's regime. 'It was one of the greatest moments of my life,' the head of the Egyptian Organization for Human Rights told me. 'I was in the office but I had to run home to watch the television. I felt so relieved and emotional. That statue was a symbol of all the repression in the Arab world.'

Kassem, who has campaigned for years for democratic change, said he'd recently come to the unhappy conclusion that it would not come from within the Arab world. 'There are 22 members of the Arab League and not a democracy among them,' he said. 'The main obstacle to change is our own rulers. The coalition took on the worst of them and threatened the others and they're responding. Egypt is now proposing to abolish state security courts and hard labour and set up a higher council for human rights. It may be cosmetic but it might at least allow civil society to begin to work.'

In the weeks after the war, Kassem's views weren't popular at Cairene dinner parties or in a wider Arab society that had become increasingly anti-American. But he remains determinedly optimistic that an 'opportunity' has been created. 'Of course the Americans are not doing it for us,' he says. 'But I don't care if the devil brings democracy, as long as it's in my interests. I think that finally change will come to this region. The statue is the equivalent of the collapse of the Berlin Wall.'

I'd been in Baghdad when that statue of Saddam Hussein was unveiled on his sixty-fifth birthday in April 2002, as Israel was re-occupying the West Bank. Sensing, perhaps, that it could be Saddam's last birthday as leader of Iraq, the regime turned the day into a show of defiance. In the face of ever-louder American threats to remove him, they were billing the celebrations for the 'beloved leader' as the biggest and best the country had ever had, despite the mood of gloom in the rest of the Arab world over events in the Palestinian territories. Buses were laid on from every corner of Baghdad for a 'million-man march' in his honour. But then, confusion. On the evening of his birthday, Saddam abruptly announced that, in fact, there'd been no celebrations – they'd been cancelled because Palestinian 'brothers' were dying.

The Iraqi leader had always been a vocal champion of the Palestinian cause. He'd won Palestinian hearts when in 1991 he announced he wouldn't pull Iraqi troops out of Kuwait until Israel withdrew from the West Bank and Gaza. And from the Gaza Strip to the refugee camps of Syria and Lebanon, there was now dismay at his defeat. 'I always felt he was using us for his own ends and interests,' said a Palestinian cameraman friend. 'I didn't feel sorry for him personally when he went. But I felt that we as a people were lost. We're weaker now than ever. There's no one to defend us and we'll be under even more pressure to succumb to the Israelis.'

Few Palestinians were as upset about Saddam Hussein's demise as Ibrahim Zaanen, a leader of the Arab Liberation Front in the Gaza Strip. His group had been distributing Iraq's 'aid' to the Palestinians – $25,000 to the family of each suicide bomber. They'd made their last payments on 21 March, the day after the war on Iraq began. Portraits of Saddam still hung on the walls of Zaanen's office in Gaza's Remal region in the weeks after the fall of Baghdad. 'It's not just us that's been harmed,' he said. 'It's all Palestinians. Israel will now take advantage of what's happening in Iraq to try to force the Palestinians to compromise on their rights.'

It was an almost unanimous view in the towns and refugee camps of the West Bank and Gaza. Few Palestinians had any faith that the 'road map' for peace being pushed by George W Bush and Tony Blair would actually lead to the Palestinian state they'd dreamed of for decades.

In Syria, too, there were now major question marks about the future. The government in Damascus had expected, and hoped, that the war would last longer than it did. For weeks, Syria's official media had praised the 'brave resistance' of Iraqis against 'British–American imperialist aggression'. But as the battle moved closer to Baghdad, the warnings from Washington had been growing louder. Syria was accused of aiding Iraq militarily, harbouring fleeing officials of the Iraqi regime, giving haven to terrorists, human rights abuses ... the list went on. So, when Baghdad fell, Syrian officialdom knew that the consequences could be profound. As Saddam Hussein's statue was brought down, state-run television pulled the plug on its live coverage of the war and cut to a programme about Islamic art, while Damascene intellectuals wondered in whispers whether Syria's own statues, too, might one day fall.

Less than a month after Baghdad had been taken by American troops, the US Secretary of State, Colin Powell, who'd earlier called on Syria to 'embark on a different and more hopeful course', visited Damascus. As Mr Powell lectured Syria on the 'new strategic situation' in the region, Damascus responded by closing down some anti-Israeli groups. American pressure was proving difficult to resist, backed as it was by the threat of the military stick that had just beaten Saddam Hussein. And other Arab leaders feared their turn would come.

'There must be an urgent and extensive Arab initiative to study the Iraq experience,' came an appeal in the Egyptian government-owned daily, *al-Ahram*. 'Not only to protect Syria, but to stop the American plan that is now moving like a knife through butter.'

It had begun with Saddam Hussein, but no one knew where, or how, it would end. The quick collapse of his rule had changed how the former Iraqi dictator was seen in the Arab world virtually overnight. Some called him a 'traitor' and said he'd struck a deal with the Americans. For most, he was just one more leader who was, in the end, nothing but bluster, who was more concerned with retaining power than anything else. Most Iraqis had known it all along.

In the infamous Abu Ghuraib jail on the outskirts of Baghdad, a giant painting of Saddam, with the title 'Leader of the Arabs', has now been defaced by bullet holes. In the weeks after the collapse of his regime, the overpowering stench of death hung in the air around the portrait as relatives dug up the remains of political prisoners who had 'disappeared'. One man trying to find his dead brother told me: 'We're all glad that Saddam is gone, that the nightmare is over. We just feel bad we didn't do it ourselves. But perhaps it would have been impossible, given the nature of his regime.'

And however happy they were to have been freed from the clutches of Saddam Hussein, Iraqi after Iraqi told me they didn't want to see a prolonged American occupation. Nor did Arabs outside Iraq. It had been the presence of American troops in Saudi Arabia, home to Islam's holiest sites, that had fuelled Osama bin Laden's jihad.

From his offices at Jordan's biggest newspaper, Imad Hmoud, editor of *al-Rai*, warned: 'It'll be a huge risk for the Americans and the British to keep their troops in Iraq for a long time. Because this will lead to violence and terrorism.'

But if they pulled out quickly, leaving a stable, democratic Iraq, and were able to find a fair solution to the Israeli–Palestinian conflict, the optimism of the Egyptian civil libertarian Hisham Kassem might not be misplaced.

The chief editor of *al-Watan* newspaper, Jamal Khashoggi, believed that, with the Saudi royal family now talking of political reform, the Arab world could be on the verge of a new beginning. He told me that support for his fellow countryman, Osama bin Laden, was born not out of hatred for America so much as a 'lack of hope'. 'We Arabs had reached a dead end,' he said. The fall of Saddam Hussein's statue in Paradise Square was, for him, 'the end of an era of dictatorship'. But he cautioned: 'All my optimism depends on what the Americans do now – and how the Iraqi experiment proceeds.'

In the immediate aftermath of the war, however, few ordinary Arabs were hopeful. They were mostly still shell-shocked, struggling to digest the significance of the political earthquake that had just erupted in the region. And for Arabs the real test will be not only in Iraq but Palestine – the Middle East's long-festering wound.

CHAPTER TEN

THE NORTHERN FRONT AND THE KURDS' ENDGAME

Jim Muir

158 *Jim Muir is Teheran Correspondent and has been based in the Middle East for more than 25 years. During the war he reported from the north of Iraq on the Iraqi Kurds' participation in the conflict. He was with cameraman Kaveh Golestan near the village of Kifri when Kaveh was killed by a land mine. Here, he examines the difficult relationship between Turkey and the Kurds, and its implications for American strategy.*

As we sat in the folding, camel-coloured hills and looked down on Kirkuk, Shaikh Ahmad Askari must have felt a long way from his home in Greenway, Pinner, on the outskirts of London, where he had left his wife, Shabow, and their four children in the hope of witnessing the liberation of his home city. 'We were forced out of Kirkuk 27 years ago, and I've always dreamt of coming back,' he said. 'Now, perhaps, my dream may be about to come true.'

Tantalizingly, Shaikh Ahmad's quarter was tucked away behind a ridge, out of sight of our vantage point. We could see traffic glinting as it moved past the oilfields in the shimmering haze on the outskirts of the city, but not the centre of Kirkuk itself. Would Shaikh Ahmad be able to find his home, and would it still be in one piece? That would depend on the fate of the northern front, where hostilities had only just begun in earnest. Kirkuk was still firmly in Iraqi government hands.

It was 30 March, and the war in the south had already been underway for ten days. But here in the north there was still no sign of a major coalition offensive building, no massing of thousands of troops, no marshalling of armoured columns. However, the fact that we had been able to get as far as the foothills overlooking Kirkuk showed that things were at last starting to move.

Three days earlier, without forewarning, Iraqi troops had silently abandoned front-line positions they had held at Chamchamal, 20 kilometres away to the east, and fallen back all the way to the outskirts of Kirkuk itself. It was a clear sign that the Iraqi forces were not in good shape. There had been some coalition bombing along the front line, though not much. Not a shot had been fired at them on the ground by the Kurdish Pesh Merga fighters, who for the past decade or more had manned the other side of the line at Chamchamal, which divided the government-held area from the Kurdish-controlled north.

But, the long-awaited northern front was going to have to take a very different form from that originally envisaged by American planners. Under Plan A, there would have been a serious thrust from the north to match, and meet up with, the push from the south. Shortly after the bombs started falling, 62,000 US troops, including the 4th Infantry Division, should have been thundering down the main road from Turkey with heavy tanks and other hardware. Mosul, barely 60 kilometres from Kurdish lines, should have been the first big Iraqi city to fall. As things turned out, it was the last. Now, there would clearly be no fat arrows arcing southwards to join up with the other US forces closing in on Baghdad from the Kuwait side. It was going to have to be Plan B – Northern Front Lite. And Late. It would be a combination of American air power and special forces, and the lightly armed Pesh Mergas.

The reason for all this, of course, was Turkey. Under Plan A, it was to have provided the springboard for the northern offensive, opening land corridors and providing base facilities for US troops and equipment brought in by sea and air. But public opinion in Turkey was running strongly against the impending war and was deeply opposed to allowing US troops to use Turkish soil. The access issue had to be approved by the Turkish parliament, which faced a massive dilemma. If it abided by the will of the people, it risked alienating a major NATO partner – and losing up to $26 billion in American grants and credit guarantees that was to have been part of the deal. In the end, though, that is precisely what it did. On 1 March, the Ankara parliament narrowly voted down the government's proposal, precipitating what could only be seen as a disaster for Turkey's relations with the US, and compounding an already drastic economic situation.

Hanging in the balance throughout that turbulent period was the difficult triangular relationship between Washington, Ankara and the Iraqi Kurds. The Kurds had risen up against Saddam Hussein at George Bush Senior's urging in the wake of the 1991 Gulf War, only to be chased by the Iraqis into the mountains where they perished in their thousands. Their tragedy prompted Western intervention in the form of a US–British–French air umbrella protecting a Kurdish 'safe haven' north of the 36th parallel. There, the Iraqi Kurds were able to run their own affairs quasi-independently, albeit in an historically and geographically tenuous situation.

This Kurdish 'experiment' in democracy and self-rule was watched by the Turks with mixed feelings and growing unease. They had their own large and restless Kurdish minority. To see Iraq's Kurds living free and prosperously next door in autonomy – or, even worse, independence – was not at all to Ankara's taste.

As the US-led war against Iraq came closer, Ankara's anxieties about the Iraqi Kurds began to rise sharply. A regime change in Baghdad, which Turkey really did not want, was obviously on the way. This opened up the distinct prospect of instability, which Ankara feared the Kurds might seize on to take further steps towards independence, despite their many public protestations to the contrary. Nor did Ankara fully trust American intentions across the border in Kurdish Iraq. It was resentful, even jealous, of the close relationship between Washington and the two main Kurdish leaders, Masoud Barzani of the Kurdistan Democratic Party (KDP) and his ally and rival Jalal Talabani of the Patriotic Union of Kurdistan (PUK).

After getting off to a good start by sponsoring elections and setting up a joint government and parliament in 1992, the two Kurdish factions had plunged into a violent and bloody internecine struggle in the mid-1990s, which divided their region and institutions between them. The KDP was left ruling the western sector and the mountainous Turkish border area, with Arbil as its main city, and the PUK the east, based on Suleimanieh. Two leaders, two administrations – even two non-connecting mobile phone systems.

Turkey had tried to enhance its regional primacy by sponsoring peace moves between the warring Kurdish factions in 1997. But Ankara's bid failed, and was supplanted by a much more successful peace accord, sponsored by and signed in Washington in September 1998, drawing the US directly into the heart of Iraqi Kurdish politics and aggravating Ankara's suspicion and jealousy.

So, as preparations for war gathered pace, the Americans rapidly discovered that the hoped-for access to Northern Iraq via their NATO ally was by no means to be taken for granted, and that even minimal co-operation would be hedged with conditions and demands that would ultimately prove impossible to meet.

Things began to come to a head in the first week of February 161 when American, Turkish and Iraqi Kurdish officials met in Ankara. Although war was still six weeks away and theoretically might not happen, the assumption was that it would, and Turkey wanted some ground rules set.

It insisted a clear red line be drawn around the Iraqi government-held cities of Kirkuk and Mosul. In addition, Turkey wanted the Kurdish Pesh Merga forces to stay where they were, defending their own area. And they should not try to instigate popular uprisings in the two cities, as happened in 1991 when largely Kurdish Kirkuk rose up, and fell under Pesh Merga control for a couple of days before Saddam's forces struck back and the Kurds fled to the mountains.

Kirkuk, in particular, is demographically sensitive and a potential tinder-box. Although it's generally acknowledged to have a Kurdish majority, some Iraqi Turkomans – and Turkey – claim their community is bigger. Under Baathist rule, Baghdad tried to change the demographics by displacing tens of thousands of Kurds and Turkomans and replacing them with Arabs shipped in from the south. There is also a sizeable Assyrian Christian minority.

Even more seriously, the Kurds were told that Turkey would send troops across the border, not to fight the Iraqi army, but supposedly to pre-empt a flood of refugees heading out of Northern Iraq as happened in 1991. And the linkage was clear: if Turkish troops were not allowed in, Turkey would say no to America.

The US was still desperate at this stage to win Turkish approval to open up the northern front and was seemingly unaware of

Kurdish sensitivities about Turkish intentions. So it had apparently agreed in principle to the Turkish proposal, though details – the size and deployment of the force, and under whose command it should be – remained to be worked out. The Turkish troops would steer clear of Kurdish towns and cities, and would also keep out of Mosul and Kirkuk unless the Pesh Merga moved in.

But the idea of Turkish troops crossing the border to pursue Ankara's own agenda was anathema to the Iraqi Kurds, and especially to Masoud Barzani's KDP, which controlled the areas the Turks planned to move into. Even a modest military advance would cut the KDP off from its vital land access not only to Turkey, but also to Iran in the east and Syria in the west.

At follow-up military talks in Silopi in southern Turkey ten days later, supposedly to fine-tune the plan and agree on details, the Turks found the KDP polite but adamant in rejecting the fundamental principle of Turkish intervention. I saw Masoud Barzani at his headquarters in the summer station of Salahuddin, in the hills above Arbil, the day after those talks with the Turks. He was bristling with indignation. Our exchange, conducted to the howling of a spectacular blizzard raging outside, went like this:

'We told them that we absolutely reject the entry of any regional forces to Kurdistan,' he said. 'We said, if there were to be a security problem or a mass exodus beyond our ability to cope, we'll ask you to help us by all means.'

'But there's an agreement in principle between the US and Turkey on their troops going in,' I pointed out. 'That's their business,' he replied. 'If there's an agreement between them, it doesn't concern us. We're not bound by any such agreement between the US and Turkey on intervention.'

Salahuddin was preparing to host a vital meeting of the Iraqi opposition, with US participation. It was to be the last such gathering before the war, and the aim was to reach an understanding on Iraq's political future after Saddam. But it was repeatedly delayed, as the US administration struggled to define its relationships with its NATO ally Turkey and with the Iraqi Kurds, who formed the backbone of the Iraqi opposition. The Turkish issue dominated not only the run-up to the opposition meeting, but also the conference itself when it finally got underway on 26 February.

Kurdish fears were aggravated by increasingly clear signs from Ankara that providing relief to Iraqi refugees was far from the main motive for intervention. On 23 February, the Turkish foreign ministry issued this statement: 'The Turkish army will enter the region to prevent an exodus, to prevent the Kurds from establishing a free Kurdistan, to prevent them entering Kirkuk and Mosul, and to protect the Turkomans. We don't want a clash between Turkey and the Kurds, and for that reason we are sending lots of troops to the region as a warning.'

Turkish military briefings at the time reflected Ankara's belief that Washington had tilted towards the Kurds, that the latter would be emboldened to go for independence, that there would be an ethnic bloodbath against the Turkoman people when the Baghdad regime fell, and that a 'little war' (Turkey v the Kurds) would inevitably have to follow the 'big war' (the US v Iraq). Hence, heavy intervention was needed. Reports circulating in Northern Iraq gave credence to suspicions that Turkey intended to swamp the KDP area with troops and disarm the Pesh Mergas.

For the Kurds, equally convinced that Washington was tilting towards Turkey in the hope of winning northern-front access, it was time to start ringing the alarm bells. In a calculated move, one of Masoud Barzani's top aides, Hoshyar Zebari, appeared at a news conference in Arbil on 23 February, attended by scores of international reporters gathered for the opposition meeting and the expected war. 'We will oppose any Turkish military intervention,' Zebari declared. 'This is a decision. Nobody should imagine that we are bluffing on this issue. This is a very serious matter. Any intervention, under whatever pretext, will lead to clashes.'

So the special US presidential envoy to the 'free Iraqis', Zalmay Khalilzad, whose delayed arrival held up the conference, found himself doing a pretty fair impression of a man walking a tightrope in a gale. In a written statement after the conference began on 26 February, he referred to 'our Kurdish friends' but 'our Turkish allies', and called on the Kurds to 'support the US and their allies the Turks, to liberate Iraq'.

But at a private news briefing the same day, he spelt out what turned out to be a position of firm principle, to which Washington was to adhere in the stormy weeks ahead. 'We'd like Turkey to be part of the coalition, but we're against any unilateral move by any country into Iraq,' he said. 'Our position is abundantly clear, I cannot make it clearer: no movement by any power into Iraq, unless it is fully co-ordinated with the coalition, period – and withdrawal when the coalition withdraws. Coming together, leaving together.'

The problem for the Americans was that Ankara never had any intention of joining the US-led coalition against Baghdad, but was making *any* co-operation with the coalition contingent on a Turkish troop entry that would be in pursuit of Turkey's own perceived strategic interest.

So Washington stood to see two of its supposed allies at each others' throats instead of teaming up against Saddam Hussein. After the vote in the Turkish parliament, Plan A was already down the drain. But if the Kurds were obliged to turn north to face the Turks, there would be no Plan B either, and the northern front would be left in total disarray.

Tensions rose sharply. At anti-Turkish demonstrations by the Kurds in both Suleimanieh and Arbil in early March, the Turkish flag was burned. On 7 March, the Turkish army carried out its biggest troop movement for years, massing thousands of soldiers on the border with Northern Iraq.

For the first three weeks of March, US officials struggled to salvage something from Ankara. On 20 March, the day the Americans carried out their first strike on Baghdad, the Turkish parliament finally approved the use of Turkey's airspace by coalition aircraft.

But the Turks remained insistent on sending their own troops in as the price for any coalition access. Its policies in chaos, the government in Ankara went into stress overload and sent out a series of contradictory signals. On the night of 21–22 March, it even announced that it had sent troops across the border unilaterally, which turned out not to be true.

At a final round of talks in Ankara on 25 March, the Americans admitted failure. A US diplomat was quoted as saying the discussions were dominated by 'mutual incomprehension'. At this point, Washington essentially gave up on the Turks and turned in earnest to Plan B: bypassing Ankara and working directly with the Iraqi Kurds and the estimated 80,000 Pesh

Mergas, who suddenly became the second-biggest coalition troop contributor. For the Kurds, the most important battle had been won before the fighting even started. No announcement was made, but a clear signal was sent, and received, by both Ankara and Baghdad.

On the night of 26 March, the US 173rd Airborne Brigade arrived via an unnecessarily spectacular and well-publicized air-drop over the Kurdish airfield at Harir, 30 kilometres north of Arbil. After months of discretion, the US began working openly with the Iraqi Kurds. US aircraft ferried in special forces units from Jordan across the western Iraqi desert, avoiding Turkey alto-gether – despite this being a risky route. The northern front was underway at last. After all the delays, uncertainties and political wrangling, events began to move with bewildering speed. Within hours of the 173rd's airdrop, Iraqi troops staged their sudden withdrawal on the Chamchamal front on 27 March. In subse-quent days, similar pullbacks were carried out on other fronts around Kirkuk and Mosul.

But the first serious ground action was not directed against Iraqi troops. There was other business to get out of the way first. The Ansar al-Islam had been identified and proclaimed by Washington as a terrorist group linked to both al-Qaida and the Baghdad government. From the belt of valley and mountain terrain it controlled, abutting the Iranian border in the far eastern sector of Iraqi Kurdistan, it had also been a thorn in the side of the Iraqi Kurds, and especially the PUK, which held most of the adjacent territory.

The Ansar had long been engaged in clashes with the PUK, and was blamed for a number of actions deemed 'terrorist', including the assassination on 8 February of a senior PUK figure, Shawkat Hajji Mushir, and a car bomb attack on a PUK check-point on 22 March in which Australian cameraman Paul Moran was among four people killed.

It was an article of faith for both the Americans and the PUK that the Ansar had to be wiped out, and it made sense for that to happen before turning to the Iraqi front as the Ansar were a dan-gerous enemy to have at their backs. Small numbers of US special forces and liaison officers had been in the Kurdish north for months, discreetly scouting front-line positions and identifying potential targets. They had done their homework on the Ansar. As the bombing and missile campaign got underway in other parts of the country on 21 March, the Ansar were also hit hard. Scores of bombs and missiles struck their area that first night, killing at least 70 people. They included many members of a distinct, but geographically and politically overlapping, faction, the Islamic Komola.

A week later the long-planned ground operation was launched. At least 5000 PUK Pesh Mergas, with small numbers of US special forces, moved into the rugged Ansar-held pocket along several axes. The special forces also manned hilltop vantage points and called in strikes from US jets circling in a clear blue spring sky. By dusk, the back of the Ansar's resistance had been broken. It had become a mopping-up operation.

The same formula – small numbers of elite US special forces working with larger numbers of Pesh Mergas – was then turned on the Iraqi army. Mixed teams operated behind Iraqi lines, identifying targets – military bases, security headquarters, Baath Party centres – in and around Kirkuk and Mosul for coalition jets to bomb, which they did with generally impressive accuracy. There were some skirmishes and special operations by the US special forces and Pesh Mergas, but no concerted offensives.

In the end, as the Kurds had always predicted, the cities simply imploded and collapsed. The trigger was the fall of Baghdad on 9 April, which seems to have knocked any remaining stuffing out of the Iraqi resistance. Within a matter of hours, the defences of Kirkuk simply melted away. By the next morning, 10 April, the Pesh Mergas found they could just ride into the city virtually unresisted. They were given a hero's welcome by a populace largely delighted to see the end of Baathist rule. The general sentiment was expressed in a message daubed on one of the city's walls: THANK YOU MR BOSH AND BLEAR.

But it had not been meant to happen that way, and things rapidly got out of hand. The city became a looter's paradise, with people streaming in from Suleimanieh and Arbil – horns and Kurdish nationalist music blaring triumphantly. Government and other properties, including the city museum, were stripped.

PUK Pesh Mergas – led by Mam Rostem, a tough, cheery veteran and Kirkuk exile – were widely blamed for jumping the gun. But the PUK later won credit for stabilizing the situation by sending police and city engineers in from Suleimanieh to impose security and restore utilities. The PUK leader, Jalal Talabani, later told me his officials had seized nearly 800 looted vehicles which would be returned to their owners. Eventually, small numbers of US special forces moved into Kirkuk, and the 173rd Airborne was rushed in to secure the oilfields.

But, because of the sudden crisis in Kirkuk, US forces were ill-prepared for what followed almost immediately in Mosul, about 200 kilometres away to the north-west. The story there went differently, though the result was the same. Rather than simply disappearing without warning, the Iraqi defence and security establishment, seeing the writing on the wall after the collapse of Baghdad, agreed to surrender the city in order to spare it further punishment.

Through military and tribal intermediaries, contact was made with the KDP and, through it, with the Americans. It was agreed that the US would call off the bombing of Mosul, which it did at 3 p.m. on 9 April, and that the city's defenders would then lay down their arms and go home, which they did a few hours later.

So the city, defenceless, awaited the Americans. But nothing happened apart from the arrival of a small contingent at Mosul airport. Insurrection and wholesale looting broke out, first in the mixed but probably Kurdish-majority eastern side of town, and then in the more populous Arab quarters on the west bank of the Tigris. All public buildings, including hotels, the university, and again the city's museum, were ransacked. So too were the 17 palaces in Saddam's forest complex on the north side of the city. On one of the compound's gateposts, a local wit daubed the legend: HOUSE FOR SALE.

Both local people and the KDP, whose Pesh Merga played the same lead role in parts of Mosul as their PUK counterparts had in Kirkuk, blamed the Americans for the breakdown. KDP officials said the US commanders had held back both their own forces and the Pesh Merga regulars under their command, insisting on an irrelevant formal capitulation from an Iraqi 5th Army Corps which had already disintegrated.

Mosul took longer to stabilize than Kirkuk, and also seemed much more likely to be a source of continuing problems because of its quite different makeup. Even the Kurds would not dispute its large Sunni Arab majority, which found itself without leadership after the demise of the Baath Party. The Party had few more loyal strongholds.

'Saddam's rule was strong, and the vacuum is big,' I was told later by retired Iraqi army general Ali Jajawi, who played a key role in Mosul's surrender. 'Islamism is starting to appear, alongside Arab nationalism. If the US stays and there's no central government, we fear things will get quickly worse.'

168

Back in Kirkuk, I met up with Shaikh Ahmad Askari. He had found his house, and it was in one piece, though the Arab family who had been living there had damaged electrical fittings, plumbing and other fixtures before they fled. 'When I first came into the house I felt very happy, because it's my home, and I have a lot of childhood memories from here,' Ahmad told me as he showed me proudly around the house and its vine-covered courtyard. 'There's a lot of work to do to fix the place up. Then we'll have to decide whether to move the family back here. It won't be easy for my kids to switch from the English school system.'

Many other exiled Kurds and Turkomans were trying to reclaim homes that they had been driven out of as part of Baghdad's Arabization policy. The dangers were clear, but the Americans, increasing their grip on Kirkuk and Mosul as days went by, seemed aware of them. US forces announced that on 23 April they had intercepted attempts by Turkish military intelligence to smuggle arms in aid consignments to the Kirkuk Turkomans. The Americans had won agreement from the Kurdish factions to give up attempts to dominate the city, and seemed little inclined to indulge Turkish provocations. But on 23 April, the Turkish army also began to withdraw the thousands of forces they had massed on the border, signalling an easing of tension. 'I think the Turkish danger has passed,' the KDP leader Masoud Barzani told me that same day. 'It will become an Iraqi question, as an independent country, rather than a Kurdish one.'

Well might the Kurds hail this as their greatest victory. Even after giving up Kirkuk, they had made huge territorial gains, over-running an estimated 30,000 square kilometres of terrain, from Jebel Sinjar on the Syrian border to Mandali on the Iranian side. They had expanded their area of control by about two-thirds and reunited all parts of what they regard as Iraqi Kurdistan.

'This is the real Iraqi Kurdistan now,' said the KDP's Hoshyar Zebari. 'We have shown the Turks there have been no waves of refugees, no independent Kurdish state, no massacre of Turkomans. All their arguments have been shot down one by one.' 'We came out of this war the real winners,' he added. 'We made a clear-cut commitment from the beginning that we'll be with you [the Americans] as long as the Turks don't come in. If they do, we'll have to turn north. The Turks shot themselves in the foot.'

169

The Kurds were fully committed to cementing their autonomy within a federal, united Iraq – a concept for which they had long since won the agreement of all factions in the broader Iraqi opposition. Within days of the war in the north being over, their leaders began moving to Baghdad to join a struggle over the country's political future that they were well placed to influence strongly. Their cohesion and experience contrasted favourably with the political turmoil prevailing among both the Shia and Sunni Arabs.

'This victory of Iraqi Kurdistan will help all Kurds to be more realistic, to think about what's possible, and not to be idealistic; to seek democracy and human rights in the framework of a democratic country,' said PUK leader Jalal Talabani, when I asked him to sum up what the whole affair had done to the primordial Kurdish dream of independent statehood. 'A dream is a dream,' he added. 'But we must live with reality. We have achieved tangible things for our people.'

As for the Turks, they were left with little choice but to retire and lick their wounds. The Iraqi Kurds were well aware that they had to live with their Turkish – and Iranian and Syrian – neighbours, while the US would one day pack up and leave. But they were confident that the Americans would be around for 'the long haul', and optimistic that Turkish attitudes to the Kurdish issue would change as Ankara faced the imperative of getting into Europe.

CHAPTER ELEVEN

'ALL ABOUT OIL'?
THE ECONOMICS OF WAR

Evan Davis

170   *Evan Davis is Economics Editor. He joined the BBC in 1993, having previously worked at the Institute for Fiscal Studies and the London Business School. In this chapter he discusses the relationship between war and economics.*

Something surprising happened on the fifth day of the war, a long way from Baghdad. The New York Stock Exchange made an unexpected decision: it removed the reporting credentials of two business journalists from al-Jazeera Television. No longer would Ammar Sankari or Ramsey Shiber be allowed to use the broadcast facilities at the Exchange for al-Jazeera's daily stock exchange report.

Ammar had turned up at about 11.30 a.m., as usual, to be told the Exchange was cutting back on broadcasters; he would have to hand back his badge. 'They have their own reasons, I guess,' he told me. It was an odd decision. Surely, during a period when Arab resentment of American action was escalating the US would want to reach out to Arab broadcasters. The reason given was that the Exchange's media facilities were congested. But no other international broadcaster had been summarily ejected. 'Does the decision have anything to do with al-Jazeera's coverage of the war and the fact it showed US military prisoners?' I asked the press office. 'It's impossible to say that thought wasn't in the mind of those looking at this question,' they replied.

Perhaps we shouldn't read too much into an incident that may reflect no more than some overzealous, misapplied patriotism.

But this could be the first-ever case of a stock exchange punishing a foreign broadcaster, simply because it has taken a view of a general news story which doesn't happen to fit that of the host country. It raises the question of whether the US generally is now only willing to engage with the rest of the world on its own terms.

* * * * * *

At the time of the first Gulf War, it was said that if Kuwait produced broccoli the West would never have gone to war to end the Iraqi occupation.

This is probably true. A desire to stop Saddam gaining too much control of the energy market, and threatening other suppliers, played a large part in the West's resolve to curtail his ambitions. It was convenient that Saddam's invasion of Kuwait provided such an easy pretext to fight him, and meant there was a fortunate coincidence between upholding international law and the promotion of Western interests. It's tempting to jump from the assertion that we choose our diplomatic and military causes with a careful view to our own material interests, to the more simplistic and less plausible idea that wars are about economics. The main problem with this second argument is that it is probably less true now than it has been for most of human history. The more affluent we are, the more we have to lose and the less we have to gain by fighting. In economic jargon, peace is a 'superior good', one that you value more as you get richer. Advanced Western nations live comfortably, they're not short of the basic goods for survival, and in general they don't risk the terror of war simply to secure higher living standards, better cars, designer clothes – or cheaper petrol.

In the past, many wars did involve clashes of economic interests. Empires were built and defended for economic reasons. The first 19th-century Opium War, between Britain and China, was prompted by the British East India Company asking for government help after the Chinese destroyed 20,000 chests of opium in an effort to reduce addiction. It was an economic war, which ended with the Chinese paying a £21-million indemnity, the cession of five ports for use by the British and the award of a 150-year lease on Hong Kong.

As the 20th century progressed, however, the incidence of such classic economic conflicts declined. Even if one accepts that the first Gulf War was economically motivated, most recent wars involving Western nations have not been: the Second World War, the Korean and Vietnam Wars, the Falklands and Kosovo conflicts, and the latest war in Afghanistan.

The Second World War, for example, cost the US the equivalent of 130 per cent of one year's national income, the Korean War 15 per cent and the Vietnam War 12 per cent. These figures obviously exclude the far higher cost of war in terms of casualties. Such expenditure of resources could not possibly be justified by the importance to the US economy of, for example, Vietnam.

Indeed, in some recent conflicts, such as that over the Falklands, economics was used as an argument *against* fighting: the cost was simply disproportionate to any possible benefit. (For the amount it spent on the conflict, the British government could have simply given each citizen of the Falklands about £1 million.)

So what has changed to render wars less economically motivated than they used to be? Recent decades have seen an enormous growth in trade and economic integration. Of course, the world was economically integrated prior to the First World War – Britain was a huge investor overseas, more globalized than the US is now. But the type of integration so pervasive today is rather different. In the West we no longer import raw materials and export finished manufactured goods in the way we used to. Instead, we import finished manufactured goods of a kind similar to those we export, and we invest overseas in operations very similar to those we run at home.

While we love to claim that the West is 'competing' with other global blocs – that China will 'overtake us', for example – the truth is that national economic interests coincide to a greater degree than ever. We are, after all, operating within a framework of international rules and norms that takes us beyond the battle for basic resources – land, water, fuel or diamonds. Put simply, it doesn't make sense for the Americans to bomb Chinese shopping malls if Americans own the shops in them.

But what about oil, with its peculiar role in lubricating the global economy, figuratively and literally? We certainly use a lot of it. The world consumes about 75 million barrels a day. The US uses about 20 million of these, a little over a quarter of the total and obviously a disproportionate amount. But America is a significant producer of oil too, so on a per capita basis it only imports about a third more oil than, say, France.

Because oil is so important for Western manufacturing, and such a major component of the average consumer's weekly spending, it has dramatic economic effects. If oil prices rise, companies either take a big hit in their profits – with consequences for the stock market and for their investment plans – or they have to pass their increased costs on to consumers in the form of higher prices. That leaves consumers worse off in real terms. If they in turn try to avoid the pain of a reduction in spending power by demanding inflationary pay rises, the authorities simply have to restrain economic growth – thereby making workers less confident about asking for more money. The result is quite possibly a recession to keep inflation down.

173

Oil price rises for non-oil-producing countries are painful in one form or another. The International Monetary Fund estimates that a permanent $5 increase in the price of a barrel of oil knocks about a quarter of one per cent off national income in industrialized countries. The West clearly sees an economic interest in lower oil prices, and thus in maintaining the global supply.

And so to Iraq, which is thought to have the second-biggest known oil reserves in the world – about 10.7 per cent of the total. (By comparison, Saudi Arabia has 24.9 per cent while the US has about 2.9 per cent.) There are estimates that put Iraq's reserves far lower. The US Department of the Interior's Geological Survey, for example, suggests that Russia has bigger reserves. It is also arguable that, under Saddam, Iraq exaggerated its oil production in order to secure bigger quotas in OPEC. However, as the more optimistic figures for Iraqi oil are generally used in public discussion, it is no wonder that people think oil plays an important part in the motivation for Western 'meddling' in the Middle East.

Ever since 1908, when Anglo–Persian Oil (later BP) was created, the West has kept its proverbial snout in the Middle Eastern oil trough. For example, Anglo–Persian dominated Iranian oil production between the wars; British and American troops occupied southern Iran during the Second World War, in response to Soviet incursions further north; in 1951, the radical Iranian prime minister Mohammad Mossadegh nationalized the oil industry, but within two years he had been overthrown in an Anglo–American operation that restored the pro-Western Shah's powers; in 1956, the British and French seized the Suez canal, fearing that Egypt's control would be used to restrict oil exports to Western Europe. So oil did motivate Western policy in the 20th century. We should not be surprised that it is suspected of doing so in the 21st.

* * * * * *

174   The shifting nature of the arguments used to defend the second Gulf War only served to enhance people's sense that here, too, oil was the real, unstated motive. But it is worth examining suspicions about this war more closely.

The main case was that America's voracious appetite for gasoline to fuel excessively large cars meant the US wanted a lower oil price, and that the best way to get it was to promote an increase in Iraqi supplies. A more subtle variant was that Washington was worried about the stability of Saudi Arabia and the security of its oil exports, and wanted a large alternative supplier in the region, ready to take over if necessary. A third argument was that George W Bush was motivated by a desire to hand out lucrative business deals to his buddies in the oil business, and thought he could parcel up oil redevelopment contracts in Iraq if he succeeded in controlling it. Others blamed US corporations generally, rather than oil companies in particular. If the US could secure a reliable long-term supply of oil, its businesses would have a global competitive advantage over the rest of the Western world.

None of this is very credible. Take, for example, the argument about Bush's oil buddies and the specific promotion of oil company interests. A look at the share price of Exxon shows that it actually fell throughout 2002 as the crisis in Iraq developed. Similarly, if the President was trying to help American corporations with this war, the collapsing stock market hardly seemed to justify his trouble. Why would he spend up to $75 billion – the predicted cost of the war – to benefit big business? It would be an extraordinary gamble. A cynic might suggest that it was cheaper to buy votes through tax cuts than through bribes to big Republican supporters: $75 billion would finance a one-off handout of about $275 to each American citizen.

It would be more plausible to argue that $75 billion was a worthwhile price for cheaper oil in the long term. As the US spends, very roughly, about $130 billion a year on imported oil, the cost of the war begins to look more modest. Indeed, if the war was seen as an investment, it would probably be worth pursuing if it could secure a permanent five per cent cut in oil prices, worth about $7 billion a year – a healthy return on a $75 billion outlay.

But even here, it's doubtful that a politician would take such a huge gamble for such a return. There was always the risk that the Iraqi oilfields would be torched by retreating Saddam supporters, or that Saudi Arabia would erupt into militancy following a US invasion of a neighbouring country. The war might achieve the precise opposite of what was intended.

In addition, the conflict came at a terrible time for the global and US economies. It had the predictable effect of pushing oil prices *up* for a period, as war-induced nervousness about supply grew. And that increase in prices occurred during a second year of lacklustre growth, with confidence tumbling and nerves already rattled by the fear of terrorism. If I had been the American president and purely motivated by economic benefit, I would not have chosen to go to war in 2003.

Besides, the workings of oil markets are rather complicated. An increase in the supply of oil in one area, while clearly pushing the price down, leads to a decrease elsewhere. While OPEC countries do not 'control' the oil price, they do have some effect on it, mainly because they have the bulk of the world's excess capacity so they can raise or lower supply more easily than most other producers. If Iraq produces more oil, the Saudis will produce less. Evidence for this came at the OPEC meeting in Vienna in April 2003, at the end of the war, when the organization announced cuts in oil production amounting to two million barrels a day in response to a fall in the post-war oil price.

There's one other reason to doubt that the war was about narrow economic interests: Iraq's oil is a long way from being developed. Its industry is run down and its short-term capacity limited. As Daniel Yergin of Cambridge Energy Research Associates told the BBC on the subject of doubling Iraqi production, 'making that leap to 5.5 million barrels a day would come sometime after 2010'. That would not even increase global supply by four per cent. In the meantime, Iraq will do well to build up production to that level, even slowly. It's not often that politicians take huge gambles for potential benefits seven years down the road. George W Bush would have to be an unusually long-sighted politician to take such risks to benefit a successor.

If none of these arguments that the war was not 'all about oil' seems persuasive, consider this: the easiest way to secure large supplies of oil from Iraq, and lower prices, would always have been to ignore Saddam's misdeeds, lift sanctions and let the oil flow freely again. This isn't to deny that the US may try to exploit its position after the war, or that it may apply pressure on Iraq to undermine OPEC by increasing production. It is also quite possible that the US was aware of possible benefits when it went to war. It's simply to rule out the narrow view of US economic interests as the prime motivation.

But, if not about oil, were there other economic motives for the war? Reconstruction contracts perhaps, or support for the defence industry? Again, these might have been factors behind US decision-making, but it would be wrong to put much weight on them. Ultimately, the cost of war – and reconstruction contracts awarded to American companies – is met by the taxpayer. What Washington politicians gain from handouts to their corporate friends, they could lose in having to impose higher than necessary taxes on their voters. And for every defence-style industry that gains from war, some other industry loses from it. In the case of both Gulf Wars, the airlines suffered most. American airlines were in a precarious position already. They'd been granted $15 billion of government support after September 11, and were voted another $3 billion in April 2003 during the war itself.

* * * * * *

It is too early to make assertions about the economic effects of this war, but this is the right time to outline what we should look for. One important effect would be a retreat from the global consumer era of the latter half of the 20th century. It was an era of American domination – indeed, the words 'globalization' and 'Americanization' are often interchangeable. Will this continue? Will, for example, Arab discontent at US policies lead to a boycott of American products? Of course there will be isolated consumer boycotts. There are already products like Mecca Cola, launched by a French entrepreneur, Tawfik Mathlouthi, who wanted to give Muslim consumers the chance to drink cola without supporting the big US drinks companies. It was all about combating 'America's imperialism and Zionism by providing a substitute for American goods', Mr Mathlouthi told BBC News Online. But the forces of technology and deregulation that have propelled trade into such fast growth cannot so easily be reversed.

177

A second effect to look for will be within Europe, and in particular in the debate on the euro. There can be no doubt that many in Europe see the euro as a means to counter the power of the US dollar as an effective global currency. Many on the left, particularly those concerned with green issues, have been sceptical about the euro, viewing it as a device for promoting more globalization. But equally the left is concerned about the power of the United States. How will these different factors play in the debate?

It may be that the drive to European integration is a casualty of war and the divisions that preceded it. Voters in the UK, for example, might be more suspicious of France and Germany, and less keen to sign up to new European initiatives. However, it's possible that the opposite will happen and new coalitions will emerge. It's interesting that in the aftermath of war, the environmental campaigner George Monbiot wrote an article in the *Guardian* that ended with the words: 'Those of us who are concerned about American power must abandon our opposition to the euro.'

The third, and most important, effect could be a United States that is more assertive in global economic institutions, especially the World Trade Organization. The current round of trade talks, launched in Doha, Qatar in November 2001, is seeking a large-scale extension of the rules of world trade, with the particular aim of helping poor countries. European intransigence over the issue of agricultural subsidies is a major difficulty, as the Common

Agricultural Policy often excludes poor nations from European food markets. For its part, the United States has concerns over protecting its pharmaceutical industry as third-world countries try to use cheaper generic equivalents of Western drugs. It's unlikely the Doha round will be successful without movement on this issue. The more general question is whether the US will respect the decisions of the WTO in constraining its trade policy. The risk is that, in the post-war climate in America, the WTO will simply be dismissed as no more than an extension of the supposedly 'discredited' UN.

A fourth effect to look for is a change in overseas aid policy. The United States is not one of the world's most generous contrib-utors to poor countries – on a proportional basis, it would need to triple its official aid to match the UK. For the US, the original bud-geted cost of the war in Iraq ($75 billion) was equivalent to over five years of its aid budget. And American official aid is already highly politicized – with Russia, Israel and Pakistan among the biggest recipients. It is easy to envisage that, post-war, the US will be more nationalistic and less concerned with how its policies look to the rest of the world. But it's also possible that Washington will feel it needs to supplement its military prowess with a softer and gentler policy in civilian matters, and that it needs to buy friends with a more generous trade and aid strategy.

Certainly, after the September 11 attacks, the US did play a more multilateral role in the world, raising its aid budget and throwing its weight behind the Doha trade round. America felt it needed friends and was willing to pay for them. But much of the political goodwill since then has evaporated. This may be because the weaker US economy has made spending money on friends seem unaffordable. Whatever the reason, will post-war America become more multilateral, more unilateral or (least likely) more isolationist? One thing that can be said with certainty is that there are enormous parallels between its military and economic policies. In both, the US is unrivalled in size and stature. With a national income of about $10 trillion, the US economy is roughly the same size as those of Japan, Germany, the UK and France combined. So we can fairly conclude that whatever the US chooses to do economically will matter for the rest of us.

The Iraq conflict raises two basic questions: first, is there a heightened sense of US national interest, fuelled by the war and the diplomatic stand-off that preceded it? (in a sense this is the question raised by the withdrawal of al-Jazeera's accreditation by the New York Stock Exchange); and, second, will a world economic order that has created unprecedented wealth be sustained, advanced or harmed? The major economic concern is not the war itself, but the nationalism it has encouraged in the United States and the consequences of this for the global economy.

179

CHAPTER TWELVE

VOX POPULI – WORLDWIDE WAR-TALK ON THE WEB

Paul Reynolds

180 *Paul Reynolds is World Affairs Correspondent for BBC News Online. He was New York, Brussels, Jerusalem and Diplomatic Correspondent before being posted to Washington from 1998 to 2001, and is a specialist on international affairs. With the internet now a significant forum for public opinion, his chapter surveys the sometimes impassioned response to the war from around the world on the BBC News Online website.*

The war in Iraq produced a new phenomenon: the ability of people around the world to join in a debate on an international issue of war and peace. The internet was used even more than after September 11. The BBC website News Online had 33 million page impressions on the first day of the war, 20 March – three times the normal traffic. 'People turned to the internet for news as never before,' said News Online Editor, Mike Smartt. Governments and the media found that their agendas were being influenced by what was bubbling up in the emails that flooded the websites of news organizations. Questions were being raised that needed answers.

The messages came in such numbers and with such force that they could not be ignored as simply the ramblings and rantings of the frustrated, though there were plenty enough of those. Patterns were thrown up and issues revealed. And there were some surprises.

The internet has proved in this war to be a good source of information about public opinion worldwide. But the very volume of emails was itself an obstacle to understanding and analysing them since they covered so many subjects at one time.

It helped that specific questions were invited in online pro-grammes, but in the next war or crisis perhaps there should be an attempt to narrow them down even more so that comments can be channelled and collated more easily. There might also be a more systematic effort to track changes in opinion.

BBC News Online alone received 241,225 emails for the three-week period from 19 March to 9 April. The largest number – 27,229 – came on the day the war actually started. The com-ments were solicited both as general remarks about the war and as specific questions for guests on talk shows and phone-ins. Even in the period after the war they were coming in at the rate of about 15,000 a day.

Vicky Taylor, BBC News Online's Interactivity Editor, said: 'At the start a very strong majority was against the war. It was 80/20. Then that changed as the war developed and it ended up at roughly 60/40 against.' She said that there had not been much organized emailing. 'There were some peace groups but there was nothing on a big scale. Nor did governments get involved. And the spread of messages was global. We had them from Antarctica to Alaska.'

Broadly, four conclusions can be drawn from an analysis of the emails. First, a majority opposed the war. Second, the majority was smaller at the end of the war than it was at the beginning. Third, opinion could change further depending on what happens in Iraq in the future. And fourth, stereotypes do not always apply.

This last point emerged from emails sent to the BBC Arabic Service. Hosam El-Sokkari, Head of BBCArabic.com, said that opposition to the war in the Arab world was not as strong as might have been expected. He ran a twice-daily phone-in programme and received some 16,000 emails from right across Arabic-speaking countries. He commented on the sometimes surprising results:

'Not everyone was anti-war or against the United States,' he said. 'Nor were all Arabs in favour of Saddam Hussein and his regime. I was surprised at the diversity and maturity of views. This went far beyond what we expected. They were not the kind of views which are normally dominant in the Arab media, which come from the elite. We had cab drivers, carpenters, handymen, and refugees – many of the people who don't normally get a voice in their own media. There was one call from Mosul in Northern Iraq. In fact, the man called three times. His comment was that the United States had been safeguarding Muslims so why were some Arabs denying him the right to welcome the Americans.'

What was immediately noticeable about many emails was their directness, particularly when they were sent in as questions. People tend to ask far ruder and tougher questions than do even the most forthright of the professional interviewers in the mainstream media. And the interviewee could not complain about being treated badly, for this was the voice of the people.

182   Take, for example, a question on one BBC online programme put to Sharif Ali bin al-Hussein, the man who would like to be King of Iraq. He is a descendant of the Iraqi royal family which was installed on the throne by the British and overthrown in the coup of 1958. It was on the day when gold-plated guns had been found and filmed in the home of Saddam Hussein's son Uday. So the question from Kay Sutton in Kenilworth, England, was: 'How do we know that Iraq won't slip back to becoming a dictatorship again with you handing out golden guns to your family and friends?'

It was a good question, which prompted the reply: 'The only way to do that is not to have power in personal hands and that's why civilized nations have institutions ... personally I know that I wouldn't be doing that.'

* * * * * *

Let's therefore look at the range of the opinions expressed and at some of the implications.

On 15 February, when war was already probable, BBC News Online published 24 pages of emailed comments to a joint programme broadcast by the BBC World Service and National Public Radio in the United States. A typical anti-war comment came from Ansaruddin in the Bahamas (emailers do not have to give their full names and addresses). It was just after US Secretary of State Colin Powell had given his presentation to the UN Security Council in which he alleged that Iraq had weapons of mass destruction.

'Powell did not convince anyone about any solid evidence. The slide show is poor and lacks any strength. Saddam does not pose any threat to his neighbours and least of all to the USA. The Arab League says that Saddam is not a threat to them. He has been contained for the last twelve years. Remember the Soviet Union was contained for over sixty years until it crumbled. There is no hurry to go to war now; let the inspectors do their jobs and let them have sufficient time. Nobody wants war. More than seventy per cent of the world is against war now. It causes untold miseries. War at any time and anywhere is evil.'

Note the tone in this message. It is tinged with emotion but is reasoned and quite measured overall. It could have been delivered by the French Foreign Minister, Dominique de Villepin, who made rather similar remarks to the Security Council himself. Other emails later on would be far more angry.

183

But other messages that day in February also reflected the nuances of world public opinion. There were several from the United States opposing any war. Jeff commented: 'The reason the US is concentrating on Iraq is that it does not want to deal with the North Korean problem right now. North Korea has threatened to use nuclear weapons in front of the world and defied the US openly but the US is not in a position to deal with them or intimidate them and any attempt to do so might cause great embarrassment. Saddam is a safer bet; he is weaker, does not threaten so much and certainly does not have nuclear weapons.'

And there were some from Arab countries sympathetic to the United States. Ghaly Sahfik commented from Egypt: 'Enough appeasement of tyrants. When will the world act to stop such a dictator? The British just discovered deadly chemicals in Manchester. What are you waiting for? The US is not advocating war, but sometimes war is the only solution.'

There was also a pro-American view from Europe. Chad Weidner wrote from Ghent in Belgium: 'I am amazed at how easily Europeans criticize America. Some say this war is for oil. Do people really believe that the US is willing to spend some 200 billion dollars, as well as to send men to die, for the possibility of slightly cheaper oil … How long must we wait to remove Saddam?'

So even before the war there were interesting undercurrents, not all of which were picked up in the main media which tended to think that all Arabs were against America, all Americans were against the Arabs and all continental Europeans were against war.

During the war itself, the tone of the emails got stronger. Islamic opinion, in particular, hardened. Amnah from Pakistan commented: 'Today, we support Saddam Hussein (and the Iraqi people), not because of his past but for the fact that he is fighting for freedom for his land and because he is the one standing firm against the American and British evil. The Americans are only oppressors; they don't even know the meaning of humanity, not to talk of human ethics. The government of the USA is devoid of all moral values.'

There were also specific charges against members of the Bush administration. Nasser al-Thekair from Jeddah in Saudi Arabia raised the oil issue: 'To say that Americans and British are fighting for the Iraqi people is an insult to the average human intelligence. Rice, Cheney and Bush being ex-officials in oil companies makes it very interesting as to what are the real reasons behind this invasion.' The same writer made another contribution at a different time: 'The question to be asked: what does the Muslim world think of the US now? Trust me, you don't want to know the answer.'

A message from Bert in Louvie, France, said: 'It is a scary scenario what the US is implementing. It is the fear of the US for the Muslim population to run the Middle East and beyond. This is the reason for this war. The US is obsessed by losing control as the world's policeman.' And from YK in Malaysia came a question: 'I am pro-peace, not pro-Saddam. I am pro-diplomacy and still believe that the war is unnecessary. I believe there are a lot of people who think this way. The world wants to disarm Saddam and there are many ways to skin this cat. Why is war the only option?'

The casualties caused among civilians was a particular point of anger. Ravi from India was outraged at the comment on the BBC by General Patrick Cordingley, who fought in the first Gulf War, that 'we must harden our hearts'. 'If Iraqi civilians die, we must "harden our hearts". Would the General say the same if US and UK civilians were killed? Would your esteemed readers from the

184

West "harden their hearts" the next time Osama strikes and kills and maims their loved ones?'

From Armagh in Northern Ireland, Robin Ballantine said: 'Anyone that supports this war has to take responsibility for its consequences. I for one could not ever accept responsibility for the deaths and injuries of those caught up in it, especially the children, in the misguided belief that this will somehow increase my own safety. Shame on those who do, for this is a war of shame and misuse of power. There never was any credible threat from the start. How many lives must be destroyed before those responsible learn? Will they ever learn?'

And Bob Wallace from the UK complained about double standards when the US and British governments protested about the bodies of prisoners of war being shown on television. 'How can we complain about pictures of dead soldiers killed in a war which we started and yet day after day we see pictures of dead, innocent civilians killed by our bombs … that's the outrage.' 185

But again, among the emails, there is a counter-view about civilian casualties. This one came from Michael Lee in Singapore: 'Nobody likes war. People get killed no matter how careful you try to avoid hitting civilians. Everyone is looking at the USA as the big bully because they are the ones with the smart bombs. However it is not right to keep putting the blame on the USA if Saddam chooses to hide his army in his civilian population. Of all the fighting and wars around the world, I cannot think of another country that put in so much effort to avoid civilian casualties as the USA has in this war.'

As the war went on and it became clear that the Americans and British were going to win, so the supporters of military action began to make themselves heard more. This perhaps partly explains why the proportion of people opposed to the war began to fall. The duration and nature of the war might also have contributed, since it was neither as long nor as bloody as some had feared or predicted. Helen from the UK wrote: 'Scenes of jubilation in Baghdad as well as Basra and Umm Qasr etc. have now been reported. Perhaps now the peace protestors can admit they got it wrong.'

Roy McCrerey from Atlanta, USA, made the same point:

'The way this war is shaping up, when all's said and done, there's going to be an awful lot of people who owe Tony Blair and George Bush an apology. It will be very interesting to see if any "anti-war" people will have the guts to admit they were wrong (just as they were in the last Gulf War).'

Pavitra Hembron of Jaipur, India, also supported the war: 'In fact the Americans and the British are doing a great service to the posterity of the Iraqis and to humanity at large. The sacrifice made by the youth of these two countries is indeed laudable.'

Iraqi exiles emailed in and naturally expressed pleasure at the removal of Saddam Hussein who had been responsible for their exile in the first place. One of them, Farhard-Shkak Hawlery, said from London: 'It's crucial that Iraqis will run the country. However the Iraqi nation needs support at this stage to set up the administration. UK and US have liberated Iraq from the dictatorship and the killer (Saddam). As an Iraqi we should not forget the campaign "Iraqi Freedom". This will stay in the memory of each individual Iraqi (Arabs and Kurds) forever. Finally, the current government in Northern Iraq (Kurdistan) has shown that the Iraqis are able to practise the democracy.'

* * * * * *

As the fighting ended, so attention turned to post-war Iraq. The emphasis switched from whether the war was right or wrong, to the future of Iraq. The dominant theme was that Iraq should be run by Iraqis. This was something both sides could rally round. There was the clear and firm rejection of any American role from Mohammed in New Zealand: 'Anyone but America.' Omari Jackson in Liberia did not want to criticize the Americans: 'It goes without saying that Iraqis should run their country. The US and UK have made it possible today for Iraqis to work as one including the Kurds.'

But from Tahir Parvaiz in Islamabad, Pakistan, came a comment more hostile to the Americans and a signal of the antagonism to the United States in parts of the Islamic world: 'Irony is at work with USA whenever it tries to create governments protecting its interest but public reaction is totally against it. I think America is not learning from what happened in Afghanistan when it attacked it. The effects on Pakistan are still there and people showed their reactions in elections. Unless America stops interfering in Muslim countries, America will continue to face problems. The greatest problem which is creating distrust among Muslims against America is the Palestinian issue.'

Opinion was not unanimous that the United Nations should take the leading role in the reconstruction of Iraq. Indeed, that idea goes against the concept that Iraqis themselves should be in charge, so perhaps it is not surprising. What is a bit surprising is to read emails attacking the UN. Omari Jackson's email from Liberia went on to say: 'Had it not been for Great Britain, rebels would have wiped out the people of Sierra Leone. Just see what the United Nations failed to do in Liberia. As a result it will be disastrous for the United Nations to play a major role in Iraq.'

187

The issue of weapons of mass destruction (WMD) was very much commented on. After all, this was the reason the US and UK gave for going to war, yet people were wondering why none had been found in the days and first weeks after the war. Both countries issued dossiers before the war claiming that Iraq had these weapons. There was a good deal of scepticism. James Scobbie asked from Scotland: 'Frankly who will believe the USA and UK if they "find" weapons but prevent anyone else from looking? They may turn out to be as forged as their previous "dossier".'

There were calls for the United Nations inspectors to return. Joe Lisa of the USA wrote: 'The UN should be the ones to look for any illegal weapons. It has been already proved that the US and UK have been fabricating evidence on WMD before the war and therefore cannot be trusted to give a true account of any findings.'

The Palestinian issue was another theme among emails and one that signalled Arab and Muslim frustration with the West. This was one reason why Tony Blair pressed President Bush to become actively involved in trying to get a settlement between Israel and the Palestinians.

But an underlying dissatisfaction with the status quo in the Arab world is also revealed in some of the messages. It is not only the Americans and British who get attacked. This email from Saqib Khan in London speaks about the lack of democracy across the Middle East: 'Throughout the Middle East, the Arabs are either ruled by kings, sultans, emirs, sheiks or undemocractically elected presidents and have been denied the choice of who should govern them and under which system. Iraqis are no different to other Arabs and introducing democracy would be an uphill struggle considering their sectarian, provincial animosities. I think that the majority of Iraqis would wish to live under one flag and united and that would be possible, if the religious and regional leaders were to sit together and find a platform to start viable dialogues and serious negotiations.'

* * * * * *

There was one interesting attempt to check some people's opinions before and after the war to see if they had changed. BBC News Online invited volunteers from readers to take part in debates just after the war had started and just after it had ended. Thirteen took part in the first debate and ten of those came forward for the second.

For the first debate, the proposition was that 'going to war was the wrong thing to do'. Of the thirteen participants, seven were against the war and six were in favour. These kinds of small, self-selected groups rarely represent the exact balance of wider opinion and are not intended to do so. They are designed to reflect the arguments. It was a disparate and international group. Against the war were: an editor from New York, a salesman from Russia, a secretary from the Netherlands, a legal worker from Washington DC, an engineer from Stockholm, a man from Zambia and a woman from Lebanon. In favour were: an administrator from Belgrade, a student from Frankfurt, a software specialist from Hampshire, England, a manager from Scotland, a student from the United States and a customer service agent from Yorkshire.

Sydney, the New Yorker, led off the debate, arguing that the war was wrong: 'The ramifications of this unprovoked, unsanctioned "pre-emptive" war of aggression will resound through the globe in the years to come. A misfit assortment of reasons have been presented as to why this military adventure must go forward. None has stuck.'

Janaki Mackenzie from the Netherlands was also against the war: 'This millennium is about "lessons learnt". We are working towards globalization. South Africa's transformation has taken place by dialogue, compromise and negotiation, relatively peacefully, so we know it is possible. War may have sometimes achieved some level of success but hopefully we have grown out of using violence to achieve this.'

Adam Sofronijevic, from Belgrade, brought in personal experience to back up his support for the war: 'I was in Belgrade during the US-led intervention in my country in 1999. Within 500 metres of my home, there were more than 30 explosions. But they caused no damage whatsoever to my house. We were bombed. But now we are free. Going to war was the right thing to do.'

In the follow-up debate, only one person actually changed their mind. Dave Bennett, a telecoms engineer from Stockholm, said first time round: 'Saddam Hussein is hiding something. That is one thing we can all be sure of. But we haven't seen any significant proof of it ... UN sanctions have weakened his country even further and caused more misery for his people. The UK and US are the threat.' But in the second debate, he said this: 'To be honest, I was mostly undecided whether the invasion was the best solution. My fear was that it would become long and painful. However, seeing the statue of Saddam Hussein being pulled to the ground was the turning point. I see pictures of Iraqis celebrating and stamping on pictures of Saddam. I see images of the torture chambers he used. All these things tell me that so far we have made the right choices.'

His comments are worth noting, for their emphasis on the short duration of the war and the sight of Iraqis celebrating helps explain the shift that the online emails reflected. There is an absence of concern about the failure to find weapons of mass destruction. The Lebanese contributor, Alexandra Ahmad, was more equivocal after the war. For her, the war will only be justified by the results of the peace: 'What remains now is a situation that no one can predict the outcome of. Therein lies the real test for the coalition.'

Her comment is an indication that the final assessment of the war will depend on how Iraq develops from now on. For Arabs this will be particularly important. But Janika MacKenzie declared: 'My mind has not changed at all.' And Salik Farooqi of

189

Washington also firmly kept to his opinion: 'One cannot "liberate" those that one has oppressed.'

Online voting accompanied these debates, in which anyone could take part. There were 8313 votes after the first discussion, of which 6497 agreed that war was wrong and 1816 did not. The percentages were 78 per cent against the war and 22 per cent in favour. There was a much smaller vote after the second debate, which discussed the proposition that 'going to war was a price worth paying for the liberation of Iraq'. Perhaps people were suffering from war fatigue by then and so did not bother to vote. A total of 1254 votes were cast: 804 against the war and 450 in favour. The majority against the war was 64 per cent to 36 per cent. This change (from 78 per cent to 22 per cent first time round) reflects the emails tracked by BBC News Online's Vicky Taylor, who said that the majority opposing the war was reduced by the end of the fighting. The shift, however, did not overturn the majority against the war.

One side issue has been the row between the United States and France and this, too, has been reflected in the emailed comments. Quite often they did not rise above the level of insult. Mike Daly from the US wrote: 'As an American, I don't care what happens to France. They made a decision and they have to pay the consequences of their decision. It's clear that something was going on between Iraq and France. You have to question a leadership that would choose a third-rate country over a superpower.'

However, from Thierry in France came this: 'I feel sorry for people who always agree with their friends. I feel even more sorry for people who can't stand a friend to disagree with them. This row didn't affect my relationship with my American friends and I would be surprised if it was to affect any of the numerous friendship relationships that have tied two countries for more than two centuries.'

And, again showing that the picture is not all black or white, came a message from an American, Doland Marritz: 'What a petty, bullying, vindictive country I live in. Please believe it when I say that not all Americans are like this, but a disturbing number are, including the one at the top. Yeah, that one, the guy that lost the popular vote in the last election.'

There were also more personal emails, one of which paid

tribute to Kaveh Golestan, the Iranian BBC cameraman who died when he stepped on a mine in Northern Iraq. The BBC received this email from Azin Valy in the United States: 'I met Kaveh when I had just lost my father and he consoled me by sharing his vision of life and death through his incredible photographs and stories of the Iran–Iraq war ... He was a great source of inspiration to me through his work, courage, dedication, gentility, humbleness and his love for Iran ... He will not be forgotten.'

* * * * * *

The voices that found their outlet on the internet were not those of the powerful. They were not always those of the articulate. My assessment is that they came from a broad spectrum of people with access to the internet. And to judge from the countries they came from, they would not always have had the opportunity to speak out at home. But they were voices that had to be heard. And they were heard. Questions that came in from people on the internet or the phone found their way to government ministers and other figures as they sought to justify their policies. My own experience was that the questions from the public were often more powerful than ones thought up in the calmness of the studio. At other times, though, the questions were too general and lacked enough bite on one particular point, thereby allowing the interviewee off the hook. If you are asking about weapons inspectors, for example, it is better to be quite technical and specific.

The implication of this process is quite profound. As the techniques get more and more refined and the technology improves, so the gap between the governing and the governed will narrow. And it is a process that cuts across national borders. The international aspect of the email phenomenon during the Iraq crisis was very marked. The Russian Foreign Minister, Igor Ivanov, and the British Foreign Secretary, Jack Straw, had to answer to a world audience.

And as the debates among the readers themselves demonstrated, the dialogue is between people as well. This is one area that could easily be expanded by, for example, asking for comments from specific groups on a set subject. The Israeli–Palestinian

191

issue is one that might lend itself to this. Indians and Pakistanis might debate Kashmir. Groups that rarely talk to each other might find in the internet a forum for debate, though naturally they might find it a forum for abuse as well. Some external monitoring will therefore sometimes be necessary.

There are also political implications. Ronald Reagan predicted correctly that one of the factors that would bring down the Soviet system was its inability to withstand modern methods of mass communication. East Berliners could see from television the standard of living in West Berlin. Communication across the internet is currently restricted in countries such as China but this will become more and more difficult; just as dissidents found ways to spread the word with old technology in the past, so they will with new technology in the future.

This trend will undoubtedly continue and it will develop in other ways, too. Already the BBC has started accepting and encouraging photographs from the public. This opens up the possibility of direct reporting without the intervention of professionals, as already happens to a degree after a major event. Eyewitnesses come forward and their personal reports online are often the most vivid accounts of incidents such as earthquakes or tornados.

'Watch this cyberspace' will increasingly be the motto.

CHAPTER THIRTEEN

PROMISE AND FEAR – IRAQ'S FUTURE IN THE BALANCE

Allan Little

Allan Little is Paris Correspondent, following postings in Moscow and   193
Southern Africa. He spent several years reporting and writing on the
break-up of the former Yugoslavia and the end of Communist rule in
Eastern Europe. He also covered the first Gulf War from Baghdad. This
time, he reported extensively from Kuwait and again from Baghdad once
the city had fallen. Here he examines how the first months since the fall of
Saddam have shaped the new Iraq.

The bomb that killed Ayatollah Mohammed Bakr al-Hakim was so powerful that the Islamic cleric was torn to pieces in an instant. Close to 100 people died with him, as they filed out of the mosque at one of Shia Islam's most holy shrines – the burial place of Imam Ali in the city of Najaf in the Euphrates valley. The Ayatollah had, minutes earlier, delivered a sermon warning against the resurgence of forces loyal to Saddam Hussein. Their strategy, he said with chilling prescience, was to target the religious leaders of the country.

Hakim had been back in Iraq for less than three months, after spending more than 20 years in exile in Iran. His homecoming, on 15 May, had seemed to herald a new era. His party – the Supreme Council for the Islamic Revolution in Iraq (SCIRI) – had the potential for huge support. Under his careful leadership it was steering popular sentiment towards an accommodation with the American and British occupying forces. While condemning the occupation and criticizing the Americans and the British for failing to bring security to Iraq, the SCIRI had nonetheless joined the governing council set up under the auspices of the occupying powers. Hakim had preached the need for co-operation with the US in moving towards a modern – and moderate – Islamic government in Iraq.

Almost certainly this is why he was killed. Within 48 hours, as hundreds of thousands of Iraqis took to the streets to mourn their lost leader and to blame America for failing to protect him, Iraqi police had arrested four men. Two, they said, were Saddam Hussein loyalists. And, crucially, two were Saudi nationals. This pointed to an extraordinary and unforeseen new alliance of hugely destabilising potential – an unholy union of unreconstructed old Baathists and Islamic militants from other parts of the Arab world.

In the eyes of those committed to waging holy war against America and its allies, the removal of Saddam Hussein transformed Iraq. Almost overnight the country that had for decades persecuted Islamic leaders with torture, execution and exile, had become a magnet for Islamic militants everywhere – the latest stage on which the jihad could be prosecuted. The territory of Iraq had been, under Saddam, a no-go zone for Islamists. Now, under the American occupation, its borders were porous, its terrain ungoverned and possibly ungovernable.

The portents for this were there almost from the beginning. In the days after the liberation, people of Baghdad pointed out with rage that the one government building protected by the Americans during the orgy of looting that swept through the country was the Ministry of Oil. Everything else – hospitals, schools, government ministries and, famously, the National Museum of Iraq with its irreplaceable antiquities – had been plundered. US officials played this down: it was only natural that after so many years of oppression under Saddam Iraqis would now use their freedom to let off steam. Defense Secretary Donald Rumsfeld likened the mass pillage to the behaviour of English football fans at an international soccer match.

But American troops would soon start to pay for what seemed to be a woeful misreading of the post-war security needs of Iraq – and pay for it in lives. By the end of August, the number of American soldiers killed since President Bush formally declared the cessation of major military operations exceeded the number killed during the war itself. The evidence was that morale among the ranks was deteriorating. GIs were posting their complaints on websites and emailing news of their dissatisfaction to families back home. Private Isaac Kindblade of the 671st Engineer Company posted this on the internet: 'Somewhere down the line we became an occupation force in [Iraqi] eyes. We don't feel like heroes any more ... The rules of engagement are crippling. We are outnumbered. We are exhausted. We are in over our heads. The President says "Bring 'em on". The generals say we don't need more troops. Well, they're not over here.'

President Bush, heading for a re-election year, faced a growing chorus of dissent. How was it that a campaign designed to make the world *safer* for Americans had so manifestly had the opposite effect – turning Iraq from a country where Islamic terrorism had once been so ruthlessly crushed into a country where terrorists could wreak so much havoc, not least against Americans, with apparent impunity?

Iraqi police linked the Najaf bomb to that which had killed the UN Special Representative, Sergio Vieira de Mello, just over a week earlier. De Mello's death was a painful blow to the United Nations. The 55-year-old Brazilian had spent more than 30 years in the organization. He had, said one of his closest colleagues, devoted his entire life to the service of humanity. He'd worked in many of the most dangerous and intractable conflicts throughout the world and was widely held to be a future UN Secretary General. He was the most senior UN official to be murdered in a terror attack since the 1940s.

The two assassinations were part of a series of events that prompted a rethink in Washington DC. In early September, the Bush administration relented on its long-standing hostility to the involvement of the United Nations in Iraq. Washington tabled a motion at the UN calling for a multi-national force under American command.

France could not disguise its glee. It was – for Paris – a vindication of the position it had adopted all along. 'Bush looks for a way out', the left-wing daily *Liberation* trumpeted on its front page. An editorial declared with satisfaction that this was, at last, the beginning of a volte-face by Bush. 'Military victories,' the paper said, 'have no lasting effect if they are not followed by the victory of political and moral legitimacy.'

Both France and Germany immediately rejected the US plan, on the grounds that it was too little, too late. The role the plan envisaged for the UN was not sufficient. President Chirac and

Chancellor Schröder said the plan did not do enough to ensure that real political power would be handed over to the Iraqi people – to a legitimate Iraqi government – as soon as possible. And that word 'legitimate' lay at the heart of Franco-German concerns. Without substantial UN involvement – in effect a wresting of the levers of political control from the US by the UN – there could be no legitimacy in Iraq's unfolding political process. Both France and Germany now felt themselves to be in a strong position to extract a high political price for any support they might eventually give to the Americans.

For the first time since he declared the end of major hostilities, President Bush was looking weaker by the day – a weakness which might well have motivated the administration's change of heart about the UN. The influential Congressional Budget Office (CBO), which carries out independent policy analyses, sent a letter to the anti-war senator Robert Byrd saying that if the US stuck to current plans the troop deployment in Iraq would have to be reduced from 180,000 to between 38,000 and 64,000 by the end of 2004 – not a realistic prospect for an occupation army already struggling in a rapidly deteriorating security vacuum. The alternative, the CBO said, would be prohibitively expensive. It would bring the cost to the US of the Iraqi occupation to $29 billion a year. In fact, that proved to be an underestimate. In early September, in his first national address since declaring that America's mission in Iraq had been 'accomplished', the President said he would ask Congress for $87 billion to continue the occupation and the rebuilding of Iraq. 'Enemies of freedom are making a desperate stand there,' he said, 'and there they must be defeated. This will take time and require sacrifice.' Congressional leaders were stunned. The sum would increase the nation's federal budget deficit by almost 20 per cent at a single stroke.

Little wonder then that President Bush sought to find ways of bringing troops in from other nations – even if it meant his embarrassing about-turn on UN involvement left him open to criticism from Democratic candidates seeking to exploit growing public anxiety about Iraq. Former Vermont governor and leading anti-war campaigner Howard Dean said the President was now having to go back and ask for the support of the very people he had casually humiliated in the run-up to war.

* * * * * *

In the days after the fall of Saddam, one could see small moments of liberation – for liberation is what it was – all the time in Baghdad, gestures by which ordinary Iraqis tested the nature and limits of their new freedom. One such moment occurred in our car as we drove to Friday prayers.

My Iraqi translator and I were talking about Saddam, about the regime, its calumnies and brutalities. 'The son,' he said. 'Uday. I want to see him captured. The Iraqi people will eat him if they catch him. You know they say he was a sex maniac. Well I can tell you he raped my cousin. He saw her in the street and he ordered his bodyguards to fetch her and he raped her. He must be punished.'

The telling of this story to foreigners would have brought him a prison sentence a few days earlier. And then, his mood changed. 'Do you want me to speak like Saddam Hussein?' he said, and he launched into a practised and hilarious impersonation – the reedy voice, the long, lazy cadences, the unschooled Arabic, the pompous self-glorifying rhetoric so familiar from the hours of speeches and television addresses that Iraqis had had to sit through over the decades.

'I am Saddam Hussein, the president of the republic of Iraq,' he proclaimed. 'I am the shittiest president in the world! I destroyed my country! I humiliated my people! I brought poverty and war to a rich and peaceful land! These are my achievements! Did I do well?'

We all felt the power of the moment. In the old days this private little act of satire would have been unthinkable. The other Iraqis in the car would have felt that it was a test of their loyalty and would certainly have reported their friend for fear that, if they did not, they themselves would be reported for failing to report the incident. Thus did fear keep the population docile and divided against itself. But now, one by one, they relaxed and laughed and finally applauded the audacious humour of the performance.

America brought freedom of expression to Iraq on the back of an Abrams tank. But the most striking feature of Iraq after the fall of Saddam was that America itself – and not Saddam Hussein – was the first real target of that new freedom. The US troops guarding strategic buildings were dumbfounded. This was not supposed to

197

happen. They thought of themselves as liberators and expected to be welcomed by a people glad to be rid of an old and cruel tyranny.

But America brings so much baggage to the region – baggage that is well understood in the streets of Baghdad but about which American soldiers know little. Iraqis have a very developed understanding of the role that America has played, over the decades, in their country's misfortune – especially those who served the hated regime. I met a former major from the Mukhabarat, Saddam Hussein's feared security police. It had been his job to spy on politicians and professors, journalists and scientists, policemen and engineers: to compile dossiers that could then be used, when it was politically expedient, to destroy the lives of innocent people. I asked him whether he felt no shame that he had spent so much of his life in so ignoble a career.

'And you?' he said, holding my gaze and speaking slowly, deliberately. 'Do *you* feel shame? Listen to me. I have a wife and a family. If I fail to do my job, if I turn against the regime, they will be killed. It is very clear. What is your excuse? Who do you think created Saddam Hussein? Britain, America, France, Russia. He's your guy. You made him. He's your son.'

As we've seen, this relationship goes back more than 40 years, even before the coup that brought the Baath Party to power. James Akins was a senior diplomat in the US embassy in Baghdad. 'There's no doubt that there was CIA involvement in that coup,' he told me. 'We celebrated the Baath's seizure of power. We thought they were the great secular hope for the Arab world. Sure some people were rounded up and shot but these were mostly Communists and we didn't much care about that.'

Saddam Hussein became president in 1979, and in the aftershock of the revolution in Iran was soon America's key ally against militant anti-Western Islamism. In 1983 President Ronald Reagan sent a special envoy to Baghdad to meet the Iraqi leader in person and to discuss further co-operation. And, of course, the envoy's name was Donald Rumsfeld.

All this is well known in Baghdad. So comfortable was Saddam Hussein in his relations with the United States that he appears to have believed, in 1990, that Washington would swallow his invasion of Kuwait. He expected to be denounced. He expected con-

198

demnation. But everything he knew about America and its allies – all his experience of dealing with the reality of American power – told him that he would get away with it.

Four days after the invasion he summoned the deputy US ambassador to a meeting and, through him, made Washington an offer: the US would agree not to try to liberate Kuwait, and in return Iraq would supply cheap oil to America and undertake not to attack the oil fields in Saudi Arabia. He expected Washington to go on denouncing him in public while, behind the scenes, covertly acquiescing in this plan.

And so, 13 years later, American soldiers in Baghdad were in a state of bewilderment, unable to work out why Iraqis were so spectacularly ungrateful for what was, after all, an audacious and high-risk act of liberation. Arab hostility to American power is too deeply embedded, and cannot be explained away as what one observer has described as the 'road-rage of a thwarted Arab world – the congenital condition of a culture yet to take full responsibility for its self-inflicted wounds'.

American power in the region has not, until now, been noted for its willingness to side with the forces of progress, reform, liberation or democracy. The Arab world is routinely thought of as unstable and, of course, there is a sense in which it is. But in terms of the way political power is distributed in Arab society, instability is far from the problem: in this sense, the Arab world is stable to the point of chronic stagnation. There has been no significant regime change in the region for more than 30 years. Apart from the civil war that tore Lebanon apart, not a single Arab government has been removed since Hafez al-Assad came to power in Syria in the early 1970s. And American power has underwritten that stability.

Fouad Ajami of the US Council on Foreign Relations puts it like this: '[American] power has invariably been on the side of political reaction and a stagnant status quo .... Few Arabs would believe this [is] a Wilsonian campaign to spread the reign of liberty in the Arab world. They are to be forgiven their doubts, for American power, either by design or default, has been built on relationships with military rulers and monarchs without popular mandates. America has not known or trusted the middle classes and the professionals in these lands. Rather it has settled for relationships of convenience with the autocracies in the saddle, tolerating the cultural and political malignancies of the Arab world.'

One day, shortly after the liberation of Baghdad, I found myself in an angry crowd of demonstrators. They had been whipped up to boiling point not by intemperate anti-American speeches from Shia clerics, but by the sight of something that seemed to confirm their worst fears about American intentions. Muhammed Zubaidi, a member of the US-backed opposition group, the Iraqi National Congress, had appeared with a group of sharp-suited bodyguards and a loud-hailer outside the Palestine Hotel, which was now ringed with razor wire. He had, earlier in the week, declared himself (illegally) the governor of Baghdad. As he spoke, US troops stood between him and the crowd beyond the razor wire: he was separated from the very people he aspired to lead. Zubaidi tried to address the crowd but nothing he said could be heard above the din. This, to the crowd, was a perfect illustration of what was happening to their country. It seemed to them that America was here to install a new regime, to impose a new government on Iraq which would be protected by American power just as, they believed, Saddam Hussein's regime had for so long enjoyed American approval.

One man in the crowd screamed at me in fury. He was evidently educated – educated enough to be talking to me in effortless English. 'America is the enemy of Islam! It is written in the Holy Koran!' he shouted.

This deeply anti-American sentiment was compounded by Iraq's descent into lawlessness. At night, small-arms fire rang out across the darkness of the city. By day, armed men sold machine-guns in the street for as little as $40 apiece. A month after the Americans entered Baghdad, buildings continued to burn. The real damage to Iraq's civilian infrastructure was the result, not of British and American bombing, but of looting. Many of the main urban centres, including the capital, were still living without electricity, clean water, and – most dangerously – security. In the poorer areas, the streets ran with raw sewage. There were cases of cholera. How did the Americans so disastrously misread what would happen in the wake of the collapse of the old regime? Months after the fall of Saddam, most Iraqis were still without regular water and power supplies, and violent crime remained rife. Iraqis ruefully compared the failure of the occupying powers to restore basic amenities with the speed with which the old regime had rebuilt the country after the bombardment of 1991.

The occupying force did score some extraordinary successes, very quickly. Many leading members of the ousted regime were captured, or handed themselves over. The Americans had a 'most wanted' list of 55 senior figures – the famous pack of cards. The former deputy prime minister Tariq Aziz had negotiated his own surrender. Saddam's detested cousin Ali Hassan al-Majid – known as Chemical Ali for his part in the gassing of the Kurdish village of Halabjeh in 1988 – was captured. And, most significantly of all, Saddam's sons and putative successors, Uday and Qusay, were killed in a shoot-out with American troops in a house near their father's home town of Tikrit. When news of their demise reached Baghdad, resentment against the American occupation did not stop local people from celebrating by firing automatic weapons into the air. The capture – or deaths - of so many senior Saddam loyalists could not have been achieved without the co-operation of many Iraqis who had contact with, and knowledge of the whereabouts of, the former leaders of the ousted regime. It was evidence of the highly nuanced response many Iraqis had to the presence of the Americans: they may have denounced the occupation in public, but privately they were ready to seek an accommodation and to co-operate.

* * * * * *

In the weeks after the removal of Saddam, the single most impressive political 'fact on the ground' was the response of the country's clerics. They reacted instantly to the complete absence of civil authority by filling the vacuum themselves. Two powerful political forces were at play: the first of these was a politicized Islam, free and off the leash after decades of persecution; the second was a United States apparently determined to impose democracy from the top down. The question was whether these two forces could reach an understanding with each other – or whether they were bound to clash.

For this is another striking feature of post-Saddam Iraq – the extent to which the clergy have mobilized popular support in pursuit of overtly political goals. In the mosques, banners drape the walls.

201

They are in English as well as Arabic – a conscious and deliberate appeal to an audience beyond Iraq. Their message is consistent across the country: 'No to Saddam' and 'No to America' in equal measure. 'Iraqis must choose their own government' – a *sine qua non*. And, most significantly and consistently, 'The Honourable Scholars are the True Representatives of the People'. The latter is a challenge to the legitimacy of those would-be leaders most closely associated with the United States – men like Ahmed Chalabi, the leader of the Iraqi National Congress. He had spent more than four decades in exile, clearly had no power base inside the country and was entirely dependent on American patronage.

202   Wherever anything remotely resembling civil authority re-established itself in the weeks following the collapse of the old regime, it emanated from the mosques. The imams organized the armed guards at hospital gates; the imams drew up rotas for volunteers to clear the stinking refuse from the streets; the imams sent teenage boys to road intersections to keep the traffic moving in the absence of traffic lights. It became clear that the Islamic clergy were the only figures of authority who commanded the respect, and indeed loyalty, of the public. The street demonstrations they organized were not only well-orchestrated in the slogans they chanted, they were also well-stewarded, by armed men who, from a discreet distance, maintained discipline. Thus, after decades of persecution – and possibly because of it - political leadership had fallen into the laps of the Islamic clergy like a ripe fruit.

Something of the nature of this new force was discernible even in the early days. Despite the anti-American feeling expressed on the streets, the signals coming from the mosques were moderate, conciliatory, and highly pragmatic in their approach to the outside world – the West in general and America in particular. The Supreme Council for the Islamic Revolution in Iraq co-operated with the top US civil official in the country, Paul Bremer. But that approach cost Ayatollah Mohammed Bakr al-Hakim his life and strengthened the hand of those who seek conflict – rather than accommodation – with the American and British occupation.

This Islamic involvement was much less sectarian than many outside observers had feared. At Friday prayers the imams spoke the language of Iraqi unity. Their appeal was not to specifically Shia or

Sunni traditions, but to a powerfully expressed Iraqi patriotism. Their call, initially at least, was for brotherhood between Iraqis - Sunni and Shia, Muslim and Christian, Arab and Kurd.

The fault line running through Iraq's newly empowered religious leadership was not that between Sunni and Shia. If anything it was *within* Shia Islam, which claims the adherence of more than 60 per cent of the population. Ferocious rivalries emerged. Leading clerics had what amounted to city-state power bases. Power and authority in this community was locally entrenched and highly segmented. Some leading clerics had organized, in effect, private militias. The enmity was, in places, deadly. The pro-American cleric Abdul Majid al-Khoei was murdered by a mob days after returning to his home city of Najaf. That mob was loyal to the 30-year-old Moqtadir al-Sadr, the son of a leading Shia cleric assassinated on the orders of Saddam Hussein in 1999. These rivalries within the Shia community have yet to play themselves out. When they do, they will have a decisive role in the country's future.

203

The emerging Iraq may not be what America intended when it launched its war: a stable, secular democracy that would enable it to redefine its relationships in the world's most important oil-producing region. The United States wants to wean itself off its

unhealthy dependence on Saudi oil, in part at least because, as September 11 showed, Saudi Arabia is not only where the oil comes from, but is also the homeland of most of the perpetrators of the US terror attacks.

Can America plant the seeds of a Western-style democracy in the soil of Arabia? And if it can, will they take root? Some of the signs are good. Iraq is well endowed, materially and culturally. It has water. It has fertile agricultural land. It can feed its people. It has a strong, independently minded and well-educated urban middle class, whose links with the democracies of the Western world (especially the English-speaking ones) have been laid down and strengthened over generations. And, of course, it has oil.

* * * * * *

I'm not the first Western visitor to have been struck by the instinctive civility of ordinary Iraqi people. No matter how great the suffering they endure, and even in moments when they're experiencing the most intense grief, it seems indestructible.

During the first Gulf War I visited a suburb of Baghdad called Amariyah with a handful of other Western reporters. A civilian air-raid shelter had just been struck by bunker-busting penetration bombs fired by US aircraft flying invulnerably high overhead. As I arrived, the bodies of more than 300 women and children were being pulled from the smoking ruins.

I found myself surrounded by husbands and fathers, learning for the first time that they'd lost their entire families. One man showed me the civil identity papers of six people: a wife and five children, each card with a photograph except the youngest, that of a child of nine months whose picture had never been taken.

I tried to imagine what would happen if London were being bombed by the Iraqi air force, and a group of Iraqi reporters had the nerve to turn up at a moment like this. I couldn't believe that they would survive the popular fury. Yet at no time did I feel myself to be threatened, and though I felt a kind of reflected shame, there wasn't even a time when I felt blamed by those around me.

When you ask Iraqis why they behave like this, the question surprises them. We know that it is not you who has done this to us, they say. You are our guest; you are with us here. This attitude strikes foreigners throughout the Arab world. But it seems especially marked among Iraqis, who have, arguably, greater cause to resent and indeed blame outsiders for the suffering they have endured.

Two questions still intrigue me. How could this instinctively and enduringly civil people produce such a pathologically brutal tyranny? And how is it that their civility has survived the cruelty that Saddam Hussein inflicted on them for so long?

* * * * * *

The ziggurat at Ur is a pyramid-shaped structure that rises above the mud flats of the Euphrates. Ur is the oldest city in human history. One day, its old stones will be properly excavated and it will, no doubt, surrender whatever secrets still lie buried there in the mud. It is said to be the birthplace of Abraham – the Abraham of Jews, Christians and Muslims. The Euphrates valley is where human beings invented agriculture and began to live in one settled place. It is where human beings learnt to live together in cities. It is where they developed scholarship and commerce. It is where they invented that precious repository of cumulative experience – the written word. Saddam Hussein and his predecessors have stood between the Iraqi people and this extraordinary heritage for decades.

A month after his removal, there were indeed fresh excavations in Iraqi soil. But these were not sites of biblical antiquity. They were sites of some of the worst atrocities in living memory. The bodies of tens of thousands of people massacred on the orders of Saddam Hussein were being dug up by relatives. They combed the earth for the dead as though sifting through rubble, trying to identify their own loved ones from a jumble of bones, skulls and semi-decomposed clothing. These were the dead of the 1991 Shia and Kurdish uprisings, which occurred after the expulsion of Iraq's army from Kuwait. In March that year, Saddam Hussein had come closer to being toppled than ever before. His retribution was swift and decisive. In the south, it was led by his infamous cousin, Ali Hassan al-Majid. Iraq's opposition leaders believe that he was responsible for the deaths of as many as 300,000 people.

But it was not Saddam Hussein's human rights record that provided the impetus for the war. It was launched in the face of world-wide criticism, mainly because Britain and America insisted that

Baghdad had weapons of mass destruction and that these were ready to be used at just 45 minutes' notice.

Yet months after US and UK troops took control of the country, and after dozens of sites had been inspected, almost no suspicious material had been produced. Nor did the British or US governments seem unduly concerned about this. At one stage the British Foreign Secretary, Jack Straw, admitted that weapons of mass destruction might never be found and that this was 'not crucially important'. He pointed out that the Iraqi regime had had plenty of notice to destroy the material. In a further 'clarification', the Prime Minister's spokesman maintained that the legality of the war did not hinge on the discovery of weapons of mass destruction, but on Iraq's failure to comply with the UN resolutions on weapons inspectors.

However the row over whether such weapons had ever existed was to lead to the biggest political crisis of Tony Blair's six-year premiership. In a report on early morning radio, the BBC reporter Andrew Gilligan said a senior intelligence source had told him that the dossier published by the British government in advance of the war had been 'sexed up'. In particular, the claim that the Iraqi dictator had access to WMDs that could be deployed 'within 45 minutes' was unreliable. It had been inserted into the document, Gilligan reported, even though the government 'probably knew that it was wrong'.

The Prime Minister's Director of Communications, Alastair Campbell, exploded with fury. This, he said, was an unprecedented attack on the integrity of the government and of the Prime Minister. He demanded an apology. The BBC – anxious to demonstrate that despite being publicly funded it was nonetheless editorially independent of the government – said the accusation had not been made by the BBC but by Gilligan's source, who was both credible and senior. The Corporation refused to apologise and insisted that it had been right – given everything else that had thus far been revealed – to place the accusation in the public domain.

The government demanded, unsuccessfully, to know the name of Gilligan's source. It then announced that an official of the Ministry of Defence (MOD) had come forward – in confidence – to say that he had spoken to Gilligan, but that he did not believe he could have been the source for the report in question. The Ministry of Defence later confirmed to the media that the official was scientist Dr David Kelly, highly respected for his expertise on disarmament and weapons of mass destruction, who had worked as a weapons inspector in Iraq.

Dr Kelly was summoned to give evidence to the Parliamentary Foreign Affairs Committee. Two days later he walked into a remote corner of rural Oxfordshire, five miles from his home, and apparently committed suicide. His body was found the next day. He had swallowed pain killers prescribed for his wife's arthritis and had cut the artery of his left wrist with a pocket knife he had had since his days as a Boy Scout.

207

The Prime Minister was told of Dr Kelly's death in mid-air, on a flight to Tokyo. Mr Blair had just been in Washington where he'd received a rapturous reception from both houses of Congress who had awarded him the Congressional Gold Medal, in recognition of his support 'in trying times'. It was an extraordinary honour; no British prime minister had received it since Winston Churchill. It should have been a moment of triumph for Tony Blair. Instead he found himself ordering a judicial inquiry into Dr Kelly's death.

In the midst of a raging political storm the inquiry, led by Lord Hutton, sat in the neo-Gothic splendour of London's ancient Royal Courts of Justice. Amid its thousand rooms and three miles of corridor, Court Room 73 was an oasis of calm, careful, forensic precision. Lord Hutton ruled that the proceedings should not be televised; Dr Kelly's family had made the request because, it was reported, they did not want the death of their loved one turned into a form of entertainment – a daily soap opera of revelation and counter-revelation. For daily revelation there was to be. The inquiry systematically dissected the original Gilligan report, the BBC's decision to defend him, the government's decision to reveal Dr Kelly's identity, and the circumstances that led to his death. Neither the government nor the BBC was expected to emerge from the inquiry without criticism.

Tony Blair was not the only one in the firing line. President Bush also came under intense scrutiny. His respected Secretary of State, Colin Powell, had gone to the UN Security Council in February to make the case for war. He'd produced aerial and satellite photographs of Iraqi sites which, he insisted, were known to house Saddam's secret WMD programme. But after taking control of the country the US refused to readmit the UN weapons inspectors, even though the Security Council resolutions authorizing (indeed requiring) their presence in Iraq were still in force. This created the supremely ironic situation of the Baghdad authorities continuing to block the work of the inspectors – not, this time, at the behest of Saddam Hussein but at that of George W Bush.

Administration officials, from the President down, spoke increasingly of other issues in seeking to find retrospective justification for military action. They reminded the world of Saddam's human rights record, of the massacre of tens, possibly hundreds, of thousands of Iraqis in 1991, of the mass graves uncovered in the weeks after the end of the war. France and Germany could not conceal their satisfaction at the growing discomfort Bush and Blair were suffering.

* * * * * *

What then of America's credibility as a power determined to bring democracy and open government to a region that has never enjoyed either? The US has decades of foreign policy to live down, decades in which it has propped up corrupt and unpopular regimes, decades of speaking about America as the home of democratic values while pulling the feet from under democratic aspirations in countries governed by undemocratic client regimes.

Saudi Arabia is the clearest example. America's relationship with the House of Saud has been seen throughout the Arab world as a cynical 'oil for guns' arrangement. Washington's decision in the aftermath of the war in Iraq to remove its forces from the Prince Sultan Air base near Riyadh was highly significant. It marked the start of the fundamental redrawing of Washington's relations with the region and its intention to distance itself from the House of Saud, for whose interests, of course, it is not good news.

In the aftermath of September 11, Americans were genuinely bewildered to discover that much of the world hated their country. To them, America was, after all, the world's most dynamic democracy, the place that took the values of the 18th-century Enlightenment, turned them into a working political system and enshrined liberty in a system of laws. At home, Americans experience the state as a benign force, as the protector of their right to life, liberty and the pursuit of happiness.

The problem for the United States in its new zeal to 'export' democracy is that it has, for much of its history, appeared to believe that it can do 'life, liberty and the pursuit of happiness' at home, while exporting something quite different.

It is like ancient Rome. Within the walls of the imperial citadel the state meant one thing, while on the barbarian fringes of the empire, indigenous people experienced the might of the state quite differently. There, it did not bestow liberty, or even aspire to. Rather, it meant the application of force in ruthless pursuit of Roman self-interest, unaccountable to any system of law. Thus, today, an America that was brought into existence by challenging the arbitrary exercise of power is seen by many as exercising arbitrary power itself.

If Washington really does, this time, intend to 'export' democracy – the same values and liberties enjoyed by Americans – then the world will indeed have changed.

INDEX